Contemporary Debates on Nationalism

Also by Umut Özkırımlı

Theories of Nationalism: A Critical Introduction

Nationalism and its Futures

Contemporary Debates on Nationalism

A Critical Engagement

Umut Özkırımlı

First published 2005 by
PALGRAVE MACMILLAN
Houndmills, Basingstoke, Hampshire RG21 6XS and
175 Fifth Avenue, New York, N.Y. 10010
Companies and representatives throughout the world

PALGRAVE MACMILLAN is the global academic imprint of the Palgrave Macmillan division of St. Martin's Press, LLC and of Palgrave Macmillan Ltd. Macmillan® is a registered trademark in the United States, United Kingdom and other countries, Palgrave is a registered trademark in the European Union and other countries.

ISBN-13: 978–0–333–94772–2 hardback
ISBN-10: 0–333–94772–x hardback
ISBN-13: 978–0–333–94773–9 paperback
ISBN-10: 0–333–94773–8 paperback

This book is printed on paper suitable for recycling and made from fully managed and sustained forest sources.

A catalogue record for this book is available from the British Library.

A catalog record for this book is available from the Library of Congress.

10   9   8   7   6   5   4   3   2   1
14   13   12   11   10   09   08   07   06   05

Printed in China

*O güzel insanlar
o güzel atlara binip
gitmediler.
Bütün çirkinliklere inat
bizimle birlikte
yaşıyorlar,
yaşayacaklar.*

To my father, Atilla Özkırımlı

Contents

Tables

Preface

In his famous poem, *Ithaca*, the distinguished Greek poet Constantine P. Cavafy (1863–1933), writes:

> When you set out on your journey to Ithaca,
> pray that the road is long,
> full of adventure, full of knowledge
> The Laistrygonians and the Cyclops,
> the angry Poseidon – do not fear them:
> You will never find such as these on your path,
> if your thoughts remain lofty, if a fine
> emotion touches your spirit and your body.
> The Laistrygonians and the Cyclops,
> the fierce Poseidon you will never encounter,
> if you do not carry them within your soul,
> if your soul does not set them up before you.

The journey of this book has indeed been long. I have met the Laistrygonians and the Cyclops quite a few times on the road, as it has not always been possible to keep my thoughts lofty. A number of people helped me carry on during those difficult times. Among them, my friends and colleagues in the Department of International Relations at Istanbul Bilgi University, and Taner Berksoy, the Dean of the Faculty of Economics and Social Sciences, deserve special mention as they relieved me from some of my duties in the last two years to enable me to complete this book. Steven Kennedy has been not only a patient and understanding editor, but also a perceptive guide and a constructive critic throughout. Colleagues from all around the world, notably Erica Benner, Craig Calhoun, John A. Hall, Fred Halliday, Michael Hechter, John Hutchinson, Spyros A. Sofos, Nira Yuval-Davis and the anonymous Palgrave Macmillan reviewer, have been extremely generous with their time, and read the initial draft of the manuscript, helping me to improve it in ways that I could not even imagine. I owe special thanks to Seda Yüksel and Erol Ülker for going through the whole text at a later stage and alerting me to the needs of my potential readership. In a more personal vein, I must thank Sema and Can Yüksel, and the members of the Arın family, especially the late Suha Arın who took a personal interest in seeing this book completed, for offering much valuable support when it mattered most. I must also thank my friends in London, my sanctuary, in particular Spyros, Roza, Can, Aybige and Burcu, for their companionship and, more importantly, for reminding me that the Laistrygonians and the Cyclops are in fact in my soul. I am particularly grateful to a friend of mine who fought these imaginary giants alongside me, even when they proved to be invincible – the road to Ithaca is indeed long and arduous, but I shall get there, I give you my word on it. Finally, my mother and father, the perpetual sources of the fine emotion that touches my spirit and my body . . . Thank you for all the good things you have done, most importantly for the 'hope' you have implanted in me. I shall do my best to live up to it.

I completed the final draft of this book on 14 January 2005. A week later, on 22 January, my father, the literary historian and writer Atilla Özkırımlı, passed away, leaving behind more than 20 books, an encyclopaedia and hundreds of students whom he helped to find their own Ithacas. As for me, the road has only become longer and more arduous . . .

The author wishes to thank Ted R. Gurr, Monty Marshall and the Center for International Development and Conflict Management for granting permission to reproduce copyright material from *Peace and Conflict 2003: A Global Survey of Armed Conflicts, Self-Determination Movements, and Democracy*; and Coşkun Aral for permission to use material from his *Sözün Bittiği Yer* on the jacket. Every effort has been made to trace all the copyright-holders, but if any have been inadvertently overlooked, the publishers will be pleased to make the necessary arrangement at the first opportunity.

1
Introduction

The nationalists have no country. This is not just an eccentric attempt to capture the reader's attention by turning a famous aphorism on its head. Paradoxical and puzzling as it may seem, this pithy statement encapsulates two important insights on nationalism, which have provided the impetus for this book.

The first insight concerns the disparity between the claims to nationhood and the realities on the ground, and tells us that the idea of a 'pure', homogeneous nation is a fiction. Homogeneity may indeed be the nationalist's ultimate dream, as Ernest Gellner's famous definition of nationalism as 'a political doctrine which holds that the political and national unit should be congruent' reminds us (1983: 1). Yet such correspondence has been an aberration, not a constant, in human history. Rulers of most premodern societies did not share the norms of those over whom they ruled; 'and, typically, there were several sets of norms, given the presence of many and varied ethnic groups within most territories' (Hall 2003: 16). The idea of a pure, homogeneous nation continues to be a deceptive and dangerous fiction in the modern world, where no state is a nation in the sense in which nationalists use the term. Ethnic and cultural pluralism continues to be the norm, and the content and boundaries of the nation are ceaselessly contested by those who are not considered to be, and in most cases do not consider themselves to be, part of the officially defined nation. In short, national homogeneity, in the sense of a complete congruence between national and political units, has always been a pipe-dream.

The second insight, on the other hand, draws our attention to what unites various nationalisms, rather than what divides them.

1

We have already seen that we should think of nationalism in the plural or as a site where different constructions of the nation contest and negotiate with each other. What unites these different views is a particular language, a cluster of claims that are commonly made in describing nations. Nationalism is in this sense a form of discourse, a way of seeing and interpreting the world. The discourse of nationalism asserts that humanity is divided into distinct nations, each with its own separate past, present and destiny. Human beings can only fulfill themselves if they belong to a national community, the membership of which remains superior to all other forms of belonging – familial, gender, class, religious, regional, and so on (Suny 2001a, 2001b). The discourse of nationalism is also universalist (in theory, if not in practice): it presupposes a system of nation-states in which each nation has a right to self-determination. All nationalisms, however varied their internal nature, draw on this common frame of reference to make their demands (Calhoun 1993, 1997). In other words, the discourse of nationalism is what defines diverse movements, ideologies and policies as 'nationalisms'.

Combined, these two insights show us that nationalisms are not as internally homogeneous and externally heterogeneous as nationalists would have us believe. The 'immaculate nation' of the nationalists has never existed: the nationalists have no country as they know it!

Context

The idea of a homogeneous and unique nation may well be a fiction of the nationalists; yet as a frame of reference and a principle of social and political organization, nationalism is ubiquitous. Given that, it is striking that nations and nationalism have been a peripheral concern of social and political theory for much of the twentieth century. It is only in the last two decades that the academia has emerged from its long slumber and begun to explore nationalism and its paraphernalia. The upshot of this belated interest has been an avalanche of books and articles on nationalism, the publication of a number of specialized academic journals and the establishment of research centers, institutes and degree programmes in various universities across the world.

The revival of interest in nationalism has been prompted by the convergence of a number of trends in world politics. Chief among these is the proliferation of ethnic conflicts in many parts of the world in the wake of the euphoria of 1989. As Marshall and Gurr remark in *Peace and Conflict 2003*, the biennial report of the Center for International Development and Conflict Management (home to the Minorities at Risk Project), ethnonational wars for independence are commonly considered to be the main threat to international peace and regional security in the post-Cold War period. The report documents 70 armed conflicts for autonomy or independence waged by territorially concentrated ethnic groups since the 1950s, without counting the peoples of former European colonies. These conflicts, the report informs us, spiked sharply upward at the end of the Cold War, from five ongoing wars in the 1950s to a maximum of 48 in 1991 (see Table 1.1). Yet the report also notes that the number of these conflicts has declined even more precipitously, to 22 ongoing conflicts as of the beginning of 2003, a smaller number than any time in the last quarter-century. What is more, fighting in most of these conflicts is low-level and de-escalating – thanks to a marked increase in local, regional and international efforts to contain or settle wars of self-determination.

Table 1.1 Armed conflicts for self-determination and their outcomes, 1956–2002

Period	New armed conflicts	Ongoing at end of period	Conflicts contained	Conflicts settled or won
Before 1956		4		
1956–60	4	8	0	0
1961–65	5	12	0	1
1966–70	5	15	2	0
1971–75	11	23	0	3
1976–80	10	31	2	0
1981–85	5	35	0	1
1986–90	10	41	2	2
1991–95	16	39	7	11
1996–2000	2	28	7	6
2001–2002	3	22	9	0
TOTAL	72		29	24

Source: Marshall and Gurr 2003: 30

In short, the real picture is more complicated than the everyday media clichés would have us believe.

There are two reasons for this. The first is what Brubaker and Laitin call a 'coding bias' in the ethnic direction. Noting that the actual instances of ethnic and nationalist violence remain rare measured against the universe of possible instances, they draw our attention to the impact of prevailing interpretive frames. Today, they argue, 'the ethnic frame is immediately and widely available and legitimate; it imposes itself on, or at least suggests itself to, actors and analysts alike'. This generates the coding bias in question:

> Today, we . . . are no longer blind *to* ethnicity, but we may be blinded *by* it. Our ethnic bias in framing may lead us to over-estimate the incidence of ethnic violence by unjustifiably seeing ethnicity at work everywhere and thereby artifactually multiplying instances of 'ethnic violence'. More soberingly, since coding or framing is partly constitutive of the phenomenon of ethnic violence, not simply an external way of registering and coming to terms with it intellectually, our coding bias may actually increase the incidence . . . of ethnic violence. (Brubaker and Laitin 1998: 428)

The second factor complicating the picture concerns the prevailing tendency to locate nationalism on the periphery, seen by many as the seedbed of atavistic feelings and primordial hostilities. Nationalism, in this view, becomes the property of 'others', not of 'us'. 'Our' nationalism is 'patriotism', a benign and necessary force, a kind of battery capable of storing power for future use without needing to be active all the time. Yet, as Billig maintains, this accepted use of the word 'nationalism' is misleading, as it overlooks the nationalism of the established nations where there is a continual 'flagging', or reminding, of nationhood. 'Nationhood provides a continual background for their political discourses, for cultural products, and even for the structuring of newspapers' (1995: 8; for the image of 'battery' see Canovan 1996: 3).

This takes us to the second major trend of the post-Cold War period, namely the revival of nationalism in the Western world. This may take not only the form of separatism and regionalism as mentioned above, but also of increasing xenophobia against immigrants, evidenced by the startling electoral successes of a string of radical nationalist parties in many European countries (see Table 1.2). Billig's observation is valid here as well: most analysts in the West explain the sharp increase in ultranationalist votes by the tendency of voters to perceive the ever-growing number of immigrants as the source of the social and economic ills that bedevil them, thus turning a blind eye to the myriad ways in which nationalism is reproduced. In fact, for them, immigrants are the 'usual suspects' even in the case of mounting ethnic unrest, a tendency Appadurai wittily calls 'the germ theory of ethnic strife'. This theory takes Western democracies to be fundamentally mature and civilized, but now at risk as they have become host to populations, typically from the Third World, that carry the primordial bug – 'the bug, that is, that makes them attached in infantile ways to blood, language, religion, and memory and makes them violence-prone and ill-equipped for participation in mature civic societies' (Appadurai 1996: 143).

We might add to this the terror and violence caused by the collision between various ethnoreligious movements and a bellicose American nationalism (see Juergensmeyer 2002 and Lieven 2004)

Table 1.2 Electoral results of radical nationalist parties in national parliamentary elections in Europe, 1996–2003

	1996–99		2000–2003	
	Votes (%)	*Seats*	*Votes (%)*	*Seats*
National Alliance, Italy	15.7	93	12	99
Pim Fortuyn's List, The Netherlands	–	–	17	26
Freedom Party, Austria	26.9	52	10	18
Flemish Block, Belgium	9.9	15	11.6	18
Progress Party, Norway	15.3	25	14.7	26
National Front, France	14.9	1	11.3	–
Danish People's Party, Denmark	7.4	13	12	22

– what Tariq Ali (2002) calls 'the clash of fundamentalisms' – and we have the big picture: a global kingdom where nationalism enjoys untrammelled sovereignty.

No account of the contemporary political/cultural landscape would be complete, however, without mentioning two other trends, hailed by many as insurgent forces that undermine the global reign of nationalism, namely globalization and identity politics. The story is a familiar one: the nation-state is besieged from on top by the growing interdependence of the planet and from below by the rediscovery of long-forgotten cultural (read subnational) identities. These two counter-trends are mutually reinforcing, with globalization both provoking and facilitating identity politics, and identity politics encouraging the growth of transnational solidarities. Thus we live in a postmodern world, a world in which we are all strangers (Bauman 1998, Kristeva 1993). This has led to the crystallization of new forms of identity and community, mostly in the absence of territorial bases. Diasporas are the emblems of such formations, or in the words of Tölölyan, 'the exemplary communities of the transnational moment' (1996: 428). It may be too premature to write an obituary to the nationality principle, but it no longer constitutes the only, or the most important, form of belonging as it did for most of the twentieth century.

This story may be suggestive at first glance, but it needs to be qualified in important ways. It is indeed true that one of the distinctive features of our time is the demand by various groups for the political recognition of their distinct identities. The opportunities provided by globalization, notably increasing geographical mobility and dramatic advances in media and communication technologies, make it easier for members of minority cultures to keep in touch with each other and their home countries, hence to resist assimilation and mobilize for greater public recognition. However, it is not clear why this should be seen as a threat to nationalism. Most of the demands for cultural recognition are also instances of nationalism, perhaps on a smaller scale, and stripped of the territorial component. The culture that needs to be recognized is in most cases an 'ethnic' or 'national' one. Hence demands for public recognition of cultural distinctiveness may be a threat to majority nationalism, but certainly not to nationalism *per se*, as the groups that seek recognition draw on the same discourse to frame their demands.

As for globalization, it is now well-established that the relationship between nationalism and processes of globalization is not a zero-sum game (see for example Waters 1995; Holton 1998; Held *et al.* 1999; Scholte 2000). Globalization not only undermines, but also reinforces, nationalism both by provoking nationalist reactions and by facilitating (different types of) nation-formation (Hutchinson 2003; Guibernau 2001; Held 1996). More importantly, as Sassen notes, 'the global does not (yet) fully encompass the lived experience of actors or the domain of institutional orders and cultural formations; it persists as a partial condition'. However, continues Sassen, this 'should not suggest that the global and the national are discrete conditions that mutually exclude each other. To the contrary, they significantly overlap and interact in ways that distinguish our contemporary moment' (2000: 215).

Finally, diasporas may be transnational in the sense of extending across state borders, but they usually insist on being nations of a sort themselves (Goldmann *et al.* 2000: 12). Diasporas have been very active in the generation of nationalist ideas and movements, and continue to be active participants of ethnic and national conflicts in the 'homeland' – leading Benedict Anderson to coin the term 'long-distance nationalism' (1998: chapter 3; see also Yuval-Davis 2003: 139–41). Hence the picture of diasporas as 'the exemplary communities of the transnational moment' is at best a partial one.

To sum up, contemporary trends in world politics make it clear that it is too early to write nationalism off as an outdated form of consciousness. Whether we like it or not, 'being national is the condition of our times', as Eley and Suny remark in the Introduction to their 1996 reader, and the need to understand nationalism is more pressing than ever.

Aims

Very broadly, this book aims to critically engage with the fast-growing theoretical and normative literature on nationalism in order to make better sense of the challenges it poses at the onset of a new century. More specifically, it has three objectives: to offer a critical overview of the contemporary debates on nationalism; to sketch the contours of a theoretical and normative approach that would enable us to question the claims of nationalism; and to identify and discuss some of the alternatives to nationalism. Three interconnected claims will guide my analysis of these issues. First, neither nationalism nor its widespread emotional appeal should be taken for granted, but problematized and studied carefully. I shall argue that this could best be done through a 'social constructionist' approach which enables us to identify the contingent, heterogeneous and shifting nature of nations, thus sensitizing us to the central role of reproduction in sustaining nationalisms. Such an approach contributes to our understanding of nationalism in four concrete ways:

- It helps us to unearth the historical nature of nationalism and produce a theoretical account of the social and political processes through which national identities are constructed, sustained and contested.
- It allows us to discover which interests are secured in and by particular constructions of nationhood.
- It alerts us to the waxing and waning nature of nationhood, thereby enabling us to assess the degree of success of particular nation-making projects.
- It increases our sensitivity to the institutional and discursive mechanisms through which nationalisms are maintained, and just as importantly, resisted or challenged.

Second, nationalism cannot be understood properly without taking its normative dimension into account. There are two rather obvious reasons for this. First, as a quarter century of feminist, post-structuralist and postmodernist theorizing has made it all the more clear, our analyses are intimately tied up with our current political concerns and normative judgements – and this is nowhere more true than in the case of nationalism. More importantly, however, nationalism is itself a normative principle, or an ethical doctrine; it states a view about how the world should be organized. Yet very few of the existing sociological accounts of nationalism engage with its normative dimension, leaving this to political theorists and philosophers. This is equally true of the classics of nationalism studies and of the growing number of readers and introductions to the field (see Spencer and Wollman 2002 and Day and Thompson 2004 for partial exceptions). The problem with much discussion of nationalism in the field of political theory, on the other hand, is exactly the opposite: they are, for the most part, impervious to the insights of contemporary debates in sociology and political science. I shall cross over this disciplinary divide and complement my theoretical analysis with an evaluation of the normative claims of nationalism, thereby bridging the gap between the two literatures.

Third, we need to adopt a critical stance towards the existing nation-state order. Many of the problems that have preoccupied thinkers and activists of all political persuasions for centuries are still with us, be it economic inequalities, wars or intolerance. The track record of nationalism in solving these multifarious problems has not been terribly encouraging. It is thus reasonable to believe that without a radical rethinking of the system of nation-states and a careful consideration of its alternatives, we shall not make headway in solving the problems humanity continues to face. This is all the more important in today's highly globalized world, where the successful resolution of the most urgent problems requires a greater level of international cooperation.

Some of the specific questions I shall address in this context are:

- What is nationalism? What are the different types of nationalism?
- Where does the theoretical debate on nationalism stand today? What are some of the issues that continue to bedevil the theory of nationalism?
- How can we best make sense of nationalism? What kind of approach could enable us to engage critically with appeals to nationhood?
- What are the normative claims of nationalism? What is 'national partiality'? Is national partiality compatible with principles of universal justice and equality?
- Are nations moral communities? What are the problems with the project of rehabilitating nationalism?
- Is it possible to talk of 'good' and 'bad' nationalisms? What is 'liberal nationalism'? Can the liberal nationalist model work?
- What is the relationship between multiculturalism and nationalism? Can multiculturalism offer an alternative to nationalism? What are the chances for constructive dialogue between different cultures?
- What are the implications of the processes of globalization for

nationalism and nation-states? What are the prospects of cosmopolitanism in an increasingly interdependent world?
* Can we envisage a world without nations? What are the major
obstacles to a postnational order?

As these questions indicate, the scope of this book is comprehensive and ambitious. It covers a number of disciplines, ranging from
sociology and political science to history, cultural anthropology
and political theory. It engages with a vast array of issues and
debates, and intends to bridge the gap between the theoretical and
normative literatures. Given this, two preliminary remarks on the
the scope of the book are in order. First, as its title reflects, the
scope of the present book is more contemporary than historical.
Hence it will not chart the historical evolution of nations and
nationalism, although it will touch upon the question of the
modernity of nations, a problem that continues to preoccupy most
theorists of nationalism. This choice of focus is deliberate, as
I believe that time is ripe for engaging with contemporary nationalisms, that is, for exploring their fundamental characteristics,
their continuing appeal and their prospects in an increasingly
globalized world, instead of tracing their roots in the haze of
history – in short, to focus on the present and the future, rather
than the past.

This will necessarily reflect on my selection of texts and writers,
the second point I would like to raise with regard to the scope of
this book. Since my aim is to provide an overview of the state of play
in the field, I shall refer to those canonical debates that remain relevant today through the eyes of their current protagonists rather
than their originators. Consequently, I shall refer to the classics of
nationalism studies sparingly, only when it is imperative. In that
regard, this book could be read as a companion, or complement,
to my first book, *Theories of Nationalism: A Critical Introduction* (2000),
which covered the classical theoretical debates in the field.

Structure

This book falls roughly into three parts. Chapters 2 and 3 cover
the conceptual and theoretical debates in the field; Chapters 4, 5
and 6 address the normative challenges posed by and to national-

ism, and provide an assessment of the future of nations and nationalisms in a globalizing world; finally, the last two chapters sketch the outline of a theoretical approach to nationalism and discuss the possibilities and the need for a postnational order.

I begin by exploring the conceptual problems that afflict the study of nations and nationalism. Thus Chapter 2 addresses two fundamental questions around which the conceptual debates swirl: are nations objective or subjective phenomena? Is nationalism about culture or politics? It then engages critically with various attempts to develop typologies of nationalism, laying special emphasis on the distinction between civic and ethnic forms of nationalism, probably the most influential distinction in the field. The chapter concludes by proposing an alternative conceptualization which stresses the discursive qualities of nationalism. Chapter 3 aims to summarize the current state of play in the field so far as the theory of nations and nationalism is concerned. Focusing in particular on issues of periodization and the nature of nations, it takes up two questions that continue to trouble theorists of nationalism: what is the relationship between premodern ethnic communities and modern nations? Are nations invented and imagined, or are they simply reconstructed out of pre-existing cultural materials? It then turns to recent developments in the field and reviews the attempts to address issues that have been glossed over by mainstream theorizations of nationalism.

Chapter 4 looks into the recent revival of interest in nationalism in Western political theory. It first outlines some of the arguments put forward in defense of nationalism and summarizes the main criticisms raised against each of them. It then wrestles with the issue of 'national partiality', the idea that we owe special obligations to our fellow nationals, and tries to assess the extent to which this claim is compatible with principles of universal justice and equality. The chapter concludes by addressing the question of whether nations should be treated as moral communities. Chapter 5 examines the thorny relationship between nationalism and multiculturalism, devoting particular attention to the question of whether multiculturalism poses a threat to nationalism, the major question preoccupying liberal political theorists in the last two decades. The chapter first sketches the contours of the liberal nationalist project with a view to bringing into focus the affinities between liberal interpretations of nationalism and multicultural-

ism. It then outlines the main arguments of liberal multiculturalism, focusing on the works of Will Kymlicka and Charles Taylor,
and offers a summary of the charges brought against them. The
chapter concludes by considering 'dialogical' models of multiculturalism that operate outside a liberal framework.

Chapter 6 discusses the implications of the processes of globalization for the future of nations and nationalism. Having provided
a brief overview of the conceptual debates on globalization, it
tackles the question of whether globalization is leading to the
emergence of new forms of political organization, thereby sowing
the seeds of the extinction of the nation-state. It then explores
the cosmopolitan project, and considers the extent to which
cosmopolitanism forms a viable alternative to nationalism. The
chapter ends by suggesting that we should conceptualize globalization not as accomplished fact, but as an opportunity to imagine
postnational forms of community and belonging. Building on
these observations, Chapter 7 sketches the outline of a social constructionist approach to nationalism. Clearing away two common
misconceptions surrounding the idea of 'social construction', it
first identifies the premises upon which such an approach is based.
It then attempts to map out the dimensions of the nationalist discourse, with a view to clarifying what distinguishes it from other,
similar, discourses. Finally, after a brief digression on the historical
debates on the need to transcend the nation-state, Chapter 8 considers some of the objections to postnational perspectives and provides a qualified defense of postnationalism.

2
What is Nationalism?

'A word is like a coin', says Guido Zernatto in his pioneering study of the history of the word 'nation', first published more than half a century ago. Every coin in the course of its history, Zernatto notes, is subjected to different changes in value. Exactly the same applies to the value of a word: 'it can at one time denote more, at another less . . . And just as for the coin, there comes also for the word the day on which it is "removed from circulation"' (2000 [1944]: 13). Nothing could describe the history of the word 'nation' better.

The etymological hunt for the roots of the word 'nation' takes us back to the Latin word *natio*, meaning 'something born'. In ordinary speech, this word referred to a group of people who belonged together because of similarity of birth. Yet the Romans never designated themselves as a *natio*, reserving the term to a native 'community of foreigners'. In this initial usage, the word possessed a derogatory connotation as these people were seen as standing outside, if not below, the Roman society (Zernatto 2000 [1944]; Greenfeld 2001).

In its original meaning of a community of foreigners, the word 'nation' was applied to communities of students in medieval universities. On the strange soil of the university cities, quips Zernatto, 'the students were just as much foreigners as were once the immigrants into Roman centers of population' (2000 [1944]: 15). Students originating in geographically related areas were defined as a nation, housed together in quarters that were also shared by their professors. These students participated in university disputes with their professors, and thus were identified with particular intellectual positions. This led to a change in the meaning of the word 'nation', which now signified more: not only a community of origin or foreigners, but also a union of purpose, a community of opinion (*ibid.*: 16; Greenfeld 2001: 252).

It was in the sense of a community of opinion that the concept was utilized in yet another context, the ecclesiastical councils of the late Middle Ages. Representatives of various princes and potentates were assembled in these councils, debating on the future of the Respublica Christiana. The different parties to the debates, sharing similar opinions on the fate of the republic, also bore the name 'nations'. This time, however, the word designated not only 'foreigners' who found themselves thrown together for a time or pilgrims who met by chance, or students. The delegates in the councils were above all deputies, representatives of cultural or political authority. This way, the word lost all its derogatory connotations and acquired a honorific and, more importantly, aristocratic meaning (*ibid.*: 18–22; Greenfeld 2001: 252–3).

In the course of time, the term 'nation' as a community of representatives, or of elites, was expanded from below with the pressure of broader sections of the citizenry 'who had come into money and esteem', and who thus wanted to draw a clear line between themselves and the lower strata. Now understood as a synonym of the 'people', 'nation' gradually acquired its modern political meaning and became a word of fashion (Zernatto 2000 [1944]: 23).

The question of exactly when this happened, that is, when the concepts of 'nation' and 'people' were equated and when the word 'nation' became common property, is a source of deep controversy among scholars of nationalism, as it relates to questions of theorization and periodization. Suffice it to say that the word 'nation' was in wide usage from the eighteenth century. The word 'nationalism', by contrast, is of more recent vintage. Hence Walker Connor, following G. de Bertier Sauvigny, believes that the word first appeared in the literature in 1798 (1994: 98). Peter Alter, on the other hand, claims that the term 'nationalism' first appeared in 1774 in a text written by Herder (1989: 4).

The aim of the following sections is to engage critically with the contemporary conceptual debates in the field. I shall begin by addressing two questions that bedevil the definition of nations and nationalism:

- Are nations objective or subjective phenomena?
- Is nationalism about culture or politics?

I shall then outline the various attempts to avoid the dilemmas these questions create by developing typologies of nationalisms, devoting particular attention to the distinction between civic and ethnic forms of nationalism, the most influential distinction in the field.

I shall conclude this chapter by proposing an alternative conceptualization of nationalism, and argue that nationalism is best understood as a particular form of discourse. I shall also contend that this conceptualization enables us to move beyond the objective/subjective and culture/politics dichotomies, and helps us unmask what is common to all forms of nationalism.

Competing Definitions of Nationalism

As Dankwart Rustow observed more than 30 years ago, 'nationalist writers have done little to clarify what they mean by nation', and thus 'have generated more heat than light' (1968: 9). This is still true today, after three decades of musing over various definitions and possible meanings, not only because the concepts of 'nation' and 'nationalism' are 'essentially contested', in that they have, like most other concepts in social sciences, several competing definitions that make the quest for the perfect meaning inevitably frustrating. It is also because politics is deeply implicated in issues of definition. After all, any definition of the nation legitimates some claims and delegitimates others (Calhoun 1993: 215). Yet the fact remains that definitions abound, and the most fundamental conceptual divide in the literature concerns the relative weight to be attached to objective and subjective elements in the definition of nations.

Objective vs. Subjective Definitions

The catalogue of objective markers used in the definition of nations is a familiar one: ethnicity, language, religion, territory, common history, common descent or ancestry (kinship), or, more generically, common culture. Probably the most famous definition of the nation based on objective elements comes from Joseph Stalin, who was regarded in the early years of the Bolshevik movement as the highest party authority on the national question. A nation, Stalin argues, is 'a historically constituted, stable community of people, formed on the basis of a common language, territory, economic life, and psychological make-up manifested in a common culture' (1994 [1913]: 20). None of the above characteristics taken separately is sufficient to define a nation, according to Stalin, and it is sufficient for a single one of these characteristics to be lacking for the nation to cease to exist.

There are several obvious problems with 'objective' definitions of nationhood – some of which have been alluded to way before Stalin came up with his famous definition. To begin with, it is not clear which characteristics a group of people must possess in order to become a nation, and how many of them. Hence Renan asked, as early as 1882:

> How is it that Switzerland, which has three languages, two religions, and three or four races, is a nation, when Tuscany, which is so homogeneous, is not one? . . . France is [at once] Celtic, Iberic, and Germanic . . . The United States and England, Latin America and Spain, speak the same languages yet do not form single nation. Conversely, Switzerland, so well made . . . numbers three or four languages. (1990 [1882]: 12, 14, 16)

The upshot is that no nation will possess all the necessary qualifications and any attempt to offer an inventory of traits will end up looking as a roster of exceptions (Bauman 1992).

The picture is further complicated by the all too often forgotten fact that objective differences between neighbouring populations are minimal. In fact, most claims to national distinctiveness are either implicitly or explicitly oriented towards very close neighbours – as the case of the Balkans has repeatedly shown (Greenfeld 2001; Miščević 2001). Ignatieff draws on Freud to explain this tendency, and argues that 'the smaller the real differences between two groups, the larger such differences are likely to loom in their imagination' (1999: 94).

Another problem with 'objective' definitions, noted by Barth, concerns the shifting quality of the cultural traits groups use in their dealings with others. The features that are taken into account, argues Barth, are not the sum of 'objective' differences, but only those which the actors themselves regard as significant. In that sense, it is better to view ethnic and national groups as 'organizational types', where individuals strategically manipulate their cultural identity by emphasizing or underplaying certain markers according to context. From this point of view, the critical focus of investigation needs to be the boundary that defines the group, not the cultural stuff it encloses (1969: 14–15).

This brings us to the issue of 'agency'. We have already seen that ethnic or national groups are not simply the product of pre-existing cultural differences, but are the consequences of organizational work undertaken by their members. Thus, 'creative political action is required to transform a segmented and disunited population into a coherent nationality' (Eley and Suny 1996: 7). This necessarily involves a conscious and deliberate effort to reduce the importance of objective differences within the group while emphasizing the group's uniqueness *vis-à-vis* outsiders (Tamir 1993: 66).

In short, all attempts to arrive at an 'objective' definition of nation are necessarily arbitrary, hence fundamentally misguided. These attempts, Bauman argues, stem from a common error of mistaking what ought to be the topic of explanation for the explanatory resource:

> it takes off from the acceptance of the 'objective reality' of the nation, de-problematizing thereby the very elusiveness and contingency of the nation's precarious existence which nationalisms try hard to conceal . . . The search for an 'objective definition' obliquely legitimizes the nationalistic claims that it is the sharing of certain attributes that 'makes a nation' . . . rather than exposing the fact that the 'commonality' itself . . . is always an artefact of boundary-drawing activity: always contentious and contested, glossing over some (potentially disruptive) differentiations and representing some other (objectively minor) differences as powerful and decisive separating factors. (1992: 677)

Given these problems, very few scholars define nations today solely on the basis of objective markers, using them instead in conjunction with subjective factors. Some of most commonly cited subjective elements in defining nations include self-awareness, solidarity, loyalty and common (or collective) will. Hence for Renan, a nation is 'a large-scale solidarity, constituted by the feeling of the sacrifices that one has made in the past and of those that one is prepared to make in the future' (1990 [1882]: 19). For Weber, it is 'a community of sentiment which would adequately manifest itself in a state of its own' (1994 [1948]: 25); for Connor, it refers to 'a group of people who believe they are ancestrally related' (1994: 212) and, more recently, for Hechter, to 'a relatively large group of genetically unrelated people with high solidarity' (2000: 11).

The key to 'subjective' definitions to nationhood is the issue of 'self-awareness'. For many commentators, until the members of a particular group are aware of their uniqueness *vis-à-vis* others, it is merely an ethnic group and not a nation. In other words, a nation only has life when it is an idea or representation in the minds of most members of the group in question (Tyrell 1996: 243). In that sense, national communities are constituted by belief; they exist only when their members recognize each other as belonging to the same community, and believe that they share certain characteristics (Miller 1995: 22).

This also sheds light on the relationship between objective and subjective elements. Objective markers do not of themselves make nations; yet they are necessary to generate the feeling of commonality that gives birth to or sustains the nation. Thus, it is not surprising that most nations seek to validate their existence with reference to ostensibly objective features. For Tamir, this is in fact a necessity since the belief that they share certain attributes may lead individuals to care more for each other and develop mutual responsibilities:

> Hence, despite the fact that one cannot claim that a certain nation exists just because its members share certain objective features (or have the illusion that they share some), it is still plausible to claim that the fact that they share these features played a constitutive role in the formation of the nation. (1996: 90; see also Lichtenberg 1997: 160)

Most writers who prefer a 'subjective' definition of nationhood accept that nations may have their ends, just as they had their beginnings. Feelings may change and bring about the dissolution of existing nations or the emergence of new ones. Nations, in other words, exist so long as their members share a feeling of common membership (Tamir 1993: 66; see also Renan 1990 [1882]). 'Subjective' definitions are not without problems however. The first problem relates to the issue of specifying the right unit. Even if we admit that a group of people becomes a nation when its members become aware of their uniqueness, the question of 'which people' still remains. In other words, why do we feel we are related to these particular people and not to others?

A second, closely related, problem concerns the issue of distinguishing nations from other, similar, groupings. Solidarity, self-awareness and loyalty characterize many other groupings, from families and religious groups to voluntary associations. Subjective feelings may be the minimum condition in defining a nation, but they do not in themselves constitute nations (Calhoun 1997: 4; Brighouse 1996).

It needs to be pointed out that both of these problems could be avoided by using objective and subjective factors in combination – arguing that only those people who already share certain attributes feel that they are related. But this takes us back to the problems associated with objective elements (which elements are necessary, how many, and so on) and reduces the formation of nations to a passage from 'nation *an sich*' into 'nation *für sich*', assuming the existence of already formed unities and common group interests (Bauman 1992: 677).

More generally, we need to ask ourselves whether nations are voluntary communities or not. In other words, is subjective identification enough? The answer to this question appears to be negative. It may seem convenient to see the nation as a product of individual or collective will. Yet can we really question our national identity at will? After all, the existence of any particular nation confronts its members as part of objective reality:

> The nation I belong to may be all in the mind, but it is not all in *my* mind and I cannot alter the situation by an act of will . . . Any particular individual confronted by a well-established convention cannot will it away . . . Nations also grow, change and decay as a result of myriad acts and opinions, but this is not to say that individuals can simply opt in or opt out. Very often, of course, national consciousness is buttressed by institutional and legal forms, the apparatus of states and citizenship. But even

where these are absent, national identities can confront individuals as solid and insuperable social realities. (Canovan 1996: 55; see also Norman 1999)

It seems safe to assume at this stage that neither 'objective' nor 'subjective' definitions are satisfactory. And particular combinations of both sets of factors are not immune to the criticisms that are raised against any one of them. Let me now turn to an issue that undermines efforts to arrive at an acceptable definition of nationalism, namely the relative salience of culture and politics in the formation of nations.

Culture or Politics?

Is nationalism about culture or politics? This simple question stands at the heart of a heated debate on the nature of nationalism. For a number of influential scholars, nationalism is primarily a political ideal, aiming at independent statehood or some form of political autonomy (see for example Motyl 1999 and Hechter 2000). Some in fact go so far as to claim that 'to the degree that a given group aims for something less than complete sovereignty then it is perforce less nationalist' (Hechter 2000: 8). In this view, national identities are 'political' identities, 'connected to the political community with which one identifies, and cultural difference is not a crucial or even necessary element' (Moore 2001: 14).

There are two potential problems with this view. The first problem is terminological. Too tight an association between nationalism and statehood may lead (and has often led) to what Connor (1994) calls a 'terminological chaos', with the term 'nation' being used as a substitute for the state, a territorial juridical unit – hence the obvious misnomers the United Nations or the League of Nations. Secondly, such a usage may become too restrictive, if it is not carefully qualified. First, groups that lack states may sometimes harbor nationalist aims. In fact, the case for statehood is often predicated on the assumption of nationhood. Second, most states today are multinational (Lichtenberg 1997: 159). This has led some scholars to opt for a cultural definition of nationalism. Hence for Tamir, the right to national self-determination stakes a cultural rather than a political claim, namely the right to preserve the existence of a nation as a distinct cultural entity. In that sense, 'national claims are not synonymous with demands for political sovereignty' (1993: 57). Connor makes a similar point, arguing that most members of national minorities are prepared to settle for something less than independent statehood (1994: 82).

Cultural definitions are also blamed for being too restrictive, this time by those who point to the dangers of downplaying the political side of the equation. According to Calhoun, for example, long-existing cultural patterns may have contributed to the crystallization of national identities, but the meaning and form of these identities have been transformed in the modern era, in the process of state formation (1997: 10). Cohen puts the same point even more forcefully: '. . . ethnicity is essentially a political phenomenon, as traditional customs are used only as idioms, and as mechanisms for political alignments. People do not kill one another because their customs are different' (1969, cited in Willford 2001: 7).

The way out of this conundrum is to see nationalism as both a cultural and a political phenomenon. As Eley and Suny point out:

> If politics is the ground upon which the category of the nation was first proposed, culture was the terrain where it was elaborated, and in this sense nationality is best conceived as a complex, uneven, and unpredictable process, forged from an interaction of cultural coalescence and specific political intervention, which cannot be reduced to static criteria of language, territory, ethnicity or culture. (1996: 8; for similar views see Delanty and O'Mahony 2002 and Cullingford 2000)

Eley and Suny's observation also points to the futility of quibbling over the issue of 'objective' versus 'subjective' definitions. It is true that most nationalisms presume the existence of a shared culture which provides the material out of which the nation is forged. Yet those prior commonalities should not be 'reified' or 'naturalized', as if they have always existed in some essential way. 'What looks from outside and from a distance as a bounded group appears much more divided and contested at closer range. Culture is more often not what people share, but what they choose to fight over' (*ibid.*: 9).

To sum up, nationalism is not about culture or politics, it is about both. It involves the 'culturalization' of politics and the 'politicization' of culture. This final point will be crucial when discussing various typologies of nationalism, the topic of the next section.

Types of Nationalism

The project of identifying different types of nationalism can be seen as a response to the conceptual debates broached in the previous section. Many writers have tended to avoid the tough choice between culture and politics or between objective and subjective factors in defining nationalism and nations respectively by associating particular types of nationalism with one or the other aspect – instead of rejecting the choice in the first place or trying to go beyond it. This gave birth to perhaps the most far-reaching distinction in the field, that between civic (variously labelled as political, individualistic, voluntary) and ethnic (variously labelled as cultural, collectivistic, organic) nationalism.

Two Types of Nationalism?

We can trace the origins of the dichotomy between ethnic and civic nationalism back to Hans Kohn's influential distinction between Western and Eastern forms of nationalism. Kohn's distinction was mainly based on geographical criteria. In the Western world, Kohn argued, nationalism was a political occurrence. It was preceded by the formation of the national state or coincided with it. In Central and Eastern Europe and in Asia, on the other hand, nationalism arose later and at a more backward stage of social and political development. In conflict with the existing state pattern, it found its first expression in the cultural field and sought for its justification in the fact of a community held together by traditional ties of kinship and status (1958 [1944]: 329–34; see Calhoun, forthcoming, for a stimulating reassessment of Kohn's distinction).

Kohn's classification has been given a new lease of life in the post-1989 period, in the wake of the collapse of the Soviet Empire and the resurgence of nationalism in Europe. In the newer version, Western and Eastern nationalisms have been reconceptualized as civic and ethnic nationalism respectively, and based upon criteria of membership in the nation (Xenos 1996: 214).

In most formulations of civic nationalism, the nation is defined in terms of a shared commitment to the public institutions of the state and civil society. According to Ignatieff, probably the most vociferous defender of the distinction, civic nationalism maintains that 'the nation should be composed of all those – regardless of race, colour, creed, gender, language or ethnicity – who subscribe to the nation's political creed'. This nationalism is civic because 'it envisages the nation as a community of equal, rights-bearing citizens, united in patriotic attachment to a shared set of political practices and values'. This nationalism is also democratic in that it vests sovereignty in all of the people (1994: 3–4).

The civic conception of nationalism is generally associated with the name of Ernest Renan and exemplified in the events of the French Revolution. The concept of nation that characterizes this form of nationalism is subjective and individualistic – hence voluntary – as it emphasizes the will of the individuals that compose it (Seymour *et al.* 1996: 2–3).

Ethnic nationalism, by contrast, emphasizes common descent and cultural sameness. Here the nation is overtly exclusive. What gives unity to the nation, what makes it a home, 'a place of passionate attachment', is not the cold contrivance of shared rights, but the people's pre-existing characteristics: their language, religion, customs and traditions (Ignatieff 1994: 4). Ethnic nationalism claims that an individual's deepest attachments are inherited, not chosen; hence membership in the nation is not a matter of will. It can only be acquired by birth, through blood.

Ethnic nationalism is usually traced back to Johann Gottfried Herder, and exemplified by German Romanticism, which arose as a reaction to the Enlightenment and to its unconditional belief in reason. It is largely based on language, culture and tradition, and thus appeals to the objective features of our social lives (Seymour *et al.* 1996: 3).

It needs to be noted at this stage that other typologies (not necessarily dualistic) of nationalism have also been suggested in the literature. Examples include state-building, peripheral, irredentist and unification nationalisms of Hechter (2000: 16–17); state-reinforcing, state-subverting and state-creating nationalisms of Mann (1995: 46); the 'triadic nexus' of Brubaker (1996), which consists of the nationalizing nationalisms of newly independent states, transborder nationalisms of external national homelands and the autonomist nationalisms of national minorities. Yet the distinction between civic and ethnic nationalisms remains the most commonly used classification in the field and most of the alternative typologies have been produced with the aim of reforming or transcending that dichotomy. It is thus imperative to engage critically with this model and identify its theoretical weaknesses before unearthing the normative project that underlies it.

A Critique of the Ethnic–Civic Distinction

The ethnic–civic dichotomy is deeply flawed in many respects. The first, and perhaps the most fundamental, problem concerns the validity of the distinction itself. Since all nations lay claim to a unique place in history and to certain boundaries, all national identities are exclusionary. In that sense, all nations are ethnic nations (Motyl 1999: 78; see also Spencer and Wollman 2002: chapter 4 and Brown 2000: chapter 3). Brubaker elaborates on this, claiming that there are two different ways of mapping culture onto the ethnic–civic distinction. Ethnic nationalism may be interpreted narrowly, as involving an emphasis on descent. In this case, Brubaker argues, there is very little ethnic nationalism around, since on this view an emphasis on common culture has to be coded as a species of civic nationalism. If, however, ethnic nationalism is interpreted broadly, as ethnocultural, while civic nationalism is interpreted narrowly, as involving an acultural conception of citizenship, the problem is the opposite: 'civic nationalism gets defined out of existence, and virtually all nationalisms would be coded as ethnic or cultural'. Even the paradigmatic cases of civic nationalism, France and America, would cease to count as civic nationalism, since they have a crucial cultural component (1998: 299; see also Calhoun, forthcoming).

This problem applies in particular to the category of civic nationalism which has a certain oxymoronic quality:

> The term 'nation' connotes a community into which a person is born, while the term 'civic' connotes a community to which a person belongs by choice or common belief. And if the common belief is of putative common ancestry, or if the choice is to believe in a common ancestry, is the national idea still civic? (Laitin 2001a: 577)

Some writers have thus argued that the idea of civic nationalism, understood as a voluntary political community that is ethnically neutral, is a myth. Gans, for instance, contends that without resorting to common culture and history, loyalty to common principles cannot be considered nationalism, let alone civic nationalism (2003: 12). Nielsen makes a similar point, noting that a purely civic nationalism exists nowhere and could exist nowhere, given the very definition of what a nation is (1999b: 125). The fragility of this distinction is further reinforced by the fact that for the large majority of the citizens of so-called civic nations, there is no choice as to national identity. They acquire citizenship by birth, and not through an act of will. What is more, entry into another 'civic' nation may be as restrictive as in the case of 'ethnic' nations. In short, 'civic nations are communities of obligation which demand allegiance and which must therefore resist voluntaristic renunciations by present members' who are obliged to abide by the decisions made by past generations (Brown 2000: 61).

Some commentators emphasize the analytical use of distinguishing between ethnic and civic nationalisms, and argue that we should continue to use them as ideal-types, rather than seeking real-life incarnations of each. Others disagree, however, claiming that the distinction creates more problems than it solves, and propose alternative distinctions which can do the analytical work that is expected of the ethnic–civic distinction without the attendant confusions. One such alternative comes from Brubaker, who distinguishes between 'state-framed' and 'counter-state' understandings of nationalism. In the former, Brubaker argues, 'nation' is conceived as congruent with the state, as institutionally and territorially 'framed' by the state; in the latter, it is conceived as opposed to the territorial and institutional frame of the existing state. According to Brubaker, there is nothing necessarily 'civic' about state-framed nationalism. It is the state that is the point of reference, not the nation, and the state that frames the nation need not be democratic. Such a conception of nationalism can also accommodate ethnic and cultural aspects of nationhood in so far as these are framed and shaped by the state. Counter-state nationalisms, on the other hand, need not be ethnic. Counter-state definitions of nation may be based on territory, on distinct political histories prior to incorporation into a larger state and so on. In that sense, counter-state nationalisms may partake of 'civic' qualities (Brubaker 1998: 300–1).

A final danger with the ethnic–civic distinction concerns our moral preferences, more specifically, our tendency to use this distinction to laud particular nationalisms while discrediting others. This takes us directly to the normative project underlying the ethnic–civic classification.

Normative Implications

Most of the existing typologies of nationalism serve both descriptive and normative goals. The ethnic–civic distinction is no exception; it is used not only to classify the different forms of nationalism that exist in the modern world, but also to distinguish morally acceptable forms of nationalism from immoral, hence dangerous, ones. In this context, the normative project of distinguishing between civic and ethnic types of nationalism becomes one of differentiating the 'good' from the 'bad', and then associating the civic-good variety with the West and the ethnic-bad variety with the 'Rest'. In fact, critics hold that the whole project is 'part of a larger effort by contemporary liberals to channel national sentiments in a direction – civic nationalism – that seems consistent with the commitments to individual rights and diversity that they associate with a decent political order'. This is deeply misleading however:

> Designed to protect us from the dangers of ethnocentric politics, the civic/ethnic distinction itself reflects a considerable dose of ethnocentrism, as if the political identities French and American were not also culturally inherited artifacts, no matter how much they develop . . . The characterization of political community in the so-called civic nations as a rational and freely chosen allegiance to a set of political principles seems unthinkable . . . a mixture of self-congratulation and wishful thinking. (Yack 1999: 104–5)

There are two obvious problems with the normative project underlying the ethnic–civic distinction. The first problem, once again, concerns the spurious nature of the distinction itself. The 'civic' identity Canadian is no less a cultural inheritance than the supposedly 'ethnic' identity Québécois. The same is true for the American or French identities: 'However much they may have come to stand for certain political principles, each comes loaded with inherited cultural baggage that is contingent upon their peculiar histories' (*ibid.*: 106). This suggests that 'civic' nationalisms also have a cultural component. It is simply not true that membership in a 'civic' nation is based on allegiance to political principles, rather than on culture or descent. Thus native-born Americans automatically acquire citizenship by descent, and cannot be robbed of it if they turn out to be fundamentalists or fascists. This also applies to immigrants who are required not only to swear allegiance to the Constitution, but also to learn the English language and American history (Kymlicka 1999a: 133). Political values may be part of a culture, but it is not the only or the most important part; no American citizen would start to think of herself as French simply because she sympathizes with the political values of the French. In short, there is no purely political conception of nationalism: all nationalisms are cultural, in one way or another.

The second problem relates to the nature of so-called civic nationalisms. Even if we grant that the distinction between two forms of nationalism is valid, there is nothing to suggest that the civic variant is inherently progressive and benign. To begin with, most of today's so-called 'civic' nations are the product of earlier unsavoury histories, a point made by Renan more than a century ago. 'Unity is always effected by means of brutality', said the French historian, pointing to the massacres of Saint Bartholomew (where thousands of Huguenots were killed) which many French citizens have forgotten today (1990 [1882]: 11; see also A.D. Smith 2001: 41). Equally forgotten is the fact that the United States was founded only after much Native American blood has been shed and owes its unity to a brutal civil war. In short, a nation that is peaceful, secure and a favourable site for liberal democratic politics today usually has a past that no liberal democrat can comfortably look into (Canovan 1996: 104).

What is more, 'civic' nations can be as intolerant and cruel as the so-called 'ethnic' nations:

> After all, American citizens have been denounced and persecuted for clinging to unAmerican political principles as well as for their backgrounds. And as George Mosse reminds us, it was the decidedly civic nation of the French Jacobins that invented many of the techniques of persecution and mass paranoia

exploited by twentieth-century fascists and xenophobic nationalists. (Yack 1999: 115–16)

Examples can be multiplied. The problem here is the tendency of
those who defend 'civic' nationalism to overlook the multinational
nature of most modern states. The dominant culture in these states
is generally the culture of the ethnic majority which controls the
political institutions of the state. Yet there are also a number of
minority groups that do not share the culture of the majority. Civic
nationalists are either impervious to the plight of these groups, or
simply reluctant to recognize the conditions that often lead to their
exclusion from the public sphere as they cling to a non-cultural
conception of national membership.

In sum, the ethnic–civic distinction is bogus, both in theory and
in practice. The normative project of associating the civic-good
variant with Western countries, on the other hand, is simply
another example of liberal self-congratulation, with little explanatory power so far as actually existing nationalisms are concerned
(Beiner 1999: 4). This should remind us that distinguishing
between good and bad, progressive and regressive nationalisms is
a highly risky undertaking and that 'we are always dealing with a
double-edged sword' (Clifford 1998: 364).

Nationalism as Discourse

The discussion in the previous sections has provided us with two
insights regarding the definition of nations and nationalism. First,
we cannot effectively define nations in terms of objective markers
or subjective feelings alone. There is no perfect list of objective
characteristics that would make a nation. The term 'nation' can be
applied to populations which claim to have a preponderance of
the characteristics any such list would include – language, religion,
territory, common history, and so on. In that sense, recognition of
nations works through a pattern of what Wittgenstein called 'family
resemblance': the characteristics possessed, or, for that matter, the
number of characteristics possessed, by particular nations will vary;
so too the emphasis placed on a particular characteristic (for this
analogy, see Calhoun 1997: 4–6). Yet it is crucial to note that it is
not the characteristics themselves that count, but the claims that

are made about them. As Calhoun reminds us, nations are largely constituted by the claims themselves, and not the actual presence of this or that characteristic, which is, in any case, difficult to ascertain and never fixed (*ibid.*). As for subjective feelings of identification, we have already seen that they do not differentiate nations from other sorts of groupings for which similar feelings exist, such as families or religious groups. In short, there is no systematic way of designating a nation:

> Any attempt to do so can only be a purely arbitrary definition. Through a combination of historical conjunctures, national boundaries have been and continue to be drawn . . . There is no systematic way in which any social theoretical discourse can justify the state of nationhood in the one case and deny it in the other. (Zubaida 1978: 53)

Second, attempts to define nationalism in terms of either culture or politics are doomed to failure. What gives nationalism its power is its ability to bring the cultural and the political together. 'Cultural struggle is a struggle about culture before it is a struggle among cultures' (Brubaker and Cooper 2000: 32). This is exactly why the project of distinguishing between different types of nationalism, depending on whether they emphasize cultural or political criteria, does not work. Such an attempt obscures that which unites all nationalisms, namely that they are both cultural and political phenomena.

Given these insights, I would argue that what we need is an alternative conceptualization of nationalism, one that moves us beyond the objective/subjective and culture/politics dichotomies, while at the same time enabling us to capture what is common to all nationalisms. I suggest that both of these aims will be achieved if we see nationalism as a particular form of 'discourse' (for similar conceptualizations see Calhoun 1997; Finlayson 1998; Suny 2001b). By 'discourse' I mean, following Stuart Hall, 'sets of ready-made and preconstituted "experiencings" displayed and arranged through language' (1977: 322; the term 'discourse' owes a lot to the work of Michel Foucault of course; see for example Foucault 1981, 2002a [1972] and 2002b [1994]; for a useful introduction to the various uses of the term, see Mills 2004). This suggests that people live and experience through discourse in the sense that discourses impose frameworks that limit what can be experienced or the meaning that experience can assume, thereby influencing what can be said or done. Hence *nationalism is a particular way of seeing and interpreting the world, a frame of reference that helps us make sense of and structure the reality that surrounds us.*

It needs to be noted at the outset that the definition I propose has strong affinities with certain conceptions of ideology, which define it as

> the mental frameworks – the languages, the concepts, categories, imagery of thought, and the systems of representation – which different classes and social groups deploy in order to make sense of, define, figure out and render intelligible the way society works. (Hall 1996c: 26; see also van Dijk 1998)

This definition also shows that nationalism is in important ways a cognitive phenomenon, which works through categories and category-based knowledge. In that sense, it is embedded in our entire view of the world – not only conferring citizenship, but also shaping the way we structure our newspapers, the way we classify literatures and cinemas or the way we compete in the Olympic games (Brubaker 2002, 2004: chapter 3; Calhoun 1997).

Such a conceptualization of nationalism enables us to transcend the objective/subjective dichotomy by showing us that nationhood cannot be defined objectively, prior to political processes. This is so, because nations are partly made by nationalism. They exist only when their members understand themselves and the world around them through the discourse of nationalism:

> 'Nation' is a particular way of thinking about what it means to be a people, and how the people thus defined might fit into a broader world-system. The nationalist way of thinking and speaking helps to make nations. There is no no objective way to determine what is a nation. There are no indicators that are adequate independent of the claims made on behalf of putative nations. (Calhoun 1997: 99)

Subjective identifications, too, are not produced in a vacuum, but are influenced by the discursive context in which people find themselves and the narratives that surround them. 'Identities, then, are always formed within broad discourses, universes of available meanings and are related to the historic positionings of the subjects involved' (Suny 2001b: 868).

This conceptualization also shows that nationalism is not just a political doctrine, but 'a more basic way of talking, thinking and acting', thereby moving us beyond the culture/politics dichotomy. As Calhoun notes, 'to limit nationalism simply to a political doctrine . . . is to narrow our understanding of it too much. It doesn't do justice to the extent to which nationalism and national identities shape our lives outside of explicitly political concerns' (1997: 11). Nationalism is not the solution to the problems that afflict world politics but the discourse within which struggles to settle the problems are most commonly waged.

Finally, the alternative conceptualization I have proposed helps us to identify what is common to all nationalisms. I have already discussed the project of distinguishing between 'good' and 'bad' forms of nationalism in the previous section, arguing that these attempts obscure their commonalities. Both positive and negative manifestations of nationalism are shaped by the common discourse of nationalism. In the words of Calhoun:

> An enormous range of otherwise different movements, ideologies, policies, and conflicts are constituted in part through the use of terms like 'nation', 'national', 'nationality', 'nation-state', and 'national interest'. The common denominator among, say, Japanese economic protectionism, Serbian ethnic cleansing, Americans singing the 'Star-Spangled Banner' before baseball games, and the way the World Bank collects statistics is a discursive form that shapes and links all of them, even though it may not offer a full causal explanation of any of them. (*ibid.*: 21–2)

In passing, let me note that conceptualizing nationalism as a form of discourse allows us to recognize the modernity of nationalisms as well, a point I shall elaborate further in the next chapter. Suffice it to say at this stage that the most fundamental difference between premodern ethnicities and modern nationalities is the discursive universe within which the latter operates. A modern nationality is only possible within the modern discourse of nationalism:

Whatever Greeks in the classical period or Armenians in the fifth century were, they could not be nations in the same sense as they would be in the Age of Revolution. The discourses of politics of earlier times must be understood and respected in their own particularity and not submerged in understandings yet to be formed . . . Earlier histories of classes and nations should be read not simply as prehistories, but as varied historical developments whose trajectories remained open. (Eley and Suny 1996: 10–11; see also Suny 2001b)

Before moving on, it is necessary to allay a possible criticism of the definition I have just proposed, namely that it is too general, hence irredeemably vague. It is indeed true that as such, the definition does not differentiate the nationalist discourse from other, similar, discourses. After all, religion too is a way of seeing and interpreting the world, a frame of reference that helps us structure the reality around us. In order to tell the nationalist discourse apart from other discourses, we need first to probe into the nature of nationalism, laying special emphasis on its socially constructed qualities; and second, to map out the dimensions of the discourse of nationalism. This will be the topic of Chapter 7, where I shall present the outline of a social constructionist approach to nationalism, with a view to identifying the main characteristics of this particular discourse. At this stage, I shall confine myself to a few preliminary remarks on the mode of operation of the nationalist discourse, in order to set the scene for the discussion in Chapter 7. I would argue that there are four different ways in which the nationalist discourse operates:

- *The discourse of nationalism divides the world into 'us' and 'them'.* Nationalism is a specimen of the family of 'we-talks', that is, of discourses that divide the world into 'us' and 'them', positing a homogeneous and fixed identity on either side. It is set apart from other discourses by its exclusivity, or its tendency to perceive the world in terms of 'friends' and 'enemies'. As Bauman remarks, identity is permanently under conditions of a besieged fortress. 'Always made-up, almost always contested, it tends to be fragile and unsure of itself; this is why the we-talk can seldom stop. Identity stands and falls by the security of its borders, and the borders are ineffective unless guarded' (1992: 678–9).

- *The discourse of nationalism hegemonizes.* Like other discourses, the nationalist discourse is about power and domination. It legitimates and produces hierarchies among actors. It thus authorizes particular formulations of the nation against others, thereby concealing the fractures, divisions and differences of opinion within the nation (Allan and Thompson 1999; Verdery 1993; Suny 2001b). It also dominates other discourses, or alternative political languages, by 'nationalizing' narrative and interpretative frames, ways of perceiving and evaluating, thinking and feeling (Brubaker 1996: 20–1). In short, we can only understand the nationalist discourse by asking 'what other forms of potential community are ruled out, placed out of bounds', and 'against what other forms of potential community are dominant projects placed' (Roseberry 1996: 83–4).

- *The discourse of nationalism naturalizes itself.* 'Nationalism treats national identity as a system of absolute values, in which the relativism of ethnic shifters has been transformed into a set of reified eternal verities' (Herzfeld 1997: 42). National values are no longer seen as social values and appear as facts of nature – they become taken for granted, common sense and hegemonic. This ultimately turns the language of national identity into a language of morality, and renders nationalism the very horizon of political discourse (Finlayson 1998: 7–9; Herzfeld 1997: 43; see also Billig 1995: 10).

- *The discourse of nationalism operates through institutions.* The nationalist discourse does not arise out of nothing, and does not exist in a social vacuum. It is produced and imposed by a whole gamut of institutions. National identity has to be learned and internalized through socialization. Furthermore, it has to be reproduced daily in myriads of small ways to retain its power.

This brief discussion sought to show that the national order is pervasive, that none of us – including those who consider themselves anti-nationalists – can avoid it. The categories and presumptions of this discourse are so deeply ingrained in our everyday language and academic theories that it is virtually impossible to cast them off. All we can do, under the circumstances, is to remind ourselves continuously to take them into account (Calhoun 1993: 214; Billig 1995: 125–7).

3
The Theory of Nationalism

When contemporary nationalists appeal to history, says the medieval historian Patrick J. Geary, their notion of history is static. They look to the moment of 'primary acquisition', when 'their people' set up their sacred territory and their national identity. This is, however, the very antithesis of history:

> The history of European peoples in Late Antiquity and the early Middle Ages is not the story of a primordial moment but of a continuous process. It is the story of political appropriation and manipulation of inherited names and representations of pasts to create a present and a future. It is a history of constant change, of radical discontinuities, and of political and cultural zigzags, masked by the repeated re-appropriation of old words to define new realities. (2002: 156–7)

To what extent does the past matter for present-day nations then? The answer to this question gets to the heart of the theoretical debate on nationalism that took off in the 1960s with the pioneering works of Karl Deutsch, Elie Kedourie and Ernest Gellner (not to mention the work of an earlier generation of historians such as Hans Kohn and Carleton Hayes who are considered by many as the founding fathers of the academic study of nationalism) and gained momentum from the 1980s onwards with the publication of the seminal works by Benedict Anderson, Eric J. Hobsbawm, Anthony D. Smith, and, again, Ernest Gellner. The major contenders in this debate are generally divided into three groups, namely the primordialists, the ethnosymbolists and the

34

modernists, depending on the answer they give to the above question and their views on the nature of nations and nationalism. For the primordialists, *the past determines the present*: nations have existed since time immemorial and they are a natural part of human beings, as natural as sight or speech. For the ethnosymbolists, *the past constrains the present*: modern nations are, in most cases, an outgrowth of pre-existing ethnic communities, and a resilient feature of the social and political landscape as they respond to real human needs. Finally, for the modernists, *the past is exploited by the present*: nations that have emerged as a direct or indirect consequence of various processes associated with modernization, appeal to the past to validate their existence in the present and project themselves into the future.

In what follows, I shall first address two questions around which the theoretical debates revolve, with a view to summarizing the current state of play in the field:

• What is the relationship between premodern ethnic communities and modern nations?
• Are nations invented and imagined, or are they simply reconstructed out of pre-existing cultural materials?

I shall devote the final, and the longest, section of this chapter to the attempts to rejuvenate the theoretical debate by addressing issues that have been glossed over by mainstream theorizations. This will also prepare the ground for the discussion in Chapter 7, where I shall outline my own approach to nationalism, which draws heavily on the theoretical edifice laid out in these works.

The Modernity of Nationalism

In a telling essay on the history and ideology of what he calls the 'nation form', Balibar observes that the history of nations is always presented to us in the form of a narrative that attributes to them the continuity of a subject. 'The formation of the nation thus appears as the fulfillment of a "project" stretching over centuries, in which there are different stages and moments of coming to self-awareness.' Such a representation constitutes a retrospective illusion according to Balibar, which is twofold:

It consists in believing that the generations which succeed one another over centuries on an approximately stable territory, under an approximately univocal designation, have handed down to each other an invariant substance. And it consists in believing that the process of development from which we select aspects retrospectively, so as to see ourselves as the culmination of that process, was the only one possible, that it represented a destiny. (1990: 338)

Yet the real picture is more complicated than the nationalist illusion would have us believe. The world system of nation-states is of relatively recent vintage, mainly a product of the last 200 years. Before that the political scene was populated by local communities and empires, which organized their political affairs on a scale smaller or larger than most contemporary states. What we would call today the 'nation' provided only one of the overlapping ways in which politically active elites identified themselves, and by no means the most important. 'Nor did a common national identity unite the high and low, lord and peasant, into a deeply felt community of interest' (Geary 2002: 19). Equally importantly, premodern political identifications did not necessarily develop into the national identifications of modern times. Hence the nationalist myth of linear destiny is just that, a myth.

Given that, we should be wary of taking the claims of nationalists at their face value. Instead, we should test them against the historical record, and focus on the continuities and discontinuities between premodern ethnicities and modern national identities.

Continuities, Discontinuities

What then is the relationship between premodern ethnicities and modern nations? For the late Adrian Hastings, it is one of continuity. Modern nations can only grow out of certain ethnicities, under the impact of the literary development of a vernacular and the pressures of the state. It is true that every ethnicity did not become a nation, but many have done so. The defining origin of the nation, Hastings argues, like that of every other great reality of modern Western experience, needs to be located in an age a good deal further back than most modernist historians feel safe to handle, that of the shaping of medieval society. Hastings contends that ethnicities naturally turn into nations at the point when their specific vernacular moves from an oral to written usage to the extent that it is being regularly employed for the production of a literature, and particularly for the translation of the Bible (1997: 11–12). Every ethnicity, Hastings concludes, has a potential nation-state within it, though in the majority of cases that potentiality will never be activated for a variety of reasons. 'But the intrinsic connection between ethnicity, nation and nationalism is not to be gainsaid. It provides the sole intelligible starting point for a theory of nationalism' (*ibid*.: 31).

Patrick J. Geary disagrees. For him, the congruence between early medieval and contemporary peoples is a myth. What we see instead is the long-term, discontinuous use of certain labels that have come to be seen as 'ethnic'. But these names were less descriptions than claims (2002: 155). The social realities behind ethnic names underwent rapid and radical transformation in each case. With the constant shifting of allegiances, intermarriages, transformations and appropriations, all that remained constant were names, and these were vessels that could hold different contents at different times. Names were thus renewable resources; 'they held the potential to convince people of continuity, even if radical discontinuity was the lived reality' (*ibid*.: 118).

Geary argues that military bands appropriated these names and used them as rallying cries for mobilizing people. In time,

> [w]ith victory and territorialization, bold claims created the reality that they asserted and, in a matter of generations, social and political groups with widely differing pasts, values and cultures accepted the victor's right to articulate for them a common past. Myths of common descent and shared history, myths molded less by indigenous oral tradition than by classical ideas of peoplehood, masked the radical discontinuity and heterogeneity that characterized Late Antiquity. (*ibid*.: 156)

The view adopted in this book is very much in line with Geary's position. As I have argued in the previous chapter, ethnic differences are only assigned significance in the age of nationalism, that is, within the framework of the nationalist discourse. This point is crucial because nationalism is not just a claim of ethnic similarity but 'a claim that certain similarities should count as the definition of political community. For this reason, nationalism needs boundaries in a way premodern ethnicity does not' (Calhoun 1993: 229). Equally important is the nationalist claim that national identities 'trump' other personal or group identities. This is sharply contradictory to medieval realities, where overlapping identification with several communities is the rule. In short, nationalism involves a distinctive new form of group identity or membership (*ibid.*).

If we accept that nationalism selects, reconfigures and sometimes recreates older identities in accordance with present concerns, then the question becomes one of the extent to which such reconfiguration involves innovation in existing identity patterns. The answer to this question obviously varies from one case to the next. It is true that nationalists do not make their history under conditions of their own choosing. In most cases, they draw on pre-existing traditions and other cultural resources to forge political unity. Yet these traditions are adapted to new circumstances and what seem like minor changes may end up altering their meanings considerably. Traditions that do not serve present purposes, on the other hand, are either overlooked or constructed as 'deviant' and relegated to the minorities (Calhoun 1997: 50, 83; see also Breuilly 1996).

In short, even if we admit that the past constrains the present to a certain degree, that past still leaves a sufficiently rich set of records as to allow for constant reinterpretation. What matters most is not the presence of premodern cultural materials but the ways in which these are selected, used and abused by nationalists, and this necessarily reflects present concerns (for a more detailed discussion, see Özkırımlı 2003 and Laitin 2001b).

The Origins of Nations and Nationalism

The above discussion inevitably brings into focus the thorny issue of the origins of nations, or, as it is widely formulated in the field, the question of 'when is the nation'. We might begin to explore this question by comparing, once again, the answers provided by Hastings and Geary, which represent the most eloquent articulations of the rival positions in the debate.

For Hastings, the origins of both nations and nationalism can be traced back to the birth of the English nation at the end of tenth century. He argues that an English nation-state existed around 1066, grew steadily 'in the strength of its national consciousness through the later twelfth and thirteenth centuries, but emerged still more vociferously with its vernacular renaissance and the pressures of the Hundred Years War by the end of the fourteenth' (1997: 5). English nationalism, on the other hand, was already present in the fourteenth century in the long wars with France. Thus, Hastings argues, England presents the prototype of both a nation and a nation-state, that its national development does precede every other. In this context, Hastings rejects once again the great divide between the premodern and the modern, claiming that the understanding of nations and nationalism will only be advanced when any inseparable bonding of them to the modernization of society is abandoned (*ibid.*: 4–9).

Not surprisingly, Geary repudiates Hastings's account. For him, there is nothing particularly ancient about the peoples of Europe: they have always been far more fluid, complex and dynamic than modern nationalists suggest. Thus the real history of the nations that populated Europe begins not in the sixth century but in the eighteenth (2002: 12–13, 16–17). More importantly, the past two centuries of intellectual and political activity have so utterly changed the ways we think about social and political groups that we cannot pretend to provide an 'objective' view of early medieval categories, unencumbered by this recent past:

> Not only is ethnic nationalism, as we currently understand it, in a certain sense an invention of this recent period, but . . . the very tools of analysis by which we pretend to practice scientific history were invented and perfected within a wider climate of nationalism and nationalist preoccupations. (*ibid.*: 15–16)

Geary illustrates this view with reference to ethnographers and historians who describe the origins of 'peoples' in terms derived from biblical and classical prototypes. This is exactly what a string of authors at the end of Antiquity and in the early Middle Ages did when they provided accounts of the origins of Goths, the Lombards, the Franks, the Anglo-Saxons, and, later, of the Serbs, the Croats and the Hungarians, claiming to convey ancient oral traditions yet casting their peoples in Romano-Christian categories. Such histories, Geary maintains, were never really 'national' histories. 'Rather they were grounded in the author's political and cultural concerns and were structured in order to advance the author's own contemporary agenda' (*ibid.*: 164–5). In past ages, people had different ways of identifying themselves and we often have difficulty recognizing the differences between these early ways and more contemporary attitudes because 'we are trapped in the very historical process we are attempting to study' and we use the terms 'people', 'ethnicity' and the like as though these words carried some sort of objective, fixed meaning (*ibid.*: 41). In short, '[b]oth in large, hegemonic states and in aspiring independence movements, claims that "we have always been a people" actually are appeals to become a people – appeals not grounded in history but, rather, attempts to create history' (*ibid.*: 37).

Geary is not the only one who stresses the historical novelty of nations and nationalism. As early as 1882, Renan stipulated that nations are something fairly new in history. Classical antiquity had republics, municipal kingdoms, confederations of local republics and empires, but not nations in our understanding of the term (1990 [1882]: 10–12). Anderson and Goodman concur, arguing that nation-states and nationalisms were unimaginable in medieval times. Political authority was shared between a variety of secular and religious institutions, and the political territories were often discontinuous, with fluid rather than fixed borders (1999: 20–1). Dunn makes a similar point and notes that nationalism has certainly not been a natural sentiment for most human beings in most of human history. Cultural chauvinism may be a common enough motif in history but until relatively recent times it has been an elite prerogative: 'most peoples in history have had their cultural chauvinism done for them' (1999: 35). Finally, Duara claims that what is novel about modern nationalism is not political self-consciousness, but the world system of nation-states. It is only with this system – globalized in the last hundred years or so – that the nation-state came to be seen as the only legitimate form of polity (1996: 157).

The discussion so far reveals that the issue of the origins of nations and nationalism cannot be settled until we come to grips with two problems that plague our analyses. The first problem is conceptual. Can we use the terms 'nation' and 'nationalism' to describe premodern realities? For those who believe in continuity between premodern communities and today's nations, we surely can. Thus Hastings claims that there has been 'a surprisingly firm continuity in usage' across more than 600 years in our language, that the sense of 'nation' was already in the fourteenth century related explicitly to a distinct language group, and that it drew on biblical and Vulgate roots (1997: 18). Now, I have already noted that the issue of when the word 'nation' acquired its modern political meaning is a source of deep controversy among scholars, depending on where they stand on the theoretical divide in the field. Yet I have also shown that for Zernatto, considered by many as the classical source on the history of the word 'nation', the term came to be widely used only in the eighteenth century. Zernatto is not alone in holding this position. Drawing on Hastings's own cherished example, Calhoun observes that

> [i]n what was becoming England in 1066 . . . it was one thing to be loyal to one's king and kinsmen when faced with Norman invaders. It was quite another, in the years that followed, to nurture English nationalism by mythologizing Camelot, making the 'Norman yoke' the focus of quasi-class complaint, and proclaiming that 'there will always be England'. Loyalty to the abstract category England was quite different from loyalty to one's actual and specific comrades. (1997: 7)

Contra Hastings, we should also note that it is not clear what the authors of premodern documents meant when they used the word 'nation'. As Verdery argues, what we should do is to explore 'which sense of nation is apt to the context in question, rather than imposing a modern sense on a medieval reality, a French sense on a Kenyan reality, or a 19th century sense on the evolving reality of today' (1993: 39).

The second, related, problem that bedevils our analyses concerns the nature of nations. Are nations an elite or a mass phenomenon? Those who stress the continuity between premodern communities and modern nations mostly rely on elite documents to support their cases. Hastings, for example, argues that for a nation to exist it is not necessary that everyone within it should want it to exist or have full consciousness that it does exist; we have a nation when a number of people beyond government circles or a small ruling class consistently believe in it. It may be true that in large parts of France many people did not speak French and had little sense of being French until well into the nineteenth century.

But, Hastings hastens to add, 'this does not prove that there was not, from a much earlier date, a French nation in existence' (1997: 26–7).

Connor takes a completely different view, arguing that nationalism is a mass phenomenon. It is of course quite impossible to say what percentage of a people must achieve national consciousness before the group merits treatment as a nation. But, he maintains, it is not enough that a group of intellectuals believes in the existence of nationhood:

> The fact that members of the ruling elite or intelligentsia manifest national sentiment is not sufficient to establish that national consciousness has permeated the value-system of the masses. And the masses, until recent times totally or semi-illiterate, furnished few hints concerning their view of group-self. (1994: 212; see also Hechter 2000: 35)

Part of the problem then concerns the difficulty of knowing what did the labours of intellectuals and activists signify for the majority of the people. It is quite likely that these have penetrated the consciousness of only a small part of the population. The crux of the matter is, once again, the discourse of nationalism. Several different threads of historical change have conspired to produce modern nationalism. Yet, as Calhoun reminds us, these threads were never simultaneously important before the modern era. The discursive formation was in full swing only at the end of the eighteenth century. Needless to say, some modern countries have histories before the discourse of nationalism; however these are only constituted as national retrospectively (1997: 9–10).

The Resilience of Nations

The final issue I want to consider in this section is somewhat more problematic as it bears on the relevance of what I have said so far. To put it in a nutshell, why do we need to dig up the origins of nations and nationalism? Or why is the question 'when is the nation' important?

A possible answer to this question might be 'to account for the resilience of nations and nationalism'. It is now widely accepted that nations have been one of the defining features of modernity, and a major actor of social and political life for almost two centuries. It is very likely that they will continue to be so in the foreseeable future. Yet do we need to trace them back in the hoary mists of history in order to account for their current power and resilience? I think not, and alternative explanations have already been proposed by a number of writers. Hence for Delanty and O'Mahony, what has made nationalism a recalcitrant force in modernity is the persistence of certain key problems (2002: xv). Poole, on the other hand, argues that the major source of the strength of national identity is its inescapability. The nationalist principle of the fusion of language, culture and polity has so deeply penetrated our conception of ourselves that it is difficult to address the question of who we are without presupposing that we already have a national identity (1999: 69). According to Brennan, nation-states are 'manageable' communities. Administratively, they continue to be ideal units for the organization of profit-making, resource extraction, and the perpetuation of unequal social relations (2001: 83). Finally, for Canovan, 'the advantage that nations have over alternative sources of collective power is that they can lie dormant without being defunct'. Nationhood, once established, functions like a battery, a reservoir of power that can slumber for a long time and still be available for mobilization. Furthermore, the power generated by nationhood is flexible and all-purpose, particularly in long-established nations (1996: 73–4).

In short, as Greenfeld notes, there is nothing surprising in the tenacity of nationalism:

> Cultural frameworks which define historical epochs, as nationalism defines modernity, change slowly, and in the life of an historical type of society, which modern society is, a hundred years is not a very long time. We can estimate the life-expectancy of nationalism by comparing it to other order-defining cultural frameworks, such as the world's great religions . . . Like the great religions of the past, nationalism today forms the foundation of our social consciousness, the cognitive framework of our perception of reality. Seen against the record of the great religions' historical longevity and continuous vitality over centuries of political, economic, and technological change, the recognition of this functional equivalence may give us a more accurate idea

of nationalism's projected life span and pace of development than would our experience with food-processors or word-processors, whose ever-changing models seem to be the chief inspiration for our model of ever-changing reality. (2000: 29–30)

In the light of this, I would argue that the question of origins is not as important as some theorists would have us believe, and not only because the answer is buried in the haze of history – after all, as Geary notes, claims can be made with impunity, since few people know any better (2002: 9). The question of whether nations existed in premodern times may be interesting from an intellectual or academic point of view, but it is not clear how the existence of such forerunners contributes to our understanding of modern nations – even if 'genealogical' continuity can be asserted (see Delanty and O'Mahony 2002: chapter 4, for a similar view). For ideological purposes, it may be effective to claim that a nation or its traditions have existed since time immemorial. Sociologically, however, what matters is not the antiquity of the tradition, but 'the efficacy of the process by which tradition constitutes certain beliefs and understandings as unquestioned, immediate knowledge, as the basis for disputing or questioning other claims' (Calhoun 1993: 222). In other words, whether nations are recent or ancient is not the point. What matters is that they are always imagined as ancient (Reicher and Hopkins 2001: 17).

The Nature of Nationalism

'History is a purely human artifact, a story we tell ourselves', says Goodin in a recent essay on the moral record of nationalism. No doubt there are some constraints on the stories we tell ourselves. Bloodlines and battlegrounds constitute hard facts about the world, whatever social construction we might ascribe them. And some stories will fit those hard facts better than others. Still, Goodin continues, which story we settle upon among the many eligible ones is largely an arbitrary choice from among that admittedly circumscribed set of almost equally viable options (1997: 98). Goodin's observations pose point-blank the question of the nature of nations, another major theoretical riddle preoccupying scholars of nationalism in recent years.

Invented or Reconstructed?

Are nations invented and imagined, or are they simply reconstructed out of pre-existing cultural materials? Needless to say, both views have their fair share of followers. Thus for Motyl, both invention and imagination presuppose the existence of pre-existing building blocks: we cannot invent or imagine *ex nihilo* (1999: 70). Miller concurs noting that there is a sense in which the past always constrains the present: 'present identities are built out of the materials that are handed down, not started from scratch' (1995: 175). In short, the kind of remaking which features in modern nationalism is nothing but a reformulation constrained by determinate parameters of the nation's past (Nairn 1998: 121).

By contrast, Hechter notes that states actively promote new traditions, such as national anthems, flags and monuments. These might seem to have existed from time immemorial, but in fact all of them are of recent vintage (2000: 64). Gillis makes a similar point, claiming that national memory is shared by people who have never seen or heard of one another, yet who regard themselves as having a common history. Changes accompanying the foundation of nations create such a sense of distance between now and then that people find it impossible to remember what life had been like only a few decades earlier:

> The past went blank and had to be filled in, a task taken up with great fervor by professional historians from the early nineteenth century onward. Their task, as Jules Michelet conceived it, was to speak for past generations, to bestow on them a national history regardless of whether they were aware of themselves as French, German, or English at the time they were alive. (1994: 7–8)

In order to get a better grasp of the views just canvassed, we need to clarify the meanings of the terms we employ. Let us begin with the term 'reconstruction'. What exactly does 'reconstruction' imply? Is a 'reconstructed' past still the same past? Now there is a kernel of truth in the view that nationalists did not simply make up the past. They have drawn on pre-existing cultural materials, even if they used them to create something completely different. To that extent, the reconstruction thesis is correct: nations are not created *ex nihilo*. But we should be careful not to overstate this point. To begin with, the reconstruction thesis should not imply that discrete, easily recognizable cultural identities already existed before – hence predated – the age of nationalism. Unfortunately, most of those who support the reconstruction thesis fall into this trap, claiming that there is ultimately an objective basis, a 'ground' which determines the form of community construction (Norval 1996: 61–2). Premodern ethnicities have their own complexities, and they are certainly not as 'natural' or 'immemorial' as is sometimes thought. There is also the question of the extent to which a reconstructed past is the same past. As Tamir notes, national movements cling 'to even the faintest evidence of historical continuity and to adopt strictly false beliefs in order to prove their antiquity and assert that the emergence of their nation was a matter of historical necessity' (1996: 94). In the process, they tend to ignore differentiating features and embrace common characteristics. As a result, the history constructed for the nation in the present may bear no resemblance to what really happened in the past. Some commentators argue that this may even be desirable in some cases. If national identities are valuable, says Miller, and if they cannot be sustained without a certain amount of mythologizing, then this is the price we must be prepared to pay (1996: 413–14).

What does 'invented' or 'imagined' mean then? It is sometimes argued that whenever traditions can be shown to be 'invented' or 'created', they must be false. However, it is not clear why this should be so. As Calhoun reminds us, all traditions are created, none is truly primordial or immemorial. Second, 'all traditions are internally contested and subject to continual reshaping, whether explicit or hidden' (1993: 223). Balibar makes the same point, arguing that

> [e]very social community reproduced by the functioning of institutions is imaginary, that is, it is based on the projection of indivivual existence into the weft of a collective narrative, on the recognition of a common name and on traditions lived as the trace of an immemorial past (even when they have been created and inculcated in the recent past). (1990: 346)

I shall elaborate on this point further in Chapter 7, when I shall discuss the idea of 'social construction' and its implications for our understanding of nationalism. Suffice it to say that the purported correlation between 'invention' and 'falsity' is in fact phoney. To say that a nation is 'imaginary' is not to consign it to the category of mere fiction: 'if it is a "dream" it is one possessing all the institutional force and affect of the real' (Parker *et al.*: 1992: 11–12).

This problem is closely related to another issue raised by the invention thesis: if nations are invented or imagined, how do we explain their resonance? Why would people willingly lay down their lives for the inventions of a handful of intellectuals and activists?

The Issue of Resonance

Before we tackle these questions it is important to issue a warning regarding the widespread tendency to take resonance for granted. As Brubaker observes, 'the strength, salience and centrality of national feeling, national identity and nationalist politics tend to be overestimated' (1998: 283). It is generally assumed that a high percentage of national populations are deeply attached to their communities, and that they are willing to make great sacrifices for those communities. Yet, as Laitin rightly argues, these are bold claims that need to be carefully justified. We would need to know, for example, how much defection and apathy should exist before a collective identity ceases to have any power. This is a reflection of a more general weakness in nationalism studies, according to Laitin, namely the lack of attention to ethnic groups or nations that have commanded little loyalty or attachment. We tend to study 'the ethnics that become nations to the exclusion of the "dogs that did not bark"'. Hence, we have no way of knowing the probability of any ethnic group becoming a nation. 'Moreover, without a sample of both national successes and national failures, we cannot assess the depth and long-lastingness of the attachment of people to their ethnic groups' (2001b: 176–7). In short, membership of any community admits of degrees and is not homogeneous in nature. In fact, it may sometimes become a subject of deep disagreement.

This reservation notwithstanding, it is still true that there are many people who are strongly committed to the communities they belong to – not only their nations – and who are prepared, under certain circumstances, to sacrifice even their lives for it. The first point to be noted in this context is that resonance is not automatic, but needs to be produced and actively promoted. As Miroslav Hroch informs us in his monumental study of national movements in Northern and Eastern Europe, a nationalist movement typically starts with scholarly inquiry into the linguistic, historical and cultural attributes of the relevant community on the part of a number of committed activists, which Hroch calls Phase A. In the next stage, or Phase B, a new range of activists emerge and try to win as many of their group as possible to the project of creating a nation. It is only in the last stage, Phase C, that a mass movement is formed, when the national consciousness becomes the concern of the majority of the population (Hroch 1985, 1993). In other words, the nation takes hold in the hearts and minds of the people only after it has been actively promoted by a small number of nationalist ideologues who take on the task of forging the nation. Hroch qualifies his position in his later work, noting that the basic condition for the success of any agitation is that its argument at least roughly corresponds to reality as perceived by those to whom it is directed. After all, says Hroch, nobody launched a campaign at the beginning of the nineteenth century to persuade the Hungarians that they were actually Chinese. National agitation therefore had to begin with the fact that certain relations and ties had developed over the centuries that united the people towards whom the agitation was directed (1998: 99–100). This appears to be just a rhetorical point however. Why would the agitators try to convince Hungarians that they were Chinese anyway? On the other hand, it is quite conceivable that they launch a campaign to persuade them that they were Slovaks. It is of course true that the agitators built on pre-existing ties and relations. But, as I have argued in previous sections, they made use of some ties, ignored others, and transformed them beyond recognition to suit present (political) needs.

It needs to be added that the success of nation-builders also depends on their capacity to monitor and sanction their dependants. Hence many people may simply respond to their calls out of fear of coercion. Such coercion may sometimes involve the direct threat of death. As Spencer and Wollman point out, the alternative in war to sacrifice might be the firing squad or to be exposed to danger in the front-line as a non-combatant. At other times, it may involve shame or abuse, which can act as powerful enforcers of the general will (1999: 113; Hechter 2000: 24).

Resonance and cultural homogenization may also be the unintended consequences of other factors such as economic and technological developments or military policies (Hechter 2000: 66–7). A charismatic leader can transform nationalism into a mass movement by linking national aspiration to a host of existing complaints. In such cases, the motivation for the masses may have little to do with a call to difference, emanating instead from a sense of physical threat, of the fear of displacement, or even extermination by a hostile other (Taylor 1999: 236–8). In yet other cases, we may love the nation simply because there is nothing else left for us to love. When the communities to which people were formerly attached – communities of kin, village, occupation, status and so on – are dissolved, individuals have nothing to turn to except the nation (Canovan 1996: 61).

These observations relate to the founding moment of the nation-state. How do we account for resonance in the present, that is, after the nation-state is founded? Once again, there are a number of mechanisms here. The first mechanism involves the inexorable process of the reproduction of nationalism, both formally, through a whole gamut of institutions including schools, the military and the media, and informally, in myriad small, taken-for-granted ways that pervade the invisible realm of everyday life. In fact, the longer the coexistence lasts, the more likely it is that the common political identity will take on a life of its own. In that sense, 'the sheer survival of a state over a long period tends to bring about a sense of common nationality among those within its territory' (Barry 1999a: 259).

This is closely related to the second mechanism which accounts for resonance, that is, the process by which nationalism transforms itself into a ground project on which the successful pursuit of all other projects depends (Tamir 1997: 232). In the words of Tilly,

> . . . the institutionalized form of nationhood builds on and reinforces non-national social relations and identities in which people invest trust, resources, solidarity, and hopes for the future. States selectively confirm, co-opt, reinforce, or even create identity-bestowing social networks within which people organize work, sociability and collective action; to some degree,

all such networks come to depend on the state's backing, or at least its toleration. To the extent that nationally and locally defined solidarities actually coincide, threats and opportunities for national identities therefore ramify into local affairs and impinge on the fates of many people. (1994: 18)

Put simply, people kill for their nation, or die for it, because they identify its life with their own. As Bauer noted as early as 1924, when we think of our nation, we remember our homeland, our parents' house, our first childhood games, our old schoolmaster, the person whose kiss once thrilled us, and from all these ideas a feeling of pleasure flows into the idea of the nation we belong to (1996 [1924]: 62).

In short, there is nothing surprising in the enthusiasm nationalism generates given its intricate relationship to our whole way of life, our 'existence' so to speak. Again, this has nothing to do with how ancient or how real the nation is. Drawing on Calhoun, we can say that what gives the nation its force is not its antiquity but its immediacy and givenness. 'Some nationalist self-understandings may be historically dubious yet very real as aspects of lived experience and bases for action' (1997: 34). They might be taken as unconscious presuppositions by people when they consciously consider the options open to them. Thus,

> [i]t is impossible to differentiate among states by showing some to be created and others not, but it is indeed possible to show that some national identities have proved more persuasive than others ... It is thus not the antiquity of Eritrean nationalism that mattered in mobilizing people against Ethiopian rule, for example, but the felt reality of Eritreanness. (*ibid.*: 35)

New Approaches to Nationalism

As I noted at the outset of this chapter, issues of periodization and origins are not the only questions preoccupying scholars of nationalism. We can witness in the last two decades the emergence of a series of studies that seek to rejuvenate the theoretical debate by addressing a whole different set of questions, thereby opening up new avenues for exploration.

There are two distinguishing features of these studies. First, they are all interdisciplinary in nature, not only in the sense of crossing the boundaries separating classical disciplines but also in their openness to new fields such as cultural studies, global anthropology, gender and sexuality, new social movements, diaspora and migration studies, and so on. Second, they all give pride of place to issues and questions that have received scant attention in earlier, more mainstream, studies. In what follows, I shall try to outline and briefly discuss the contribution of these studies to our understanding of nationalism. I shall do this by identifying four issues that have been addressed by these studies, namely blood sacrifice and violence, borders and boundaries, identity and difference, gender and sexuality. I shall examine them by concentrating on one or two representative texts in each case. I shall conclude this chapter by discussing the question of whether a general theory of nationalism is possible.

Blood Sacrifice and Violence

What binds the nation together? This question forms the departure point of Marvin and Ingle's compelling study of American nationalism. Their answer is blunt and somewhat unsettling: what makes enduring groups cohere is violent blood sacrifice (1999: 1). In the words of Marvin and Ingle,

> The creation of sentiments strong enough to hold the group together periodically requires the willing deaths of a significant portion of its members. The lifeblood of these members is shed by means of a ritual in which designated victims become outsiders and cross the boundary of the living group into death. The most powerful enactment of this ritual is war. (*ibid.*: 5)

This ritual is organized through a religion of patriotism that is deeply held and constantly recreated in stories, images, rites and legal codes. The civil religion decides on who may kill and what for, how boundaries are formed, and what national identity is (*ibid.*: 11).

We are all aware of the role of blood sacrifice in keeping the nation together, Marvin and Ingle point out, but we tend to deny it as it challenges our most deeply held notions of civilized behaviour. They introduce the term 'taboo' to describe 'the tension betweeen the violent mechanism that sustains enduring groups and the reluctance of group members to acknowledge their responsibility for enacting it' (*ibid.*: 12). To protect themselves from recognizing the source of unity, group members render violence and its symbols sacred, that is, unknowable. While violence is regularly enacted through rituals of blood sacrifice such as war, this knowledge is separated from devotees, as all sacred things are. It is also denounced as primitive, an attribute of groups in Central Europe or Asia who are always eager to use violence. What we tend to forget is that blood sacrifice is as much a feature of our society as any other now in turmoil (*ibid.*: 2, 12; on the tendency to reflect nationalism onto the periphery, see also Billig 1995).

What can we do under these circumstances? Not much, say Marvin and Ingle. For them, all enduring groups are defined by violence. In that sense, the question is not how to get rid of violence, but which set of killing rules we shall submit to. We can change groups, but we cannot remove ourselves from a system of violence as long as we are members of some group. 'Wherever we are, killing rules are in effect' (*ibid.*: 313). Given this, the choice is between recognizing our complicity or deceiving ourselves that our support is anything but deferring to the killing rules of the side whose part we take (*ibid.*: 315).

There are other writers who set great store by the role of sacrifice and violence in the construction and reproduction of nations too. Appadurai, for example, claims that full attachment, rather than coming from an authentic prior sense of shared community (whether based on language, history, soil or some other element), might actually be produced by various forms of violence instigated, sometimes even required, by the modern nation-state. Put simply, 'violence (internal violence associated with ethnic cleansing; more capillary techniques of surveillance and schooling; or external violence associated with expansion, empire and colonialism) produces full attachment, rather than the reverse' (2000: 132).

Elshtain, on the other hand, shows us how the idea of sacrifice is gendered. The child's will to sacrifice, she argues, flows from embodied ties to parents that project outward into a more generalized relationship to a femininized motherland and a masculinized sovereign state. 'The young man goes to war not so much to kill as to die, to forfeit his particular body for that of the larger body, the body politic, a body most often presented and represented as feminine' (1991: 395).

On the face of it, then, nation-states seem to feel an endemic need to mobilize their members on the basis of periodically renewed blood sacrifice. After all, as Anderson quite rightly observes, body counts are essential to nationalism, and not merely for the census and on election days (1998: 52).

Borders and Boundaries

The issue of borders and boundaries has infiltrated the study of ethnic groups quite early, with the publication of Barth's pioneering *Ethnic Groups and Boundaries* (1969). Yet it is only recently that their role in the construction of nations has been systematically analysed.

The focus of the recent studies is the way in which boundaries around particular communities are drawn. Thus Duara claims that a nationality is formed when the perception of the boundaries of a community are transformed, or when soft boundaries are transformed into hard ones. A master narrative usually seeks to define and mobilize a community by privileging a particular symbolic meaning or a set of cultural practices as the constitutive principle of the community, thereby heightening the self-consciousness of this community in relation to those around it. 'What occurs, then, is a hardening of boundaries' (1996: 168–9).

Norval, on the other hand, argues that political identities are constructed via the drawing of political frontiers, and a political frontier can only be constructed by externalizing an 'other'. According to Norval, the process of identity formation is not to be imagined in terms of an elaboration of a set of features characteristic of a particular identity. A second element is necessary, namely the positing of an 'other' which is construed symbolically in opposition to the identity of the self. 'The positing of an other is what allows for the closure which facilitates the individuation of a certain identity' (1996: 65).

Norval argues that political frontiers do not exist as the internal and closed moments of a particular discursive formation:

The establishment of and changes in political frontiers result from complex processes of interaction of different and opposing discourses – in Gramscian terms, from wars of position. The assertion that an identity is necessarily constructed with reference to an other, therefore, does not relegate the other to a position of passivity . . . That is to say, it has the capacity to call into question the very identity which is constructed through its externalization. (*ibid.*: 65–6)

This suggests that borders are not only sites of power and domination, but also of subversion. This subversion is not always symbolic. In their study of a number of actual border zones, Donnan and Wilson inform us that cross-border illegal or semi-legal activities threaten to subvert state institutions by compromising the ability of these institutions to control their self-defined domain. Such activities, they observe, do not play by state rules. They ignore, contest and subvert state power, and they sometimes force the state to rethink and change its policies (1999: 88). In that sense, borders are 'liminal' zones, where nationalization projects may be most easily resisted, and where alternative, marginal, nonnational, or transnational identities may be most easily constructed. 'The margin is a site of resistance to both state nationalization and reactive subaltern nationalization – a place within which to construct a counterhegemonic identity that is neither "us" nor "them"' (Kaiser 2001: 326).

Identity and Difference

The great social collectivities which used to stabilize our identities, observes Stuart Hall, the collectivities of class, race, gender and nation, have been deeply undermined by the social and political developments of the last few decades (1996a: 342). This led us to question the received wisdom on identity, and rethink the way in which social and cultural identities are understood and experienced.

This renewed interest in identity has altered our conceptions of identity in at least four different ways. First, we have become aware of the structure of 'identification' itself. Identity, claims Hall, is always a structure that is split; it has ambivalence within it. In that sense, the story of identity is a cover story for making us think we stayed in the same place. Yet identification is not one thing, one moment. 'We have now to reconceptualize identity as a process of identification . . . It is something that happens over time, that is never absolutely stable, that is subject to the play of history and the play of difference' (*ibid.*: 344; see also Brubaker and Cooper 2000: 14–17).

Second, we have come to realize that identities are social and political constructs. They are highly selective, inscriptive rather than descriptive, and serve particular interests and ideological positions (Gillis 1994: 4). Hence we can no longer assign them the status of a natural object. In the words of Gillis,

> [i]dentities and memories are not things we think *about*, but things we think *with*. As such they have no existence beyond our politics, our social relations, and our histories. We must take responsibility for their uses and abuses, recognizing that every assertion of identity involves a choice that affects not just ourselves but others. (*ibid.*: 5)

This has also taught us to be wary of employing reifying conceptions of identity, and accordingly of nation, ethnic group, culture and the like. 'Rather, cultures and social groups – taken at any level of analysis (local, regional, national, transnational) – are now conceptualized in terms of ongoing processes of "construction" and "negotiation"' (Handler 1994: 27).

If identities are products of processes of construction and negotiation, then they are not fixed or static but fluid and fragmented, and this is the third contribution of recent studies of identity. 'Identity is always mobile and processual, partly self-construction, partly categorization by others, partly a condition, a status, a label, a weapon, a shield, a fund of memories' (Malkki 1996: 448). We should thus conceptualize identity as a process of becoming, rather than being, 'a process never completed' (Hall 1996b: 2, 4).

The final contribution of recent work on identity concerns the intriguing relationship between identity and difference, or the importance of the 'other' for any construction of identity. Identity

> is partly the relationship between you and the Other. Only when there is an Other can you know who you are . . . And there is not

identity that is without the dialogic relationship to the Other.
The Other is not outside, but also inside the Self, the identity.
(Hall 1996a: 344–5)

In that sense, identity is within discourse, within representation. It
is constituted partly by representation. And 'the most important
effect of this reconceptualization of identity is the surreptitious
return of difference' (*ibid.*: 345–6). Nationality is not an exception. It is a relational term which is defined within a system of
differences:

> In the same way that 'man' and 'woman' define themselves
> reciprocally (though never symmetrically), national is deter-
> mined not on the basis of its own intrinsic properties but as a
> function of what it (presumably) is not . . . [A] nation is
> ineluctably 'shaped by what it opposes'. But the very fact that
> such identities depend constitutively on difference means that
> nations are forever haunted by their various definitional others.
> (Parker *et al.* 1992: 5)

Gender and Sexuality

'All nationalisms are gendered, all are invented and all are dangerous – dangerous . . . in the sense that they represent relations
to political power and to the technologies of violence' says Anne
McClintock in her penetrating essay 'No Longer in a Future
Heaven'. Nations are contested systems of cultural representation,
she argues, that limit and legitimate people's access to the
resources of the nation-state. And despite the nationalists' investment in the idea of unity, 'nations have historically amounted to
the sanctioned institutionalization of gender difference' (1996:
260). Two things follow from this observation. First, men and
women are constructed differently by the nationalist discourse;
second, as a result of the first, they are incorporated differentially
into nationalist projects.

Nations are frequently imagined through the family metaphor.
This helps them to replicate the traditional division of labour
between men and women, hence naturalize the subordination of

women within the domestic sphere. However, according to McClintock this is not the whole story. What is less often noticed, she argues, is how this allegedly natural division of labour helps resolve the temporal anomaly within nationalism, that between a nostalgia for the past and the impatient, progressive sloughing off the past:

> Women are represented as the atavistic and authentic body of national tradition (inert, backward-looking and natural), embodying nationalism's conservative principle of continuity. Men, by contrast, represent the progressive agent of national modernity (forward-thrusting, potent and historic), embodying nationalism's progressive, or revolutionary, principle of discontinuity. (*ibid.*: 263)

Women, in this context, were the unpaid keepers of tradition and the *volk*'s moral and spiritual mission. They served as 'boundary markers visibly upholding the fetish signs of national difference and visibly embodying the iconography of race and gender purity' (*ibid.*: 276).

Skurski, on the other hand, notes how women were associated with the forces of the land to be tamed and protected, while the family unit became a metaphor for the unification of the fatherland under a central authority that could defend it. 'The married couple, bound by a natural hierarchy that included the wife's dependence and the husband's enlightened authority, metaphorically imaged the education of subordinate sections of the population by the modernizing elite in a mutually engaging relationship' (1996: 377). She also claims that in the postcolonial context, women usually served as a sign of postcolonial national identities. As a marker of otherness and dependency, 'woman' has been constructed by being articulated with class, ethnic and regional hierarchies and given content by a linear narrative of history.

> From the perspective of determinist evolutionary theories of history, 'woman' configures the lowest elements in these hierarchies, to be understood as a sign of anachronism and backwardness and as an obstacle to Western progress. From the perspective of the discourse of authenticity, 'woman' also embodies the authentic and the universal, a force to be tamed

in the service of civilization. 'Woman' thus validates the role of the male elite as an agent of progress within the nation and stands for the nation's subaltern position in relation to metropolitan progress. (*ibid.*: 392)

Chatterjee in a way endorses Skurski's analysis by arguing that this was exactly how postcolonial nationalisms wanted to solve 'the women's question'. The crucial requirement in this context, Chatterjee contends, was to retain the inner spirituality of indigenous social life. The home was the main site for expressing the spirituality of the national culture, and women had to take the main responsibility of protecting and nurturing this quality. 'No matter what the changes in the external conditions of life for women, they must not lose their essentially spiritual (i.e. feminine) virtues; they must not, in other words, become essentially westernized' (1990: 243). According to Chatterjee, this explains why the issue of female emancipation disappeared from the agenda of nationalist agitation in the nineteenth century: nationalism did not want to make the women's question an issue of political negotiation with the colonial state. This also accounts for the seeming absence of any autonomous struggle by women themselves for equality and freedom. The evidence for such a struggle should not be sought in the public archives as this is not where the battle was waged. 'The domain where the new idea of womanhood was sought to be actualized was the home', hence the real history of that change can be constructed only out of evidence left behind in autobiographies, family histories, and so on (*ibid.*: 249–50).

This brings us to the second theme of the burgeoning literature on gender and nationalism, namely the differential ways in which women are incorporated into nationalist projects. No doubt, the pioneering work in this respect is Yuval-Davis and Anthias's 1989 *Woman–Nation–State*, where they identified five major ways in which women have tended to participate in ethnic and national processes, focusing mainly on their – biological, ideological and symbolic – reproductive roles. Following in their footsteps, we can identify two levels at which women are commonly used by the nationalist discourse, the reproductive and the symbolic.

A number of scholars have stressed the significance of demographic factors such as birth rate for ethnic and national projects, 'hence the pressure placed, in historically specific moments, on women to breed or not to breed "for the good of the nation/ race"', in a variety of contexts (Walby 1996: 237). As Heng and Devan rightly observe, a sexualized, separate species of nationalism exists for women:

> [A]s patriotic duty for men grew out of the barrel of a gun (phallic nationalism, the wielding of a surrogate technology of the body in national defense), so would it grow, for women, out of the recesses of the womb (uterine nationalism, the body as a technology of defense wielded by the nation). Men bearing arms, and women bearing children; maternal and/as military duty. (1992: 349)

On the other hand, women are also the symbolic bearers of the nation, and the keepers and embodiments of national traditions. The figure of woman stands as a symbol of the 'motherland', a metaphor for the body politic. This trope of the nation-as-woman depends on a particular image of woman as chaste, dutiful, daughterly or maternal for its representational efficacy (Parker *et al.* 1992: 6). Here the women's body becomes an important marker, a boundary, for the nation. Because women's bodies represent the 'purity' of the nation, an attack on these bodies becomes an attack on the nation and its honour:

> Mass rapes, such as in Bosnia . . . are about the invasion of the Other's boundaries, the occupation of the Other's symbolic space, property and territory: rape of women becomes an attack on the nation, figuring as a violation of national boundaries, a violation of national autonomy and national sovereignty. (Mayer 2000: 18)

Given their differential and unequal incorporation into the nation, it is necessary to ask whether women are as committed to national projects as men. Or as Walby puts it, 'do women's nationalist/ethnic/racial and other large-scale social projects have the same, or more global, or more local boundaries than those of men?' (1996: 238) Not necessarily, says Walby. Sometimes women support a different national project than that of men, one more committed to equality between sexes. Moreover, 'there is a difference in the extent to which men and women take up arms for nationalist projects, support peace movements and support politicians who favour military build-up' (*ibid.*: 247; see also Enloe 1989). Under these circumstances, it is not surprising that male nationalists have generally condemned feminism as divisive, urging women to hold their tongues until after the nationalist revolution:

> Asking women to wait until after the revolution serves merely as a strategic tactic to defer women's demands. Not only does it conceal the fact that nationalisms are from the outset constituted in gender power, but, as the lessons of international history portend, women who are not empowered to organize during the struggle will not be empowered to organize after the struggle. (McClintock 1996: 281)

The only way out of this political quandary is to provide a gendered analysis of nationalism. Otherwise, the nation-state will remain a repository of male aspirations and male privilege. According to McClintock, a feminist theory of nationalism should devise a four-tiered strategy that involves (1) investigating the gendered formation of male theories; (2) bringing into historical visibility women's active cultural and political participation in national formations; (3) bringing nationalist institutions into critical relation with other social structures and institutions; and (4) paying attention to the structures of racial, ethnic and class power that continue to afflict privileged forms of feminism (*ibid.*: 261). West, on the other hand, espouses a form of 'feminist nationalism' that will redefine the private and public realms as not mutually exclusive and binary but as complementary and unitary. Work and struggle for the nation will not be prioritized over family/leisure and the struggle for women rights, and women will be actors, not simply reactors. Moreover, while women struggle within specific cultures, economies, polities and societies, there will be a quickly growing internationalization of feminism (1997: xxxi).

As we have seen above, however, West's account goes in the teeth of historical evidence: why would nationalists accept such a deal? What would make them see feminism as a unifying force rather than a divisive one? In any case, why fight for women's rights within the framework of nationalism?

In passing, it needs to be noted that like gender, sexuality is also organized into systems of power that favour particular sexualities while suppressing others. As Mayer notes,

Purity, modesty and chastity are common themes in national narratives of gender, nation and sexuality . . . When a nation is constructed in opposition to the Other there emerges a profound distinction not only between us and them but also more pointedly, between our women and theirs. Our women are always 'pure' and 'moral' while their women are 'deviant' and 'immoral'. (2000: 10)

Moreover, the idealization of motherhood entails the exclusion of all nonreproductively-oriented sexualities from the discourse of the nation (Parker *et al.* 1992: 6).

In short, as Eley and Suny remind us, women are never absent from the scene of nationalist grandiosity but figure as important 'supportive' players, 'as conquerors' mistresses, wartime rape victims, military prostitutes, cinematic soldier-heroes, pin-up models on patriotic calendars and of course as workers, wives, girlfriends and daughters waiting dutifully at home – and this structure of meaning too needs to be unpacked' (1996: 27).

A Theory of Nationalism?

It may be helpful to conclude this chapter by asking whether a general or universal theory of nationalism is possible. The answer to this question appears to be negative. As Mouzelis remarks, a general as well as a substantive theory of nationalism is bound to be either true but trivial, or wrong – 'in the sense that its statements will apply in only certain conditions which, given the theory's generality, will have to remain unspecified' (1998: 163).

There are various reasons for that. First, the theoretical problems posed by nationalism are multiform and varied, and cannot be resolved through a single theoretical framework. This means that

. . . grasping nationalism in its multiplicity of forms requires multiple theories. To address a question like, 'Why do nationalist movements seem to come in waves?' will require a different theory from the question, 'Why is nationalist ideology pervasively bound up with sexuality and gender?' (Calhoun 1997: 8; see also Brubaker 1998: 301)

A second reason concerns the tension between the requirements of a general theory and nationalism's inherent particularism. The form and the content of particular nationalisms are determined by pre-existing structural conditions and the creative actions of various agents – not to mention various historical contingencies. Thus:

> Why nationalism comes to dominate in those settings where it does – or for some people and not others within an ostensibly national population – are questions that by and large can be answered only within specific contexts, with knowledge of local history, of the nature of state (and other elite) power, and of what other potential or actual movements competed for allegiance. (Calhoun 1997: 25)

On the other hand, as I have already stressed in the previous chapter, what unites various nationalisms is a particular form of discourse, which may not completely explain any specific nationalism, but helps to constitute each through cultural and ideological framing. In view of this, we might try to identify the factors that lead to the continual reproduction of this discourse, and theorize the way in which it operates. This might in turn enable us to gauge the strength of nationalism in the contemporary world. This will be the aim of the Chapter 7. Let me now turn to the normative claims of nationalism.

4

The Normative Claims of Nationalism

In an essay he wrote in 1945, George Orwell defines nationalism as 'the habit of assuming that human beings can be classified like insects and that whole blocks of millions or tens of millions of people can be confidently labelled "good" or "bad"'. For the nationalist, Orwell notes,

> [a]ctions are held to be good or bad, not on their own merits, but according to who does them, and there is almost no kind of outrage – torture, the use of hostages, forced labour, mass deportations, imprisonment without trial, forgery, assassination, the bombing of civilians – which does not change its moral colour when it is committed by 'our' side. (1968: 369)

Orwell's observations are a salutary reminder of the all too often forgotten fact that nationalism is indeed a normative principle, or a language of morality: it not only describes what 'is', but also states a view about what 'should be' the case. Hence conceptual, theoretical and normative issues about nationalism are inextricably linked. This has far-reaching implications for the way we study nationalism given that our theories are intimately bound up with our current political concerns and normative judgements. More often than not, we embark on the study of nationalism with a particular national conflict in our mind, and our view of it necessarily impinges on our general perception of nationalism. In fact, most theorists have their own favourite nations, usually their own. In view of this, Norval argues that any attempt to theorize nationalism should take the form of a genealogy, that is, it has to start from where we stand today, from our present concerns and commitments (Norval 1999; see also Tamir 1999: 77, 87).

Yet for all this, nationalism did not make significant inroads into Western political theory for much of the twentieth century. The national was generally assumed to be the limit of political legitimacy, hence a background condition of almost all political thinking. More importantly, it was presumed that the question of boundaries and membership were already settled. In other words, political theorists, while writing in terms that seem to apply to all humanity, implicitly assumed that nation-states could be taken as given (Canovan 1996: 1–2).

It is only recently that the received wisdom about nationalism began to crumble under pressure from minorities and historically disadvantaged groups who spurned the dominant national ethos and escalated their demands for the recognition of their differences (Benner 1997: 191). The upshot was a major revival of interest in nationalism in Western political theory, as writers of all political stripes began to churn out books on every aspect of this baffling phenomenon. Unlike earlier writings, however, recent discussions did not treat nationalism as a background condition, but as a positive force to be promoted (see for example Tamir 1993; Miller 1995). Following Benner, we might distinguish between two strategies employed by the political theorists of the last decade. The first, what Benner calls 'the quarantine strategy', 'is mainly prudential and directed against those who value nationhood too much'. Here a healthy dose of nationalism is encouraged as a means of guarding against the real danger, virulent nationalism. The second strategy, on the other hand, consists of 'the claim that national attachments have a positive value, and seeks to give those attachments a central and constructive role in political life'. This strategy, Benner argues, is not directed against nationalists, 'but at "universalist" doctrines which routinely downgrade national culture and specificity'. Citizens who do not have a sense of collective identity and shared purpose, the argument goes, 'are prone to political apathy, social atomization and mutual irresponsibility' (Benner 1997: 191–2). Strikingly enough, the centrality of nationhood is emphasized not only by conservatives, but also left-wing writers such as David Miller, Brian Barry, Michael Walzer and Kai Nielsen.

In this chapter, I shall engage with the second strategy identified with Benner, leaving the 'quarantine strategy' to the next chapter.

I shall thus outline some of the arguments advanced in defense of nationalism, together with an overview of the main criticisms raised against each of them. I shall then turn to the issue of national partiality, that is, the idea that we owe special obligations to our fellow nationals that we do not owe to other human beings, and expose the morally dubious nature of this claim. I shall conclude the chapter by addressing the question of whether nations are moral communities.

Normative Arguments in Defense of Nationalism

All arguments in defense of nationalism are motivated by the belief that nationalism offers a set of moral values worthy of respect and serious consideration (Tamir 1993: 95). Some of these arguments stress the instrumental value of nationalism, others its intrinsic value. In what follows, I shall first identify and discuss four instrumental arguments on behalf of nationalism, which are respectively the liberation argument, the identity argument, the cultural context argument and the public good argument, before tackling the intrinsic value argument. It goes without saying that this list is not exhaustive. I have instead preferred an ecumenical approach, confining myself to the most commonly cited arguments in the field, with a view not to lose the wood for the trees and not to make the discussion unwieldy.

The Liberation Argument

It is a well-established fact that nationalism has been an important feature of anticolonial struggles in the Third World. In fact, it would not be an exaggeration to say that the legacy of European colonialism and the subsequent process of decolonization have done much to legitimate nationalist principles in this century. Hence some commentators argue that to make no concessions to the normative force of nationalism would entail not only embracing the nineteenth century empires, but also denying the moral legitimacy of anticolonial struggles in the twentieth century (Beiner 1999: 4). Accordingly, postcolonial accounts seek to demonstrate that nationalism has been a transformative and emancipatory power in the postcolonial context. Such accounts stress the importance of the principle of self-determination for people's sense of their own worth, in accord with Berlin's following observation:

> ... men prefer to be ordered about, even if this entails ill-treatment, by members of their own faith or nation or class, to tutelage, however benevolent, on the part of ultimately patronising superiors from a foreign land or alien class or milieu. (1991: 251)

This leads to a moral dilemma because even those who are opposed to nationalism are prepared to tolerate or endorse the struggle of oppressed peoples for autonomy, even though the struggle is often fought in the name of the same 'nationalist' principles they condemn. Thus we may ask, can we do both at the same time without contradicting ourselves (Miščević 2001: 5)?

I would argue that we can, as I believe the liberation argument is problematic in at least two ways. First, why are we obliged to defend imperialism, as some say we do, when we reject nationalist principles? Or, to put the point more rhetorically, why do we need to fight evil with a lesser evil? We can perfectly oppose colonialism and imperialism on the basis of more universal principles such as human rights, equality, freedom, or simply solidarity with oppressed peoples. Why do we need to fall back on nationalist justifications? The snag here of course is one of flawed comparison: the proponents of the liberation argument make things artificially easy for themselves by judging the moral worth of nationalism against something worse, in this case imperialism.

The second problem concerns the double standards of nationalism and is best exemplified by the historical record of postcolonial nationalisms. As Connor notes, although independence movements have often been conducted in the name of self-determination of nations, they were, in fact, demands for political independence not in accord with the geographical distribution of national groups, but along the borders that delimited either the sovereignty or the administrative zones of former colonial powers (1994: 5). This led to the formation of a host of multinational states, which were, in most cases, as hostile to their minorities as the colonial empires they replaced. Thus, 'national independence is often to be had only at the price of civil wars, new kinds of repression, or ensuing problems that perpetuate the initial conflicts with the signs reversed' (Habermas 1994: 127; see also Halliday 2000a). This problem stems from a more general tendency in liberal theory that leads some to assume that there are nations out there, waiting to be liberated:

> Remove the dictator, the communist party or the military junta, and what remains will be a people: that is, an entity with enough cohesion to sustain . . . stable frontiers and internal peace, and perhaps also to establish the rule of law, representative government and . . . economic prosperity. Unfortunately, as experience has continually shown, these expectations are unwarranted . . . In case after case, national self-determination has led only to the reinstatement of oppressive rule, often worse than before, since the shattered state has to be rebuilt by Macchiavellian methods. (Canovan 1996: 107)

According to Canovan, the animosity between colonizers and colonized was sometimes enough to unify the latter and create a brief illusion of nationhood during the struggle for independence. 'Once independence was achieved, however, the new state was faced with the problem of giving substance to that illusion' (*ibid.*: 108). Since the historical record gives us few grounds for assuming that nationalist government will necessarily be good government, Canovan concludes, those who support the redrawing of state boundaries along national lines cannot reasonably argue that the benefits will outweigh the immediate costs (*ibid.*: 12).

To recapitulate, the problem with the liberation argument is that the values it cherishes are often not upheld by nationalist movements themselves, which can turn out to be autocratic and oppressive (Lichtenberg 1997: 163). As Dunn reminds us, the births of nations are often ghastly affairs, years or decades drenched in blood, leaving behind precipitates of problems that are beyond any morally plausible political solution; hence we should be wary of sentimentalizing this process (1999: 38).

How should we come to grips with oppression then, a problem that continues to beset most contemporary states? Here we have two options. First, we might simply oppose oppression in the name of more universal values, such as justice, freedom and solidarity, without succumbing to the enticements of nationalism. Second, we might constantly remind ourselves that often the cause of oppression is another nationalism, which promotes the interests of the majority at the expense of minority groups. Given this, we should refrain from curing nationalism with more nationalism (of whatever kind) and consider keeping majority nationalism in check – to forestall the crystallization of an equally nationalist defense. The crux of the matter, in both cases, is the prevention of nationalist outbursts along nonnationalist lines.

The Identity Argument

The point of departure of the second set of arguments is the idea that national membership is an important and constitutive element of personal identity (Tamir 1993; Nielsen 1999b). Two factors are generally invoked to account for the importance of national identities, namely their ability to provide a sense of continuity that enables individuals to transcend the limitations of their own existence and their centrality to human flourishing.

MacCormick for instance notes that each human being as an individual has no more than a short span of life, and can never be in more than one place at a time. For each of us, then, the 'nation' can provide a conceptual framework that allows us to perceive our existence as belonging within a continuity in time and a community in space. In other words, consciousness of belonging to a nation is one of the things that enable us to transcend the limitations of space, time and mortality in this earthly existence (1999a: 193). The nation also contextualizes human actions, making them part of a creative effort whereby culture is produced and reproduced. In that sense, nations can be said to bestow extra merit on social, cultural or political acts, and to provide individuals with additional channels for self-fulfillment:

> The respect for continuity inherent in national membership enables individuals to place themselves in a continuum of human life and creativity, connecting them to their ancestors as well as to future generations and lessening the solitude and alienation characteristic of modern life. (Tamir 1993: 85–6)

There is also another way in which the nation contributes to self-transcendence. Members of a constitutive community like the nation often view their self-esteem and well-being as affected by the successes and failures of their individual fellow members and of the groups as a whole. The achievements of others enable them to enjoy qualities that they cannot develop in themselves:

> The richness of their culture, the range of opportunities open to them, the norms, patterns of behaviour, and the values they hold, all are influenced by the activities of their fellow members, whose accomplishments influence their chances of living a fully satisfying and stable life. (*ibid.*: 96)

Another version of the identity argument emphasizes the importance of national identities for human flourishing. What we have here is the psychological claim that people need to identify with or belong to some group beyond their immediate family to flourish (Lichtenberg 1997: 160–1). Thus according to MacCormick, human beings can only become individuals, that is, acquire a sense of their individuality, as a result of their social experiences within human communities (1999a: 189). For Nielsen (1999a), on the other hand, human beings have a deeply embedded and ubiquitous interest in self-identification or self-definition. We thus need to have a keen sense of our local identities if we are to flourish. In fact, a person without a community is lost! The community we belong to may well be an accident of history, but belonging itself is essential for human flourishing, and 'the historical contingency of which community we are a part does not in any interesting or significant sense make that belonging arbitrary' (Couture and Nielsen, with Seymour 1996: 624).

In a slightly different account, Margalit and Raz explain the centrality of national membership for human flourishing by pointing to the importance of recognition. Since our perceptions of ourselves are in large measure determined by how others perceive us, it follows that membership of such groups is an important identifying feature for each one of us. Members of nations are aware of their membership in it and regard it as an important clue in understanding who they are, in interpreting their actions and reactions, in understanding their tastes and their manner (1990: 446). More importantly, membership in nations is a matter of belonging, not of achievement. 'The fact that these are groups, membership of which is a matter of belonging and not of accomplishment, makes them suitable for their role as primary foci of identification'. In other words, identity is more secure when it does not depend on accomplishment (*ibid.*: 447).

Although each of these views contains important insights, they are all defective in varying degrees. First, as Lichtenberg notes, there are questions about the universality of the need to identify with a nation-like entity or about the extent to which such identification contributes to a person's flourishing. It is true that some people feel such a need; the persistence of ethnic, religious, racial and national loyalties may serve as a proof. But there are others who do not. In any case, it is not easy to prove the existence and extent of such a need empirically. It may or may not exist; it may exist in different degrees in different people; it may wax and wane over time; and it can be satisfied by means of belonging to other groupings (more on this below). In short, much of the force of this argument depends on psychological claims that are difficult to substantiate and to which no one has definite answers (1997: 162).

Moreover, we should not forget that most people do not have a real choice about their national identity because the decision is made for them by others. As I have indicated earlier, the existence of a strong sense of identification and the resonance of a particular identity are not accidental occurrences. Most national groups work very hard to produce a sense of group identity:

> They raise children to feel a sense of loyalty and kinship. They build institutions to maintain coherence among both children and adult members of the community. They develop rituals and symbols that serve to unify the group. They celebrate their histories and build monuments to the group's achievements. They also impose sanctions on those who violate the group's norms, fail to support it sufficiently, or abandon it entirely. (Nathanson 1997: 181)

In short, there is nothing inevitable or mystical about the need to identify. Members socialized to one set of norms will be inclined to do things in the ways they have learned to do them. It becomes rational to prefer the familiar. Hence 'cultural communities are not ladders that can be tossed aside easily' (Brock 1999: 376). The second problem with identity arguments is one of scale and form of political organization. More specifically, why do we need to belong to a 'national' group to flourish? We all belong to many different groups. Why can't we flourish in these other groupings? What makes the nation so special? As we have seen, Margalit and Raz argue that what makes the nation particularly suitable as a foci of identification is that its membership is based on belonging and not accomplishment. Yet there are other sources of identification, such as race, gender, family membership and genealogy, which are not accomplishment-based. There is thus nothing distinctive about national belonging (Lichtenberg 1999: 171). Moreover, there is something 'illiberal' in basing membership on belonging, that is, on something over which people have no control – this is crucial given Margalit and Raz's commitment to liberalism. 'This is, after all, part of the reason we condemn racism and other forms of prejudice and discrimination; we believe that, to the extent possible, a person's fate should depend on her autonomous choices' (*ibid.*).

At this point, we should also ask the question 'why not the human race as the object of identification'. It may be argued that humankind is too large and too abstract to generate the appropriate feelings. But are nations small and tangible enough to serve the purpose (Lichtenberg 1997: 161; see also Nathanson 1997: 178–9)?

To recapitulate, it is implausible to claim that a person's nation is particularly important for a person's self-development and flourishing. The objection here is not that people do not need a social environment to develop, but rather that it is unclear why the required culture must be a national one. As Caney argues, this is especially true in an age of increased communication and international interdependence. Nations are not (and have never been) separate entities immune to outside influence; as a result, individuals are not simply (or even chiefly) the creations of a national culture (1996: 131–2).

This last point has been given further credence by the historical record. National identity has not always been a central component of one's personal identity. For centuries, people identified themselves in terms of a shared religion, ethnicity, language, social status, place of origin and so on, and many still continue to do so in various parts of the world. As we have seen in Chapter 3, nationalism is of recent vintage from a historical point of view, and there is nothing ontologically or existentially necessary about it (Parekh 1999: 309; see also Dunn 1999: 35).

A final problem with the identity/flourishing argument is brought up by Kirloskar-Steinbach who insists, rightly in my view, that from the fact that a person benefits from one's culture, one cannot jump to the conclusion that the culture in question needs to be protected. National membership may contribute to human flourishing. But has it proved to be equally fruitful to all its members? Is there sufficient reason to believe that the positive net results of nationalism overweigh its negative net results like chauvinism, marginalization of nonmembers, and so on (2001: 111–12)? Thus the ethical content of the culture also matters; if it promotes racism and sexism, for instance, we might prefer not to protect that culture even if it contributes to its members' flourishing (see also Brock 1999).

To conclude, we can argue, following Beiner, that the sheer possession of a given identity confers no normative authority on the kind of politics that goes with that identity:

> The question for a political philosopher here is not the relevance of identity, but how to assess the normative claims embodied in conflicting visions of identity . . . The appeal to identity by itself gives us no reason to favor the distinctively nationalist way of conferring identity, as opposed to other possibilities, such as a determinedly nonnationalist civic identity. (1999: 7)

The Cultural Context Argument

Why is cultural membership important? In answering this question, the cultural context argument draws on the liberal assumption that individuals are capable of making autonomous choices about their goals in life. But their ability to do so depends on the presence of a cultural context which provides the options from which the individual chooses and infuses them with meaning (Kymlicka 1999a: 137–8; Moore 2001: 53–4). This argument portrays individuals as reflective and autonomous but these features are dependent on the presence of a context that allows them to become strong evaluators (Tamir 1993: 35). The final step in the argument is the claim that, since a rich and flourishing culture is an essential condition of the exercise of autonomy, liberals have a good reason to adopt measures that would protect the particular cultures to which people are attached (Moore 2001: 54).

The most eloquent articulation of the cultural context argument comes from Margalit and Raz. For them, nations are 'encompassing groups' in that individuals find in them 'a culture which shapes to a large degree their tastes and opportunities, and which provides an anchor for their self-identification and the safety of effortless secure belonging' (1990: 448). Individual well-being depends on the successful pursuit of worthwhile goals and relationships, and these goals and relationships are culturally determined:

> Family relations, all other social relations between people, careers, leisure activities, the arts, sciences and other obvious products of 'high culture' are the fruits of society. They all depend for their existence on the sharing of patterns of expectations, on traditions preserving implicit knowledge on how to do what, of tacit conventions regarding what is part of this or that enterprise and what is not, what is appropriate and what is not, what is valuable and what is not. Familiarity with a culture determines the boundaries of the imaginable. Sharing in a culture, being part of it, determines the limits of the feasible. (*ibid.*: 448–9)

Margalit and Raz argue that the division of the world into a number of encompassing groups with pervasive cultures has far-reaching consequences. It means that membership of such groups is of great importance to individual well-being, as it greatly affects one's opportunities, one's ability to engage in the relationships and pursuits marked by the culture. It also means that the prosperity of the culture is important to the well-being of its members. 'If the culture is decaying, or if it is persecuted or discriminated against, the options and opportunities open to its members will shrink, become less attractive, and their pursuit less likely to be successful'. Finally, if people's self-respect is affected by the esteem in which these groups are held, then the groups, membership of which contributes to one's sense of identity, should be generally respected and 'not be made a subject of ridicule, hatred, discrimination or persecution' (*ibid.*: 449).

A broadly similar account is put forward by MacCormick who argues that human beings are not extra-social atoms coming together voluntarily or otherwise to form societies. Furthermore, individuals cannot be conceived as existing with the very nature they have independently of or in abstraction from social relationships: human individuals are necessarily 'contextual individuals'. In other words, our feelings and attachments, and commitments to other people are part of what makes us human (MacCormick 1999b: 68–9, 73, 75).

There are several objections we can raise against the cultural context argument. The first objection is conceptual. As Lichtenberg rightly points out, the view that 'nations are cultures' is highly problematic for at least three reasons. First, it is not always easy to distinguish one culture from another. In the cases of the United States and Canada, for example, the two groups share the same language and have broadly similar cultural values. Second, cultures are never pure; they contain elements of other cultures. Third, within each culture we find a multiplicity of subcultures whose members have a distinct sense of identity and belonging; the relationship between cultures and subcultures, and between the concurrent loyalties of the members may be subtle and complicated (Lichtenberg 1999: 169; see also Moore 2001: 56). In short, notions such as 'encompassing groups' are based on a holistic conception of culture that is inappropriate for dealing with the obvious pluralism in much of the world (Walker 1999: 148).

The second objection concerns the link between culture and autonomy. We have seen that for Margalit and Raz, an encompassing culture provides options from which individuals can choose, thus determines the boundaries of the imaginable. But why not broaden the spectrum and increase the number of available options by learning about other cultures? On Margalit and Raz's logic, it would seem that familiarity with more than one culture would extend the boundaries of the imaginable, providing a person with even a broader range of options. In any case, the particular culture in which we find ourselves may actually provide fewer options than a different culture would. If we are after meaningful options, then one's inherited culture may not necessarily be the best or the only one to have (Lichtenberg 1999: 171; see also Brock 1999).

More importantly, why does the culture in question need to be 'national'? National cultures may indeed provide us alternatives and guidance. But so do other cultures and communities of which we are a part. Why privilege national cultures? Margalit and Raz would probably reply to this objection by noting that most encompassing cultures today are national. After all, they candidly state that they take the existing order for granted, that is, they 'assume that things are roughly as they are, especially that our world is a world of states and of a variety of ethnic, national, tribal, and other groups' (1990: 440). Yet this picture suffers from the 'coding bias' we have identified in the introductory chapter, readily adopting the viewpoint of ethnic activists who claim that the principle site of relevant cultural differences is still the ethnic group (Walker 1999: 144–5; for a more detailed discussion, see the section on reification in Chapter 7). As we shall see in more detail later, this misses the complexity of belonging in the late twentieth century. Many people today define their goals in life within transnational and subnational contexts, as well as national ones. In short, the cultural context argument does not explain why it is important to retain one's existing culture. If culture in general is a precondition of autonomy, then it should not matter which culture an individual has (Poole 1999). In fact, today, meaningful options come to us from a variety of cultural sources. The cultural context argument

> . . . shows that people need cultural materials; it does not show that what people need is 'a rich and secure cultural structure'. It shows the importance of access to a variety of stories and roles; but it does not . . . show the importance of something called *membership* in a culture . . . We need cultural meanings, but we do not need homogeneous cultural frameworks. We need to understand our choices in the contexts in which they make sense, but we do not need any single context to structure all our choices. To put it crudely, we need culture, but we do not need cultural integrity. (Waldron 1995: 107–8)

The third objection to the cultural context argument relates to the issue of the preservation of cultures. As a number of commentators have noted, the focus on autonomy is the Achilles's heel of the cultural context argument. If culture is valuable in so far as it contributes to the exercise of autonomy, then rights to the protection of culture should extend only to those cultures that value autonomy (Moore 2001: 55). Not surprisingly, cultures do not always value autonomy. At any given time any culture will sustain practices that range from reprehensible to admirable (Johnson 2000: 408). This is because every culture is also a system of regulation. While it facilitates choices, Parekh reminds us, it also disciplines them:

> It both opens up and closes options, both stabilizes and circumscribes the moral and social world, creates the conditions of choice but also demands conformity. The two functions are inseparable and dialectically related ... While valuing the indispensable place of culture in human life, we should also be mindful of its regulative and coercive role and the way it institutionalizes, exercises and distributes power ... While appreciating that culture means much to its members and deserves respect, we should remain critically watchful of the damage it causes to some or even all of them. (2000: 156–7)

This suggests that we should focus attention less on the value of culture as such than on the origins and workings of particular norms, practices, and institutions (Johnson 2000: 408). More importantly, we should not treat the right to cultural preservation as a right to cultural stasis, that is, as a right to preserve the culture as it is at present. As Buchanan reminds us, 'what is important is that an individual be able to belong to a culture, some culture or other, not that he be able to belong, indefinitely, to any particular culture' (1995: 357).

The Public Good Argument

The last argument that treats nationhood in an instrumental fashion is the public good argument. In a nutshell, this argument takes a shared national identity to be the necessary condition for achieving political goals such as democracy and social justice (Miller 1995: 162).

Taylor for example argues that democracies require a relatively strong commitment on the part of their citizens if they are to make the necessary contributions – of money (in taxes) and sometimes of blood (in war). In other words, the democratic state needs a healthy degree of 'patriotism', that is, a strong sense of identification with the polity and a willingness to give of oneself for its sake (1999: 228). Miller, on the other hand, a stalwart defender of the public good argument, claims that democratic government cannot function unless citizens trust one another, and such trust is hard to achieve where numbers are large:

> To argue on grounds of principle, rather than of sectional interest, and to moderate my demands in order to achieve a working consensus, I must believe that my fellow participants in the deliberation are similarly motivated by a desire to reach a fair agreement. Only among people held together by common loyalties and a common identity can we expect such mutual confidence to emerge. (1996: 418)

Moore offers a revised version of this argument, taking on board the obvious objection that nationalism has often been the enemy of democratic institutions. She argues that if there is a positive, mutually reinforcing relationship between national identity and democracy, then it is not the crude one that equates more nationalism with more and better democracy; but, rather, one that suggests that a common national identity tends to promote the smooth functioning of democratic institutions, by facilitating the vertical dialogue between representative and constituent (2001: 85–7).

A shared national identity generates not only the mutual trust needed for the functioning of a stable democracy, but also collective solidarity, a precondition of distributive justice. According to Miller, in societies in which economic markets play a central role, there is a strong tendency towards social atomization, where each person looks out for the interests of herself and her immediate social network. Consequently, it is very difficult to mobilize people to provide collective goods and to get them to accept practices of redistribution from which they are not likely to benefit personally. These problems can be avoided, Miller argues, only where there exists large-scale solidarity, such that people feel themselves to be members of an overarching community. Nationality, for Miller, is *de facto* the main source of such solidarity (2000: 32).

Tamir makes a similar point, arguing that the liberal welfare state is predicated on certain 'national beliefs'. 'Charity begins at home', says Tamir, and this also makes sense in practical terms; 'we are simply better equipped to promote the welfare of the members of our own society and these attempts should therefore be given priority' (1993: 120). In short, the 'others' whose welfare we should consider are those we care about, those who are relevant to our associative identity:

> Communal solidarity creates a feeling, or an illusion, of close-ness and shared fate, which is a precondition of distributive justice. It endows particularistic relations with moral power . . . Consequently, the community-like nature of the nation-state is particularly well-suited, and perhaps even necessary, to the notion of the liberal welfare state. (*ibid.*: 121)

Not surprisingly, proponents of the public good argument remain implacably opposed to identity politics which they see as a source of instability. Suppose, bemoans Miller in a rhetorical passage, that groups were to abandon their national allegiances, identifying themselves exclusively in terms of their group membership. What would politics be like in a state composed of such groups? It would take the form of bargaining in which each group deploys the resources at its disposal to promote its material and cultural interests. No group would have any particular reason to accede to the demands of any other:

> Appeals to the common good would fall on deaf ears in these circumstances, since in the absence of a common identity or sense of belonging, each group would interpret such appeals as mere masks for the interests and perspectives of the group making them. In short this would, at best, be interest group politics with the gloves off. (2000: 77)

Hence, Miller concludes, by turning their backs on national identity which can bond citizens together in a single community, advocates of identity politics would destroy the conditions under which disparate groups in a culturally plural society can work together to achieve social justice for all groups (*ibid.*: 5).

Yet the account provided by the champions of the public good argument bristles with problems. To begin with, the argument goes in the teeth of the realities on the ground. As several commentators have noted, the evidence for the claim that a strong sense of national identity facilitates redistribution is far from clear. Moore observes that the United States, for example, has a widely shared national identity and a strong sense of patriotism, but a rather weak record on social justice. 'Indeed, redistribution from rich to poor is more effective in several nationally divided societies such as Canada and Belgium than in the United States' (2001: 82). In a similar vein, Parekh notes that the Thatcher government succeeded in boosting British national identity, but it defined its content in militarist and individualist terms. As a result, most of the country felt more enthusiastic about the Falklands War and the virtues of free enterprise than about redistribution and social co-operation. For Parekh, a shared sense of common belonging leads to redistribution only when it is fuelled by a strong social conscience, and then much of the credit for the redistribution should be given to the latter (1999: 313–15).

The same goes for the claim that a shared national identity increases commitment to a democratic state. Once again, despite the existence of a strong sense of nationhood, political participation in United States is low. Canadian nationalism is relatively weaker, but the rate of participation in national elections is higher. According to Parekh, people take part in political life for a variety of reasons such as a well-developed public spirit or a strong sense of citizenship. A shared national identity is only one of these and not necessarily the most important (*ibid.*: 318).

The second problem goes to the heart of the public good argument, and the alleged link between social justice and nationhood. The claim that a shared national identity leads to mutual trust, collective solidarity and thus redistributionist policies is tantamount to saying that these desirable consequences cannot be produced in its absence. This claim, however, is too complex and vague to be tested. As Parekh reminds us, in social life, it is not easy to extricate the influences of various factors. Moreover, since the feeling of nationhood admits of degrees and is never total, the nationalist can always retort that the feeling was not strong enough to produce the desired consequences. 'What is more, democracy, redistribution and fellow feeling are not easy to define, measure and demonstrate, and therefore, again, it is extremely difficult to decide how they are affected by the shared sense of nationhood' (*ibid.*: 313–14). For Parekh, there is little evidence to support the view that a strong sense of national identity produces a strong sense of fellow feeling or a willingness to make sacrifices. Solidarity, he claims, may remain confined to symbolic collective events or to war or simply take the form of a diffused love of the country, and not translate into the love of one's countrymen or a regard for their well-being:

> The latter requires putting others' greater needs above one's own and the willingness to make the requisite sacrifices . . . The sense of solidarity at best leads one to prefer the interests of one's fellow nationals to those of outsiders but not to one's own interests, and does not guarantee a social conscience and a spirit of altruism. This means that it is not enough to talk about a shared sense of national identity; one also needs to look at its nature and content and enrich it with moral concerns. (*ibid.*: 315)

This brings us to the third problem with the public good argument, namely the idea that the nation is the main source of solidarity and mutual trust. Needless to say, both solidarity and trust – hence commitment to liberal democratic state and its institutions – may have many different sources, not to mention the state itself. We should thus situate nationalism in relation to other sources of solidarity in this context. Here Brighouse draws our attention to the extent to which Miller neglects the disruptive effects of national identities on class solidarities, and hence on redistribution. National identity, he reminds us, is often used in capitalist democracies to persuade working people that they should moderate their demands (1996: 392). In an important rejoinder, Dahbour points to the ways nation-states undermine the real bases of community in urban, local and regional ecologies (1996: 343).

To conclude, we might argue, following Tamir, that although nationhood may be an effective way of creating solidarity and mutual trust, it is certainly not the only one. If national homogeneity was a prerequisite for democracy, Tamir points out, then very few states would be able to sustain a democratic regime, and the most vulnerable states of all would be immigrant states composed of an amalgam of ethnic, racial and religious groups. History, however, tells us that such states can develop stable democratic regimes. 'Moreover, transnational corporations, regional organizations, multicultural political systems and international institutions all prove that cultural barriers can be overcome and trust can be built among individuals of different national backgrounds' (2000: 247).

Parekh goes one step further and argues that, other things being equal, a culturally diverse society can produce most of the desirable qualities a homogeneous society possesses, but the reverse is not the case. There is no apparent reason why a culturally plural society should not develop the sense of solidarity and trust necessary for a broad moral and political consensus. This is in fact more in line with contemporary historical reality. In today's highly globalized world, no society can insulate itself against external influences. Since cultural diversity characterizes almost all societies, they must either find ways of coming to terms with and even profiting from it, or suppress or marginalize it by homogenizing themselves. The latter is very difficult because it involves an unacceptable degree of internal repression. Given this, the only choice open to any society today is to manage and draw on the creative potential of its diversity (Parekh 2000: 171). This brings us to the final argument on behalf of nationalism.

The Intrinsic Value Argument

This argument claims that cultural pluralism has an intrinsic value, that the world will be a better place if it contains a diversity of cultures. Various justifications are offered for this view. The first appeals to the familiar liberal claim that there is no single best way of living. If that is correct, then it is important that a variety of cultures exist so that people may have alternatives to the cultures in which they find themselves and dissidents may have sanctuaries or places of refuge (McMahan 1997: 123). The second justification has to do, once again, with autonomy. Individuals will not be able to exercise their right to make autonomous choices unless they live in a culturally plural environment. Thus Tamir argues that human beings can only reflect critically on their culture if there are others to which they can compare their own, from which they might learn or borrow, and into which they might assimilate. In that sense, the plurality of cultures acquires an intrinsic value (1993: 30). Third, cultural diversity is itself an impersonal value. In the words of

McMahan, 'individual cultures are worth preserving both because of their own intrinsic value and because of the contribution they make to the independent value of cultural diversity' (1997: 123). In any case, diversity and plurality are good, and a world of diverse cultures and lifestyles is more interesting than a less diverse world.

The first problem with this argument is the question of what exactly we should be protecting. As Lichtenberg puts it, what sort of entity do we have to promote if our aim is to encourage the existence and flourishing of cultures? More specifically, should we promote the existence of nation-states as the embodiment of cultures (1997: 165)? This might not be necessary as diverse cultures might thrive within other political structures so far as they remain neutral among them and committed to the protection and promotion of each. Cultural diversity, in other words, may be secured and promoted in the absence of nationalism (McMahan 1997: 124; Archard 1999: 158). On this view, the intrinsic value argument may be considered as an argument for multiculturalism rather than nationalism.

The catch here is whether a culture can secure itself without a territorial state. Unfortunately, we do not have a straightforward answer to this question. We might accept that cultures have a strong claim to their own states when this is the only way they can protect their valuable characteristics. Then the issue becomes one of national self-determination with all its attendant confusions (Lichtenberg 1997: 165–6).

Second, how should we interpret 'preservation'? Waldron, for instance, argues that there is something artificial about a commitment to preserve cultures. This often implies taking a favoured snapshot of the culture, and insisting that this version must persist at all costs, in its purity. This is dangerous, however, as it might insulate the culture in question from the very forces that allow it to operate in a context of genuine choice. How does one tell, Waldron asks, whether the gender roles defined in a given culture have value for example? He suggests that one way is to see whether the culture erodes and collapses as a way of life in a world once different ways of doing things are perceived. Thus, he concludes, the possibility of the erosion of allegiance should be the key to cultural evaluation (1995: 109–10).

A closely related problem is brought to our attention by Levy who claims that in order for the project of preservation to succeed, the culture in question must have a sufficient number of strong devotees. Unlike preserving biodiversity, however, preserving cultural diversity depends on cultivating a certain frame of mind among members of the groups being preserved. And that frame of mind is necessarily hostile to diversity at some level. That in turn, Levy notes, sharply limits the moral uses of diversity. As Tamir (and others) have argued, we ought to protect and preserve cultural diversity, because it expands our range of options and our ability to think clearly about our own culture and customs:

> But this is precisely not the attitude taken by people who are in the thick of preserving their own little piece of the allegedly gorgeous mosaic. The moral psychology of belonging to and protecting one's own group is to an important degree incompatible with that critical distance. Given that cultural communities live side-by-side with one another, that they develop in part in contrast with one another . . . treating other cultural communities as a source for ideas about living or for insights about one's own lifestyle is quickly interpreted as a kind of treason. (Levy 2000: 109)

Fourth, there is also the question of 'what kind of diversity'. As Brighouse claims, a diversity of authoritarian and fundamentalist cultures, 'coexisting uneasily only because of the heroically well-constructed design of the institutions governing their interactions', might not mean much (1996: 382).

A final problem is pointed out by Hurka who observes that cultural survival is generally valued by nationalists themselves. Thus it is above all francophone Québécois who care about the survival of French culture in Québec. And they do not care about the survival of their culture in an impartial way, or merely as contributing to a universal good such as cultural diversity. If they did, Hurka maintains, they would gladly accept the disappearance of the French culture in Québec if that somehow allowed the survival of two other cultures elsewhere in the world. What they care about specially is the survival of their own culture (1997: 145).

In conclusion, I would like to argue, drawing on Benhabib, that the goal of any policy for the preservation of cultures must be the empowerment of the members of cultural groups to appropriate, enrich, and even subvert the terms of their own cultures:

The right to cultural membership entails the right to say 'no' to the various cultural offers made to one by one's upbringing ... The exercise of autonomy is inconceivable if it entails only cultural reproduction; it must also entail cultural struggle and rejection through which the old is transformed and new cultural horizons are articulated. (1999: 56)

As Benhabib rightly argues, if our goal is the preservation of cultural diversity for its own sake, we risk sacrificing moral autonomy to aesthetic plurality. Forms of life that are unjust, cruel and authoritarian can also be beautiful or interesting. We must decide whether the aesthetic value of the plurality of cultural life-forms should take priority over the freedom, justice and dignity to be accorded to all their members, and in particular their women (*ibid.*: 57).

The Issue of National Partiality

We have now spelled out and criticized various normative arguments in defense of nationalism. The common denominator of all these arguments is their belief in the moral significance of nations. They all claim, with various justifications, that nations are ethical communities. It is now time to explore the normative implications of this claim, which in turn allows us to assess the validity of the claim itself.

What Is So Special about Our Fellow Nationals?

As we have stated at the outset of the chapter, nationalism is a normative principle, which holds that the continued existence and flourishing of the nation is a fundamental good. This requires that the members of the nation be loyal both to the nation and to one another, that they give priority to one another's interests over those of nonmembers. To put it another way, the duties we owe to our fellow nationals are different from, and more extensive than, the duties we owe to human beings as such; we are permitted, sometimes even required, to favour our compatriots over outsiders (McKim and McMahan 1997: 5; Miller 1995; Lichtenberg 1997).

The demand for partiality confronts us with two immediate questions:

- What is the basis of the demand for partiality?
- What are the limits to the degree of priority that is morally justified?

One source of the sentiment of partiality appeals to our nature as persons. Each of us is variously related to some individuals and not to others. These special relations are instrumental to or even partially constitutive of our well-being. This is most obvious in the case of relations involving love: 'Love is discriminating or selective and involves a powerful disposition to favor those who are its objects; it is therefore necessarily partial' (McMahan 1997: 112–14). These special relations, or 'constitutive ties' to use Tamir's term, are thus seen to generate special obligations. These obligations are not grounded on consent, reciprocity, or gratitude, but rather on a feeling of belonging and connectedness (Tamir 1993: 137). The most prominent example of such relations is the family. It is generally acknowledged that the relation a child bears to her parents is of intrinsic moral significance, and expressions such as 'how could she do that to her parents' illustrate well the popular perception of constitutive ties as generating special obligations. They underscore our intuitive belief that it is cruel, even inhuman, to overlook the suffering and hardships of those we have a particular reason to care about (*ibid.*: 99).

National partiality is commonly justified by comparing nations to families. It is indeed true that some forms of partiality, for example, towards one's parents and children, are morally acceptable and even a duty. 'Caring more about certain people is appropriate when one stands in certain special relations to those people' (Hurka 1997: 139). The question then is: to what extent nationhood is such a relation? Are nations families writ large, from a moral point of view?

Two other potential sources of special obligations are reciprocity and gratitude. The first one is familiar from the theory of political obligation. 'One who engages in voluntary cooperative endeavors with others normally benefits from the contributions that others make to the endeavors and thereby acquires duties of fair play to reciprocate' (McMahan 1997: 129). Goodin thinks that the best way to make sense of this is to conceptualize nation-states, within the conventional wisdom about international relations, as ongoing mutual-benefit societies:

> Within mutual-benefit-society logic, it would be perfectly permissible to impose sacrifices on some people now so that they themselves might benefit in the future; it may even be permissible to impose sacrifices on some now so that others will benefit, either now or in the future. (1988: 675)

The second potential source of special duties is closely related to the first. A nation is a collective project spanning across many generations, a community of common descent and fate:

> Members of such a community see themselves as sharing a common destiny and view their individual success and well-being as closely dependent on the prosperity of the group as a whole. They think of their self-esteem and their accomplishments as related to the achievements of other group members, and take pride in the group's distinctive contributions. (Tamir 1996: 86)

If the nation offers benefits to its members and contributes to their well-being, then there are duties of gratitude they owe to it. These include not only acquiring special responsibilities towards fellow nationals, but also contributing to the ongoing existence of the national unit, taking part in the continuous recreation of its culture, learning and respecting its traditions, and engaging in a political struggle (Tamir 1993: 88).

What are then the limits of our special obligations towards our fellow nationals? Even those who argue in favour of national partiality do not see it as an absolute right that trumps the rights of others. Thus Tamir asks, 'why are we so troubled by the idea that charity begins at home?' She believes that our aversion to favouritism is not so much related to the notion of caring for particular others as it is to the idea of conferring legitimacy on an attitude that pays no heed to the needs of nonmembers. She thus argues that we are obliged to weigh the needs of members against those of others, and favour them only if the gap between their needs and those of nonmembers is not too wide (1993: 100, 112).

Hurka makes a similar point, claiming that the basis of partiality among conationals must be an objective rather than a subjective relation, and cannot be just the fact that conationals care more about each other than about nonnationals. A purely subjective basis, he contends, could not rule out the racial partiality that most of us would find morally reprehensible (1997: 149).

Equality, Justice and National Partiality

There are several problems with the view that we owe special obligations to our fellow nationals. To start with, why do we privilege national identity against other forms of identity? Nationalism is only one form of collective identity that involves loyalty and partiality, and not necessarily the most important. As Ripstein points out, if we ground our obligations on subjective attachment, then our obligations would cease as soon as we cease to feel strongly about our fellow nationals. If, on the other hand, they stem from belonging and connectedness, and they are unchosen, as many writers seem to imply, then the basis of the obligation becomes obscure and morally arbitrary. Everyone associates with many different people on many different terms, says Ripstein: 'Why not focus on geographical proximity or economic integration instead' (1997: 216)?

Barry, on the other hand, believes that there is nothing about common nationality as such for ascribing special obligations. This is not to suggest that we may not have obligations to our fellow nationals that we do not have to others. But we shall, he believes, always discover on further investigation that this obligation arises from some other morally relevant relationship that is correlated with nationality. One such relationship, according to Barry, is common membership in a state (1996: 431).

The problem here, as some commentators have noted, is with the concentric-circle image of duty. What is wrong with this image is not that it has a center that is highlighted; rather, what is wrong

... is the *progressive* character of the decline in priority as one reaches the circles farther from the center ... Once the center has been left behind ... [there is] insufficient reason to believe that one's positive duties to people in the next country ... are

any greater than one's positive duties to people on the next con-
tinent. (Shue 1988, cited in Poole 1999: 157, original emphasis)

Brighouse endorses Shue's conclusion, and maintains that once a
universalistic standard is abandoned the particularist has to give
an account of which ties and attachments should be privileged by
theory. 'The difficulty is how to abandon universality without conceding to arbitrariness' (1996: 387). To cut a long story short, the
problem with most arguments in favour of national partiality is
their inability to single out the nation as the sole or primary object
of that partiality. The groups in which such partiality is justified are
those in which one finds oneself. Yet nothing in that argument distinguishes nation from ethnic group or from language community.
'So, if the moral argument is successful, it justifies moral consideration for all of those groups. It entirely fails to justify giving
priority to one of them' (Levy 2000: 77).

What about the claim that nations are like families? In the case
of the family, Hurka notes, there exists a special relationship
between people that is both rich and intense. The members of a
family care deeply about each other as they have lived together for
many years and have to a significant degree shaped each other's
characteristics. The relations among conationals are a far cry from
this. We have never met the vast majority of our fellow nationals
and do not know who they are; 'the causal links between our lives
are tenuous at best'. Especially worrisome is the fact that these links
do not seem closer than our links with many nonnationals (1997:
147–8). No doubt, the emotional and psychological needs met by
intimate familial relationships are very important, and a form of
social organization that does not allow for the flourishing of such
relationships would be severely impoverished. But can similar
things be said about the relationships among members of a nation,
asks Lichtenberg. 'Does a world of nations better secure people's
well-being, on the whole, than some alternative arrangement? The
blood that has been shed for the cause of nationalism is a central
reason for doubting that it does' (1997: 167).

Another problem with the idea of national partiality concerns
the treatment of nonnationals. If people are constantly told that
they should care for each other on the grounds that they belong
together, Parekh points out, and if their educational, cultural and
other institutions are designed to reinforce this message, 'their

moral imagination gets so emasculated and moral resources so depleted that outsiders will come to mean little to them'. Given this, Parekh concludes, to assert that 'healthy' nationalism need not be anti-internationalist is to be naïve in the extreme (1999: 317).

To say that our duties towards fellow members can be overriden when the 'needs of strangers are significantly more urgent than those of members' is not adequate either. As Kirloskar-Steinbach notes, in situations of crisis, one's current needs could be thought of as being more pressing than that of others. How can one then 'objectively' establish the needs of strangers (2001: 112)?

A related problem arises from the nature of membership in the nation. A person's obligations towards the nation are acquired by birth, even if she chooses not to belong to it later on in life. And from the fact that a person continues to be in a nation, it is assumed that she is a willing member and that she finds her membership valuable. What about those members of the nation who decide to leave it, say, to assimilate into another nation? Will nations tolerate them too, especially when they emphasize their own 'transgenerational, genealogical continuity' (*ibid.*: 113)?

At a deeper level, the idea of national partiality contradicts with the principle of equality, which asserts that all persons are of equal worth and as such are entitled to equal concern and respect. All forms of nationalism put great weight on the distinction between insiders and outsiders, members and nonmembers. Members have particularistic responsibilities towards each other. Moreover, they are commonly seen as passing these responsibilities on to their children. The net result of all this is a rejection of the commitment to the fundamental equality of human beings (McMahan 1997: 109; Lichtenberg 1999: 182; Scheffler 1997: 195).

Where does this leave us? A good many of those who cherish national partiality are aware of these problems, and argue that although nationalism does matter, it does not cover the whole of the moral domain. Tamir for instance argues that demands grounded in a theory of nationalism must be balanced against other moral considerations (1999: 76). The question, however, is whether (and how) nationalism can accommodate these other considerations.

It is instructive to remember at this point that nationalism does not only involve a claim of partiality, but a claim of priority. The nationalist does not ask us to choose between, say, Québec or Canada and the rest of the world, but between Québec and Canada. The important point here is that nationalism claims that the nation takes priority not only over humanity, but also over rival identities, loyalties and group affiliations. If national communities have this kind of priority over other communities, then there must be something morally distinctive about nations as such. Nations, in other words, must share some trait or traits with each other that they do not share with other collectivities. Here the burden of the argument falls on academic friends of nationalism who have been unable to identify such a trait so far (Levy 2000: 75–8).

Of course the nationalist might retreat to a more modest position and ask for a universalized partiality, which acknowledges the rights of others to be partial to their own too. Yet as Lichtenberg points out, such a position could also lead to hatred and violence. Partiality, however it is conceptualized, might amount to abdicating judgement and the need for justification. One common manifestation of this universalized partiality, Lichtenberg argues, is expressed in the saying 'my country right or wrong'. The usual interpretation is that one should defend one's country no matter what it does. And that may seem persuasive because we automatically imagine abandonment as the alternative. But this is a false dilemma:

> ... loyalty to one's country might require that one stand by it ... that one own up to one's connection and do what one can to set one's country straight. But this in no way implies that one must defend one's country no matter what it does. And in the rare case where one's country ... shows itself to be irredeemable, then abandonment may be the only acceptable course. Morally speaking, then, loyalty cannot be altogether content-neutral, blind to the nature of its object. (1997: 168)

Do We Need Nationalism?

Given all these problems, should we still cling to the idea of nations as moral communities? According to academic friends of nationalism, we should, for two main reasons. First, the majority of people are too deeply attached to their national identities to make their obliteration an intelligible goal. Second, nationalism has served and continues to serve a number of important purposes; it helps to locate us in the world; it tells us who we are, where we have come from, what we have done (Miller 1995: 184). It provides us with a principle of demarcation, and strengthens the claim that members of the state share something more than a set of institutions, 'something that evokes in them feelings of solidarity and fraternity' (Tamir 1993: 124).

Yet it would be idle to pretend that we are on the verge of some general consensus on the ethical status of nationalism. According to Miller, there are two kinds of challenges to the idea of nationalism. The first, more philosophical, challenge alleges that the idea itself cannot withstand critical scrutiny. The second, more political, challenge focuses on the practical consequences of national allegiances (1995: 12). Miller skirts around these challenges by falling back on 'complacency'. For him, political theorists are not obliged to give rationally compelling reasons for people to have national attachments and allegiances. 'What we can do is to start from the premise that people generally do exhibit such attachments and allegiances, and then try to build a political philosophy which incorporates them' (2000: 25).

'Complacency' is not the preserve of Miller, however, and constitutes a much wider problem in the field of political theory. Walzer, for example, argues that the commitment of individuals and groups to their own history, culture and identity – what he calls 'tribalism' – is a permanent feature of human social life. The parochialism that it breeds is similarly permanent. It cannot be overcome; it has to be accommodated (1999: 215). In his work on minority rights, Kymlicka makes a similar point, claiming that 'the fact that national minorities seek state recognition and use of their language and culture doesn't really need much explaining – it reflects a pervasive and *commonsensical* attachment to one's language and culture that is also found among national majorities' (1997: 64, emphasis mine).

Such unfettered complacency leads some of these political theorists to scoff at attempts to question the ethical status of nationalism. Miller's vitriolic portrayal of people who do not prioritize their national identity is worth quoting at length:

They are happy to think of themselves simply as individuals who happen to be working in this job, consuming these goods, married to this partner and so on. Questions such as 'What kind of society am I living in, and how has it come to be the way that it is?' don't matter to them. Along with this goes a view of the world as a kind of giant supermarket in which different goods and services are on offer in different places, and in which it is perfectly reasonable for individuals to gravitate to whatever place offers them the best package. On this view, national ties should count for nothing except perhaps in so far as they affect the range of cultural goods on offer in a particular place. For reasons that will be apparent, I regard such an outlook as pathological. (1995: 165)

According to Miller, a society in which everyone held such views would not be able to sustain itself. In view of this, we must either embrace a national identity and its attendant obligations and commitments, or free-ride on the backs of other people who do (*ibid.*).

What are the implications of this for the tangled world of international politics? 'Political communities should as far as possible be organized in such a way that their members share a common national identity, which binds them together in the face of their many diverse and private and group identities'. What Miller envisages is a world in which different nations can coexist peacefully. He is quick to add that he does not wish to defend the present pattern of global inequality, which bears the marks of past and present exploitation. At the same time, however, 'some degree of inequality is inevitable, and not unjust, because it is the direct consequence of a system where independent nations pursue the policies that reflect their own cultural ends' (*ibid.*: 188–92).

This complacent attitude *vis-à-vis* the existing state of affairs is nonetheless morally misguided and politically dangerous. I have already exposed the problems associated with various attempts to demonstrate the instrumental value of nationalism in the preceding sections; so I shall not reiterate them here. More generally, there are three fundamental problems with the project of rehabilitating nationalism.

First, the whole project is based on dubious premises. As Tamir notes in her discussion of the theoretical difficulties in the study of nationalism, an important characteristic of most contributions to political theory in the last two decades is their inability to successfully combine the philosophical analysis of political principles with an empirical understanding of political processes (1999: 85). Political theorists, for the most part, continue to take people's attachments to their national identities for granted, making this the fulcrum of their argument. This necessarily subverts their ability to grasp the drastic political changes that characterize our times – not to mention the theoretical problems associated with 'reification', which will be elaborated in Chapter 7. There is an element of truth in the commonplace observation that nationalism is losing its iron grip on collective identification. In that sense, Parekh's assertion that the nationalist political theorist nostalgically champions the cause of the nation at a time when it is irretrievably weakened appears to be compelling (1999: 311; this point will be further discussed in subsequent chapters).

Second, there is the problem of scale, or unit of analysis. Waldron hits the nail on the head when he expresses his frustration with the absence of a clear understanding of the concept of 'community' in the accounts of academic nationalists – by which he means the absence of any settled sense about the scope and scale of the social entity they have in mind. When they say the modern individual is a creation of community, or that each of us owes her identity to the community in which she is brought up, or that our choices are necessarily framed in the context of a community, he asks, what scale of entity are they talking about?

> Is 'community' supposed to denote things as small as villages and neighborhoods, social relations that can sustain *gemeinschaft*-type solidarity and face-to-face friendships? . . . Should we even suppose that communities are no bigger than states? If each of us is a product of a community, is that heritage limited to national boundaries, or is it as wide (as worldwide) as the language, literature and civilization that sustain us? (1995: 95–6)

We know that for many centuries, people have constructed their sense of belonging along a continuum of spatial attachments. Why should the nation have a hegemony over other sources of identity, which can also provide us with a sense of identity and belonging? What makes nations 'moral communities' at the expense of other communities to which we belong? Here nationalist theorists once again absolve themselves of any responsibility and refuse to consider in any sustained way the rival claims of other collective identities to offer normative foundations for social and political integration. Yet it is difficult to square these assumptions with the obvious pluralism in much of the world (Delanty and O'Mahony 2002: 185).

Finally, there is of course the historical record of nationalism, which gives little relief to those who wish to uphold moral values. The philosophical defenses of nationalism always work with abstract, and highly benign forms of nationalism, with no counterparts in the real world. Yet the road to successful nationhood is always very bumpy, and achieved by means that are not readily acceptable from a moral point of view. Thus, as Waldron rightly argues, the communitarianism that can sound cozy and attractive in a book can be blinding, dangerous and disruptive in the real world, 'where communities do not come ready-packaged and where communal allegiances are as much ancient hatreds of one's neighbors as immemorial traditions of culture' (1995: 113). In other words, the benefits that may flow from nationhood may be bought at too high a price in hostility to those trapped on the wrong side of the border.

What then are the options available to those who wish to operate outside the nationalist frame of reference? One option is to consider whether the emotional, moral, social and political benefits the nation supposedly confers on its members might be supplied from another source, without the attendant violence and hatred (Scruton 1999: 281). It is to this question that I now turn.

5

Nationalism, Multiculturalism and Liberalism

How can we cope with the fact of cultural diversity that characterizes virtually every nation-state today? As Kymlicka observes, minorities and majorities are at loggerheads with each other over such issues as language rights, regional autonomy, political representation, education curriculum, land claims, immigration and naturalization policy, even national symbols such as the choice of national anthem or public holidays. 'Finding morally defensible and politically viable answers to these issues is the greatest challenge facing democracies today' (1995: 1).

The last two decades saw several attempts to take up this challenge and to work out 'morally defensible and politically viable' formulae to accommodate cultural diversity. Nationalism looms large in all these discussions, owing to the profound sense of confusion concerning the exact nature of the relationship between multiculturalism and nationalism. The major question preoccupying political theorists in this context is whether multiculturalism constitutes a threat to nationalism.

In what follows, I shall argue, contrary to much received wisdom, that 'actually existing' multiculturalism does not pose a serious threat to nationalism. Theorists of multiculturalism, particularly those of liberal persuasion, take the view that we live in a world of nation-states for granted, and strive instead to design institutions that would contain nationalism's worst excesses. Theirs is a particular form of nationalism, 'liberal', 'moderate', thus hospitable to cultural diversity. This is reminiscent of what Benner calls the quarantine strategy, employed by those who seek to rehabilitate nationalism. This strategy, Benner tells us, is directed against those who value nationhood too much, and is based on encouraging a healthy dose of nationalism as a means of warding off the real danger, that is, virulent nationalism (1997: 191–2).

My aim in this chapter is to bring into focus the affinities between liberal multiculturalism and nationalism. In pursuit of this task, I shall first sketch the contours of the liberal nationalist project and review the criticisms that are raised against it. I shall then spell out the main arguments of liberal multiculturalism, drawing in particular on the works of Will Kymlicka and Charles Taylor. Following a critique of liberal models, I shall conclude by considering forms of multiculturalism that operate outside a liberal framework, laying special emphasis on 'dialogical' models of multiculturalism.

Liberal Nationalism

The mainstay of the liberal nationalist project is the belief that we should distinguish morally defensible forms of nationalism from morally indefensible forms. Liberal nationalists think that it is possible to take the illiberal sting out of nationalism, hence to find a form of nationalism that is compatible with liberal political commitments. In fact, this is the only way to fight virulent nationalism. In the words of Barber, 'pathological patriotism can be cured only by healthy patriotism, jingoism only by a pacific constitutional faith, destructive nationalism only by liberal nationalism' (1996: 36). Liberal nationalism, its promulgators add, is also an answer to the malaise of modernity, an antidote to 'the "cold" language of rights and liberties, the "shallow" and "faceless" universalism of certain liberal doctrines, and the "bloodless" cosmopolitanism of Eurocrats' (Benner 1997: 203; see also Kirloskar-Steinbach 2001).

Yet nationalism poses particular problems for liberal theory. As I have pointed out earlier, liberals are committed to the fundamental moral equality of persons. The question is whether this commitment is compatible with the demands for loyalty and partiality. More generally, can nationalism and liberalism be reconciled?

Liberals or Nationalists?

According to Yael Tamir, the most vociferous proponent of the liberal nationalist project, the answer to the above question is an unequivocal 'yes'. The liberal tradition, Tamir argues, with its respect for autonomy, reflection and choice, and the national tradition, with its stress on belonging, loyalty and solidarity, although generally seen as mutually exclusive, can indeed accommodate one another (1993: 6). Both schools of thought can agree on a characterization of individuals as agents who acknowledge that their ends are meaningful only within a social context, but who do not necessarily accept socially dictated ends unreflectively (*ibid.*: 18). Such a conception of the person embodies both the liberal virtue of self-authorship and the national virtue of embeddedness:

> It portrays an autonomous person who can reflect on, evaluate and choose his conception of the good, his ends, and his cultural and national affiliations, but is capable of such choices because he is situated in a particular social and cultural environment that offers him evaluative criteria. (*ibid.*: 33)

Liberal nationalism thus celebrates the social and cultural embeddedness of individuals together with their personal autonomy. It cultivates national ideals without losing sight of other human values against which national ideals need to be weighed, thereby redefining legitimate national goals and the means used to pursue them (*ibid.*: 79).

It is important to note at this point that for Tamir, the integration of liberal and national values precludes the possibility of granting ultimate value to national goals. Liberal nationalism does indeed suggest that individuals should be concerned with the welfare of their fellow members before they are concerned with the interests of nonmembers, but it places this argument within the framework of a universal theory. Here Tamir follows Mazzini who once declared that patriots and devoted nationalists are not to be freed from asking themselves the Kantian question: 'You must ask yourself whenever you do an action in the sphere of your country or your family . . . if what I am doing were done by all and for all, would it advantage or injure humanity? And if your conscience answers, it would injure humanity, desist' (*ibid.*: 115).

Membership in a liberal nation, on the other hand, is elective: 'individuals have a choice. They can refuse to speak the language of their community, reject their culture, and assimilate into a different culture'. Understood in this way, national obligations are nothing but the reflective acceptance of an ongoing commitment to participate in a critical debate about the nature of the national culture (*ibid.*: 88–9). In short, the political system of a liberal national entity

> will reflect a particular national culture, but its citizens will be free to practice different cultures and follow a variety of life-plans and conceptions of the good. The political entity described here differs from the traditional liberal entity in that it introduces culture as a crucial dimension of political life. Its unity rests not only on an overlapping consensus about certain values . . . but also on a distinct cultural foundation. (*ibid.*: 163)

Tamir does concede that liberal nationalism is a rather esoteric approach, given the political realities that surround us. Nevertheless, she argues that there is a long-standing – though much denied – alliance between liberal and national ideas. Why, for example, is citizenship in a liberal state a matter of birthright and kinship rather than choice? Why do liberals believe that individuals owe political loyalty to their own government rather than to the government that is the most just of all? Why does the liberal welfare state distribute resources among its own citizens, largely ignoring the needs of nonmembers? The answers to these questions, Tamir claims, direct us to the national values hidden in the liberal agenda (*ibid.*: 117). Two major issues concerning terms of membership force liberals to resort to national ideas according to Tamir. The first issue is demarcation: since liberalism cannot provide a theory of demarcation, it has adopted the national ideal of self-determination for this purpose. The second issue, on the other hand, is continuity. 'In order to sustain its character as a law-abiding and caring community, the liberal state must view itself as a continuous community rather than as a casual association of parties to a contract that could be rescinded at any time' (*ibid.*: 121). By absorbing national concepts, liberalism has thus been able to take the existence of states inhabited by specific populations for granted, and discuss ideas such as distributive justice, consent, obligations in reference to this reality. Liberals were thus able to circumvent such notorious issues as membership and immigration. 'These moves have made modern liberal theory dependent on national ideals and a national world order, thus leaving liberals little choice. Except for some cosmopolitans and radical anarchists, nowadays most liberals are liberal nationalists' (*ibid.*: 139).

Needless to say, Tamir is not the only one who attempts to reconcile liberalism and nationalism. Couture *et al.* propose their version of liberal nationalism, which they claim is fully compatible with a universalistic and internationalist cosmopolitan outlook. In fact, they believe that there are instances of liberal nationalism in the real world. Thus in our recent history Norwegian, Icelandic, Finnish and Flemish nationalisms were instances of such nationalisms and at present Catalonian, Scottish, Québécois and Welsh nationalisms are paradigms of liberal nationalism. This liberal nationalism is open and a matter of cultural achievement, residence and allegiance, as opposed to cultural nationalism which is closed, exclusionary and racist (1996: 580–602). The liberal nationalist contends that since group identity and cultural membership are key goods for all human beings, then it is something that must be recognized not only for her group, but for all human beings. Hence she will be tolerant of all other nationalisms that are themselves similarly tolerant (Nielsen 1999a). This point is also emphasized by Taylor who argues that there are qualitative differences between liberal nationalism like, for example, contemporary Québec independentism and what we now see raging in Bosnia. 'The idea that these are both manifestations of the same force but differing in virulence is a serious mistake' (1999: 241–2).

In fact, the extent to which a nationalist movement is liberal largely depends on whether or not it arises within a country with long-established liberal institutions. Flemish, Scottish and Québec nationalisms are liberal because Belgium, Britain and Canada are long-standing liberal democracies. In contrast, Serb, Ukrainian and Slovak nationalisms are illiberal because they emerged in illiberal states. 'Nationalist movements, then, tend to take their cue from the political culture around them' (Kymlicka 1997: 64).

A Critique of the Liberal Nationalist Project

If we scratch any existing account of liberal nationalism, we find beneath the surface the (in)famous distinction between 'good' and 'bad' forms of nationalism. As I have sought to demonstrate in Chapter 2, however, this distinction is fundamentally misguided. All forms of nationalism carry within them the seeds of evil and even the most moderate forms can easily be converted to virulent ones under propitious conditions. In other words, the line separating the 'good' from the 'bad' and the 'ugly' is quite thin.

This point is well-exemplified by a number of political theorists who adopt a cautious approach to the liberal nationalist project. Benner draws our attention to the recent break-up of multinational communist states, which reminded us how easy it is to cross the line between moderate and overheated forms of nationalism. She argues that already at the end of the eighteenth century, the ideals of patriotism had proved susceptible to degeneration. 'There is plenty of historical evidence that patriotism has a built-in tendency to turn angry, exclusive and belligerent under pressure'. In any case, Benner continues, most nationalists are inclined to describe themselves as patriots whose aims are essentially defensive. Thus 'the cross-breeding of idioms' continues unabated (1997: 196–7).

More importantly, history teaches us that no culture is inherently illiberal or incapable of reform. After all, all existing liberal nations had illiberal pasts, and their liberalization followed a prolonged process of institutional reform. Moreover, the liberality of culture is a matter of degree:

> All cultures have illiberal strands, just as few cultures are entirely repressive of individual liberty. Indeed, it is quite misleading to talk of 'liberal' and 'illiberal' cultures, as if the world was divided into completely liberal societies on the one hand, and completely illiberal ones on the other. The task of liberal reform remains incomplete in every society. (Kymlicka 1999b: 124)

We can conclude, with Barry, that the liberal nationalist doctrine is far too cautious to underwrite the recent uses of nationalist arguments in, say, Bosnia and Rwanda. 'Diluted poison is still poison: even if the principle of homeopathy is valid in medicine, it has no place in political philosophy' (Barry 1996: 430).

The second major problem with liberal nationalism concerns the viability of the project itself and raises the question of whether there are or can be any real world manifestations of liberal nationalism. According to Benner, it may not be as easy to reconcile liberal and national values as some political theorists have claimed. As it puts great weight on identity as a condition for the viability of the political community, national doctrine tends to override individual and cosmopolitan aspirations when these threaten the primary goals of unity and collective defense. In other words, 'constitutive questions of boundaries and membership tend to be logically and practically prior to the questions of constitutional justice that are central to liberalism' (2001: 172).

Parekh, on the other hand, finds it difficult to understand how Tamir proposes to ensure that the nation remains hospitable to diversity, given her insistence that it should also hold on to its cultural homogeneity and integrity. Since the nation as she understands it means so much to its members, Parekh notes, it is not clear why they should risk its dilution by tolerating diversity and dissent. In short,

> Tamir's liberal insistence that membership of the nation should be voluntary is difficult to reconcile with her view that the nation constitutes and structures one's identity. And while she is right to stress the importance of the right to exit, the latter is likely to prove morally and emotionally too costly to be exercised by most of its members. (1999: 307)

The whole point is succinctly summarized by Barry who points to the extent to which academic liberal nationalists find themselves attached to movements that do not fit their model because their nationalism articulates so poorly with popular nationalism. The two causes dearest to the hearts of contemporary academic nationalists, Barry claims, are those of Israel (in the case of Michael Walzer and Yael Tamir) and Québec (in the case of Charles Taylor and Will Kymlicka). However, the phenomena in these two cases obstinately fail to fit their model. According to Barry, the very existence of Israel in its present location is incomprehensible in the absence of the idea that a self-defined descent group can lay claim to a national territory even if those that it regards as its ancestors occupied it many moons ago (1999b: 133).

This brings us to the price to be paid to make the liberal nationalist amalgam work. According to Beiner, the only way the liberal nationalist project can succeed is to remove from nationalism the very things that make nationalism philosophically interesting. Defenders of liberal nationalism tend to forget that the national idea has been a potent force in the modern world precisely because it promotes ideas of national belonging, national destiny and rootedness as an alternative to liberal conceptions of life. Thus in Tamir's case, for example, the nationalist side of the equation is so watered down that the nationalism in her political theory is barely detectable. What nationalists typically want, Beiner argues, is not a vaguely defined 'public space' for the display of their national identity, but rather, control over a state to advance the cause of national self-expression. No real nationalist would accept that the ideal of the nation-state should be abandoned – as Tamir does. Beiner concludes by noting that 'any attempt to synthesize liberalism and nationalism theoretically will be forced to drop either the liberalism or the nationalism when it comes to the crunch'. The problem, in a nutshell, is how to privilege the majority cultural identity in defining membership without relegating cultural minorities to second-class citizenship (1999: 8–12).

Brock concurs, claiming that liberal nationalism can differentiate itself from morally problematic forms of nationalism only if it is rendered vacuous. It is noticeable that the sorts of liberal nationalisms outlined by political theorists are, in effect, indistinguishable from some varieties of cosmopolitanism or global humanism, if we take seriously what they say about obligations to nonmembers (1999: 368–9).

There are also more practical problems associated with liberal nationalism. First, as we stressed earlier, all forms of nationalism, including the so-called liberal nationalism, distinguish between members and nonmembers, and divide the world into 'us' and 'them'. This stress on membership can conflict with liberalism's commitment to the fundamental equality of persons. This becomes clear when we recall the principle of national partiality, which requires that the interests of members of the nation be given priority over the interests of nonmembers. Here Lichtenberg draws a distinction between a purer version of nationalism, which asserts that the welfare of outsiders does not count at all – exemplified by the standard view of international relations, in which nation-states are supposed to pursue their own interests – and a more moderate version, which stipulates that a nation may not harm outsiders but need not promote their welfare. She argues that the distinction is not very clear in practice, as the question of how the moderate version differs from the purer one depends on where and how we draw the line between the infliction of harm and the failure to promote welfare (1999: 179–82).

A second practical problem is pointed out by Parekh who draws our attention to the extent to which liberal nationalists talk of the nation as if it were an incontrovertible political reality. As a matter of fact, Parekh argues, contra Couture *et al.*, that very few states fit their description of nationhood, and those that do are increasingly ceasing to be so under the impact of globalization, multiculturalism and cultural self-assertion by such marginalized groups as women, immigrants, national minorities, and indigenous peoples:

> Very few of them possess the required degree of solidarity, cohesion, cultural homogeneity and fellow feeling. None is free from the often very deep class, religious, gender, generational, and other divisions, or the diversity of moral values, lifestyles, tastes and sensibilities . . . The unity of the state cannot be grounded in the unity of the nation as the nationalists maintain, for the simple reason that the 'nation' today is too fragmented, plural and fiercely contested to possess the kind and degree of unity necessary to sustain the state. (1999: 318–19)

A final practical problem, brought up by Kymlicka and Straehle, concerns the cases where a majority nationalism confronts minority nationalisms. If it is indeed desirable for states to be nation-states, as some liberal nationalists claim, then this seems to leave two unattractive options in countries where there are two or more national groups: either (a) split up multinational states so as to enable all national groups to form their own nation-state, or (b) enable the largest or most powerful national group to use state nationalism to destroy all competing national identities (1999: 76). According to Kymlicka and Straehle, this requires reformulating the liberal nationalist goal:

> We need to think of a world, not of nation-states, but of multi-nation states. If liberal nationalism is to be a viable and defen-

sible approach in today's world, we need to renounce the traditional aim of liberal nationalism – namely, the aspiration to
common nationhood within each state – and instead think of
states as federations of self-governing peoples, in which boundaries have been drawn and powers distributed in such a way as
to enable all national groups to exercise some degree of self-
government. (*ibid.*: 78)

In conclusion, we should note the extent to which liberal nationalist theorists suffer from the 'complacency syndrome' identified
in the previous chapter. As Canovan notes, although liberalism's
dependence on nationalism is crucial and too little noticed, it is a
matter of political contingency rather than philosophical necessity.
'In principle, it may some day turn out to be the case that con-
sensual power can be mobilized and institutionalized in other ways'
(1998: 250). The same point is made by Benner who contends that
those who put the values of nationality on an ethical par with wider
principles of justice in effect treat a historically specific, nation-
centered order as if it were the best possible order. Yet the current
constitutive and geopolitical attractions of nationhood are not necessarily ethical attractions. This means that 'if liberals strike new
compromises with nationalism, they should do so on grounds of
political and geopolitical realism, not on the misguided belief that
the "core" ethical values of nationality deserve special respect'
(2001: 173; see also Halliday 2000a).

Multiculturalism and the Politics of Recognition

One of the most distinctive features of our time is the demand by
various cultural groups for the political recognition of their distinct identities. Cultural minorities have existed in all modern
societies. Sometimes these have been created by large-scale immigration, as in the case of the United States or Australia. In other
cases, minority communities have successfully resisted the pressures towards cultural assimilation characteristic of nation-building
processes (Poole 1999). As Moore remarks, these groups were
mostly concerned with the just distribution of resources such as
money, power, status, and so on, and paid no heed to issues of identity, membership, or cultural biases of the state until relatively

recently. In the last few decades, however, a number of minority cultural or other disadvantaged groups have begun to raise their voice, claiming that the policies of the liberal democratic state have the effect of disadvantaging them. Women, gays and lesbians, minority religious, racial and ethnic groups, and disabled people have drawn our attention to the numerous ways in which the construction of the public sphere has marginalized them, arguing that, in many cases, the public sphere, which pretends to be treating everyone as an equal, is in fact based on the majority culture. This movement came to be recognized under the rubric of 'multiculturalism'. Minority nations in multinational states have similarly criticized state policies for implicitly privileging the majority national group on the territory. Not satisfied with equal citizenship rights, they have made claims for state protection of their culture or for recognition of their distinct identity (Moore 2001: 2–3).

According to Walzer, these demands came to the fore today, because the everyday encounter with otherness has never been so widely experienced: 'No one is shushing us anymore; no one is intimidated or quiet . . . The voices are loud, the accents various, and the result is not harmony' (1997: 96).

The terms 'multicultural' and 'multiculturalism' have no clear or fixed meaning. They may be used simply to record the fact that all contemporary societies contain a plurality of distinct cultural groups. On the other hand, the term 'multiculturalism' is also used to denote a viewpoint about the nature of cultural differences and about how we should respond to them individually and politically (Miller 1995: 130–1). Parekh makes a similar distinction between the two terms. A multicultural society, according to him, is one that includes two or more cultural communities. This society might respond to its cultural diversity in one of two ways, each in turn capable of taking several forms. It might either welcome and cherish it, making it central to its self-understanding, and respect the cultural demands of its constituent communities; or it might seek to assimilate these communities into its mainstream culture. In the first case, it is 'multiculturalist' and in the second 'monoculturalist' in its orientation and ethos. Both are multicultural societies, but only one of them multiculturalist. In short, 'the term "multicultural" refers to the fact of cultural diversity, the term "multiculturalist" to a normative response to that fact' (2000: 6).

Parekh also believes that multiculturalism should not be about minorities, for that implies that the majority culture is uncritically accepted and used as a yardstick to judge the claims and define the rights of minorities. Multiculturalism, he contends, should be about the proper terms of relationship between different cultural communities. The norms governing their respective claims cannot be derived from one culture alone but through an open and equal dialogue between them (*ibid.*: 13).

Before moving on, it needs to be pointed out that there are significant differences in the ways these problems arise in different societies. As Joppke and Lukes aptly summarize,

> Canadian multiculturalism is a specific response to the problem of Anglo-French biculturalism . . . In the United States, multiculturalism is race-based, and amounts to remedial action towards discriminated insiders of the national community. In Europe, by contrast, multiculturalism is directed at foreigners, most notably at postcolonial and guestworker immigrants . . . Because European multiculturalism concerns groups from the outside, towards which there is only a weak sense of historical guilt and indebtedness, it is unlikely to switch from the passive toleration mode . . . to the active restitution mode of the United States. (1999: 16–17)

As a result, there is no multiculturalism *tout court*; 'there are only specific, context-dependent multicultural problematiques; the search for a universal formula, and final judgement, is misguided from the start' (*ibid.*: 16).

Liberal Theory of Multiculturalism

As we have seen in the previous section, the main problem for the academic defenders of nationalism was how to reconcile liberalism and nationalism. The liberal debate on multiculturalism is haunted by the same specter – the specter of 'compatibility'. Put simply, is the recognition of collective cultural rights compatible with the main tenets of liberalism? The last two decades have witnessed several attempts to tackle this question. No doubt, the most influential of these is that of Will Kymlicka, whose 'liberal theory of minority rights' has become the bible of the students of multi-culturalism.

Kymlicka's point of departure is an empirical observation: most countries are multinational, in the sense that they contain two or more nations or peoples. In such multinational states, there is a majority national group and one or more national minorities (1999b: 100). According to Kymlicka, liberals believed for a long time that minority conflicts would be resolved by granting basic human rights such as freedom of speech, association and con-science to all individuals regardless of group membership. Where these individual rights are firmly protected, liberals assumed, no further rights needed to be attributed to the members of specific ethnic and national minorities. However, it has soon become clear that minority rights cannot be subsumed under the category of human rights. Traditional human rights standards were simply unable to resolve some of the most important and controversial questions concerning cultural minorities: which languages should be officially recognized in the parliaments, bureaucracies and courts? Should ethnic or national minorities have publicly funded education in their mother tongue? How should internal boundaries be drawn? Should governmental powers be devolved from the central level to more local or regional levels controlled by particular minorities, particularly on culturally sensitive issues such as immigration, communication and education? Should polit-ical offices be distributed in accordance with the proportion of each national or ethnic group in the population? For Kymlicka, the problem is not that traditional human rights doctrines give the wrong answer to these questions. It is rather that they give no answer at all. The right to free speech, Kymlicka argues, does not tell us what an appropriate language policy is; the right to vote does not tell us how internal boundaries are to be drawn, or how powers are to be distributed between different levels of government. To resolve these questions fairly, Kymlicka concludes, we need to sup-plement traditional human rights principles with a theory of minority rights (1995: 2–5).

The next step in Kymlicka's model consists of identifying the patterns of cultural diversity in a given society and the kinds of demands ethnic or national groups might make. There are two broad patterns of cultural diversity according to Kymlicka. The first arises from the incorporation of previously self-governing, territorially concentrated cultures into a larger state. These incorporated cultures, which Kymlicka calls 'national minorities', do not wish to be assimilated into the majority culture, and demand various forms of autonomy or self-government to ensure their survival as distinct societies. In the second case, on the other hand, cultural diversity arises from individual and familial immigration. Such immigrants generally wish to integrate into the larger society, and to be accepted as full members of it. While they often strive for greater recognition of their ethnic identity, their ultimate goal is not to become a separate and self-governing nation, but to alter the institutions and laws of the mainstream society so as to make them more hospitable to cultural differences (*ibid.*: 10–11).

Similarly, there are two kinds of claims that an ethnic or national group might make. The first involves the claim of a group against its own members; the second involves the claim of a group against the larger society. Both kinds of claims, Kymlicka argues, are intended to protect the stability of national or ethnic communities, but they respond to different sources of instability. The first kind aims to protect the group from internal dissent, whereas the second aims to protect the group from the impact of external decisions – for example, the economic and political decisions of the larger society. According to Kymlicka, liberals can and should endorse certain external protections, where they promote fairness between groups, but should oppose internal restrictions that constrain the right of group members to question and revise traditional authorities and practices (*ibid.*: 35–7).

Why should liberals endorse these group-specific rights? Because, Kymlicka replies, no state can be completely 'neutral' with respect to various national groups that form the society. States systematically privilege the majority nation in certain fundamental ways – for example, the drawing of internal boundaries, the language schools, courts and government services, the choice of public holidays. All of these decisions, Kymlicka argues, can enhance the power of the majority group at the expense of national minorities. Group-specific rights, on the other hand, help ensure that national minorities are not disadvantaged in these decisions (*ibid.*: 51–2).

Kymlicka is careful to admit that liberals can endorse minority rights only if they are consistent with respect for the freedom or autonomy of individuals. He does however believe that such rights are not only consistent with individual freedom, but can actually promote it. Here Kymlicka introduces the concept of 'societal culture', by which he means 'a culture that provides its members with meaningful ways of life across the full range of human activities, including social, educational, religious, recreational and economic life, encompassing both public and private spheres'. These cultures tend to be territorially concentrated, and depend on a shared language. For a culture to survive and develop in the modern world, Kymlicka contends, it must be a societal culture. Only 'nations' or 'peoples' have the capacity and motivation to form and maintain such a distinct culture. 'Societal cultures, then, tend to be national cultures' (*ibid.*: 75–80).

How are societal cultures important to individual freedom? Kymlicka resorts to 'the cultural context argument' to account for the link between individual freedom and culture:

> Freedom involves making choices amongst various options, and our societal culture not only provides these options, but also makes them meaningful to us . . . Cultures are valuable, not in and of themselves, but because it is only through having access to a societal culture that people have access to a range of meaningful options . . . The availability of meaningful options depends on access to a societal culture, and on understanding the history and language of that culture. (*ibid.*: 83)

According to Kymlicka, the attachment people feel for their language and culture is a fact to be reckoned with. The members of a nation may no longer share the moral values or traditional ways of life characteristic of the nation, but they will still have a deep attachment to their own language and culture. Indeed, Kymlicka argues, it is precisely because national identity does not rest on shared values that it provides a secure foundation for individual autonomy and self-identity. 'Cultural membership provides us with an intelligible context of choice, and a secure sense of identity and belonging' (*ibid.*: 105).

As we have alluded to earlier, Kymlicka disparages the belief that people's interest in cultural membership is adequately protected by the common rights of citizenship. The idea of responding to cultural differences with 'benign neglect' makes no sense because the members of a national minority face a disadvantage which the members of the majority do not face. In that sense, the ideal of 'benign neglect' is just a myth. Government decisions on languages, internal boundaries, public holidays, and state symbols unavoidably involve recognizing, accommodating and supporting the needs and identities of particular ethnic and national groups. Yet there is no reason to regret this fact, as long as we ensure that these unavoidable forms of support for particular ethnic and national groups are provided fairly – that is, in a way that would not privilege some groups and disadvantage others (*ibid.*: 108–15).

Kymlicka deliberately excludes the demands made by such marginalized groups as women, gays and lesbians, the disabled from the ambit of his theory, focusing instead on the sort of 'multiculturalism' which arises from national and ethnic differences. Yet the last few decades have also witnessed an escalation of demands by groups who represent practices, lifestyles and views that are different from, disapproved of, and in varying degrees discouraged by the dominant culture of the wider society. These demands form part of a wider struggle for recognition of identity and difference, or of 'identity-related differences' (Parekh 2000: 1) – the subject of Charles Taylor's widely acclaimed article, 'The Politics of Recognition' (1994).

The Politics of Recognition

Taylor begins his analysis by noting that a number of strands in contemporary politics turn on the need for recognition, which is given urgency by the presumed links between recognition and identity:

> The thesis is that our identity is partly shaped by recognition or its absence, often by the misrecognition of others, and so a person or group of people can suffer real damage, real distortion, if the people or society around them mirror back to them a confining or demeaning or contemptible picture of themselves. Nonrecognition or misrecognition can inflict harm, can be a form of oppression, imprisoning some in a false, distorted, and reduced mode of being. (1994: 25–6)

Taylor distinguishes two changes that brought about the modern preoccupation with identity and recognition. The first is the collapse of social hierarchies, which in the past formed the basis of honour. This notion of honour, Taylor argues, is replaced with the modern notion of dignity, the only one compatible with a democratic society where everyone is supposed to be equal. This in turn made 'equal recognition' an essential part of the democratic culture. The second change, on the other hand, is the emergence of a new understanding of individual identity at the end of the eighteenth century. This was the idea of an 'individualized' identity, one that is particular to 'me', and that I discover in 'myself'. Taylor calls this the ideal of 'authenticity'. This ideal states that there is a certain way of being human that is our way. This in turn gives a new importance to being true to ourselves. If we are not, we miss the point of our lives (*ibid.*: 26–30).

We need to refer to a third factor, however, in order to account for the close connection between identity and recognition. This factor is the fundamentally 'dialogical' character of human life:

> We become full human agents, capable of understanding ourselves, and hence of defining our identity, through our acquisition of rich human languages of expression . . . But we learn these modes of expression through exchanges with others . . . we are introduced to them through interaction with others who matter to us – what George Herbert Mead called 'significant others' . . . We define our identity always in dialogue with, sometimes in struggle against, the things our significant others want to see in us. (*ibid.*: 32–3)

What has come about with the modern age, Taylor adds, is not the need for recognition but the conditions in which the attempt to be recognized can fail. That is why the need is now acknowledged for the first time (*ibid.*: 35).

At this point, Taylor turns to the politics of recognition, and argues that this has come to mean two different things. The move from honour to dignity has led to a politics of universalism, which emphasized the equal dignity of all citizens, and the aim of this politics was the equalization of rights and entitlements. By contrast, the second change, or the development of a new understanding of identity, has given rise to a politics of difference, which asked us to recognize the unique identity of a particular individual or group, their distinctness from everyone else. The idea here is that it is precisely this distinctness that has been ignored, or assimilated to a dominant identity. Not surprisingly, this assimilation is the cardinal sin against the ideal of authenticity. Underlying this demand, Taylor remarks, is a principle of universal equality. Here, however, equality is described as requiring that we make people's distinctions the basis of differential treatment (*ibid.*: 37–9).

Taylor argues that these two modes of politics, both based on the notion of equal respect, come into conflict. On the one hand, the principle of equal respect requires that we treat people in a difference-blind fashion. On the other hand, we have to recognize and even encourage particularity. The reproach the first mode of politics makes to the second is that it violates the principle of nondiscrimination. The reproach the second mode of politics makes to the first is that it negates identity by forcing people into a homogeneous mould. This would be bad enough even if the mould were itself neutral. But it is not: 'the supposedly neutral set of difference-blind principles of the politics of equal dignity is in fact a reflection of one hegemonic culture' (*ibid.*: 43). Here Taylor joins Kymlicka, and asserts that liberalism is not a neutral meeting ground for all cultures, but is itself the political expression of one range of cultures, and quite incompatible with other ranges. 'All this is to say that liberalism can't and shouldn't claim complete cultural neutrality. Liberalism is also a fighting creed' (*ibid.*: 62).

In view of this, liberals must accept that we owe equal respect to all cultures. The presumption here is that all human cultures that have animated whole societies over some considerable stretch of time have something important to say to all human beings (*ibid.*: 72–3). Thus what has to happen is what Gadamer has called a 'fusion of horizons':

> We learn to move in a broader horizon, within which what we have formerly taken for granted as the background to valuation can be situated as one possibility alongside the different background of the formerly unfamiliar culture. The 'fusion of horizons' operates through our developing new vocabularies of comparison, by means of which we can articulate these contrasts. So that if and when we ultimately find substantive support for our initial presumption, it is on the basis of an understanding of what constitutes worth that we couldn't possibly have had at the beginning . . . we owe all cultures a presumption of this kind. (*ibid.*: 67)

According to Taylor, we only need a sense of our own limited part in the whole human story to accept the presumption. 'What it requires above all is an admission that we are very far from that ultimate horizon from which the relative worth of different cultures might be evident' (*ibid.*: 73).

Here I have been only able to sketch some of Kymlicka's and Taylor's complex and many-stranded arguments. Yet a more detailed examination of their contributions would deflect attention from this chapter's main purpose, which is to discuss the relationship between multiculturalism and nationalism. It is to this that I now turn.

A Critique of Liberal Multiculturalism

Does multiculturalism pose a threat to nationalism? Should we consider it as an alternative to nationalism or simply as another form of nationalism? Before embarking on a discussion of these questions, it may be helpful to point out some of the problems with liberal multiculturalism.

The first problem with most versions of liberal multiculturalism is their tendency to divide the social world into distinct cultures. As Brubaker and Cooper show, social and cultural heterogeneity is construed here as a juxtaposition of internally homogeneous, externally bounded blocs. As a result, the social world is seen as 'a multichrome mosaic of monochrome identity groups' (2000: 31–2). Thus one obvious objection to the claim that people need homogeneous cultures to make meaningful and autonomous choices is that such cultures exist nowhere, neither as minority cultures nor as the majority cultures of nation-states (Joppke and Lukes 1999: 10). This particular vision, or what Joppke and Lukes call 'mosaic multiculturalism', equates culture with territory. This is, however, a wholly inaccurate account of today's mixed-up world. It is ironical that, Joppke and Lukes add, so many people have discovered the existence of their culture just when recent anthropology has come to deny it. Drawing on Renato Rosaldo, they argue that the view of an authentic culture as an autonomous, internally coherent universe is no longer tenable in a postcolonial world. 'Neither "we" nor "they" are as self-contained and homogeneous as we/they once appeared. All of us inhabit an interdependent late twentieth-century world, which is . . . marked by borrowing and lending across porous cultural boundaries' (*ibid.*: 11).

The picture is further complicated by the fact that the proponents of multicultural policies are rarely the oppressed minorities themselves, most of whom do not have their 'own voice', but the elites who claim to represent or to speak for these groups (*ibid.*: 2). Equally importantly, as we have already seen earlier, any cultural group in the modern world would contain at least the following: identifiers, quasi-identifiers, semi-identifiers, non-identifiers, ex-identifiers, cross-identifiers, and anti-identifiers. A multicultural politics of identity is necessarily geared towards the concerns and interests of the first group (*ibid.*: 10).

Some commentators exploit this last point to reject group-based claims altogether. Kukathas, for example, argues that cultural groups are not seamless wholes but associations of individuals with differing interests. So within any minority, there are other, smaller minorities. To treat the wider group as the bearer of cultural rights is to affirm the status quo and thus to favour existing majorities. This also restricts the opportunity of minorities within the group to reshape the cultural community. According to Kukathas, liberal theory should be generally concerned to avoid entrenching majorities or creating permanent minorities, hence the need to reject the idea of group claims as the basis of moral and political settlements (1992: 114).

This is closely related to a second problem with most liberal accounts, which we might call 'the self-fulfilling prophesy problem'. As Levy points out, the celebration of cultural communities slips too quickly from 'is' to 'ought' (2000: 7–8). As a result, protagonists of multiculturalism end up naturalizing culture, seeing it as an unalterable and ahistorical fact of life (Parekh 2000: 10–11). To put it differently, they tend to fix and privilege certain group identities at the expense of others. This is inevitable according to Miller, for identity politics cannot be infinitely flexible: '[i]t must designate certain groups for recognition, fix their membership and determine what rights they are going to enjoy' (2000: 73).

A third problem concerns the cultural context argument used to reconcile the liberal ideals of autonomy and freedom with multiculturalism. We have already noted that for Kymlicka, the ability to make autonomous choices is contingent upon membership in a stable culture. Yet as Peled and Brunner rightly argue, Kymlicka provides no empirical and historical evidence to support this sweeping claim. He does not face the rather obvious fact that not all cultures foster the ability of individuals to appraise and revise received wisdoms and values critically. In fact, some cultures not only fail to do so, but regard the development of such critical faculties as a threat to the community. Moreover, Peled and Brunner continue, being an outsider to the majority culture, in other words being marginalized or exiled, may not necessarily be disadvantageous for individual autonomy as understood by Kymlicka. To illustrate this point, they refer to the case of Jewish intellectuals who have transposed themselves from an orthodox environment into their surrounding secular, non-Jewish societies, and to a number of postcolonial intellectuals who have extolled the virtues of marginality, hybridity, the diaspora, liminality, exile and even nomadism, as cultural conditions they consider empowering for critical thinking (2000: 71–2).

Kukathas voices similar concerns, and argues that the problem with stressing the primacy of importance of individual autonomy is that many cultures do not place such value on the individual's freedom to choose her ends. Instead, he proposes that the wish to live in accordance with the practices of one's own cultural community has to be respected not because the culture provides a meaningful context of choice, but because individuals should be free to associate – to form communities and to live by the terms of those associations. A corollary of this is that the individual should be free to dissociate from such communities. According to Kukathas, then, cultural communities should be looked on 'as associations of individuals whose freedom to live according to communal practices each finds acceptable is of fundamental importance'. As Kukathas points out, this liberal individualist view has the advantage of recognizing the existence of cultural groups while denying that they are in any sense 'natural' – regarding them instead as associations of individuals drawn together by history and circumstance (1992: 116–17).

Let us pause here for a while and consider Benhabib's critique of liberal multiculturalism, which offers the best way to recapitulate what has been said so far. Benhabib begins her analysis by drawing our attention to the extent to which a holistic view of cultures and societies as being internally coherent, seamless wholes has dominated recent debates on multiculturalism (1999: 45). This is particularly true in the case of Kymlicka who proposes us to focus on 'societal cultures', which he defines as 'a culture that provides its members with meaningful ways of life across the full range of human activities'. According to Benhabib, there are no societal cultures as such because any complex human society, at any point in time, is composed of material and symbolic practices with a particular history. This history, she argues, is the accumulation of struggles for power, symbolization, naming, and signification, in short for cultural and political hegemony carried out among different groups, classes, and genders. Hence 'there is never a single culture, as a coherent system of beliefs, significations, symbolizations, and practices, which extends "across the full range of human activities"' (*ibid.*: 53–4).

For Benhabib, Kymlicka's equation of societal cultures with national cultures is also problematic, since with this admission his multicultural liberalism comes to resemble varieties of nineteenth-century nationalism. He is compelled by the logic of his own argument to confuse societal culture with the dominant culture, and to plead for the preservation of such cultures. Such a definition of culture and the privileging of societal cultures marginalize other forms of collective identity formations which coalesce around different identity-markers. This is, according to Benhabib, an illiberal conclusion (*ibid.*: 55).

Benhabib is not happy with the cultural context argument either, for reasons similar to the ones specified in Chapter 5. Even if we admit that culture is valuable from the standpoint of liberalism, because it enables a meaningful range of choices, there is objectively no basis for preferring national cultures to ethnic cultures, to the cultures of religious groups, or of social movements. The value of culture for liberalism is to provide options for individual choice. To jump from this premise to the conclusion that only in societal cultures can such a value be realized, Benhabib concludes, is reifying ontology (*ibid.*).

Let us wrap up this discussion with an objection raised by Brian Barry, the most trenchant critique of recent debates on multiculturalism from within the liberal camp. Barry believes that 'multiculturalism', construed as a programme rather than as a description, is a potentially misleading way of describing claims made on behalf of a very heterogeneous set of groups with very different objectives. Endemic in the literature of multiculturalism, he argues, is the tendency to suggest that all social groups are differentiated by culture, and have distinctive outlooks, aspirations and priorities:

> This 'culturalisation' of group conflicts in many cases provides a misleading analysis of what is at issue. For example, those who object to being discriminated against in education or employment on grounds of race, gender or sexual preference may simply be demanding an equal opportunity to achieve exactly the same goods that others desire. (1999b: 129)

Often, Barry maintains, the appeal to culture is an attempt to justify either the oppression of one group by another or the oppression of some members of a group by others within the group in the name of an illiberal culture. Under these circumstances, what contemporary liberals need to do is to renew their commitment to equality of opportunity, as the demands of 'multiculturalism' begin to bite only where this condition is not fulfilled (*ibid.*: 136–8). Peled and Brunner concur, noting that what is at issue is not only cultural rights and their effects on self-respect but, equally importantly, the socioeconomic structure faced by members of minority groups and the set of practices available to them, which allow them to take advantage of the opportunities presented to them (2000: 67).

It is now time to turn to the stormy relationship between multiculturalism and nationalism. Some commentators argue that in most models of multiculturalism, the individual is connected to the larger society and state institutions not directly, as in the classic model of national citizenship, but through prior membership in her cultural group. Yet this brings with it the risk of social fragmentation. Thus one of the standard critiques of multiculturalism is its disuniting or fragmenting of national societies (Joppke and Lukes 1999: 8). Billig repudiates this view, arguing that although multiculturalism might threaten old hegemonies, which claimed to speak for the whole nation, and although it might promise an equality of identities, it is still constrained within the notion of nationhood; it takes for granted that there is a 'society', which is to be multicultural. As such, it implicitly inherits a tradition of 'us' and 'them'. According to Billig, unless identity politics can transcend the nation, the radicalism of the challenge to old images and narratives is constrained within the assumptions of nationalism (1995: 148).

Barry looks at this issue from another angle and contends that what various forms of liberal multiculturalism have in common is that they assume there to be nothing except 'my culture' and 'your culture'. It is not even 'my culture, right or wrong', because that still presupposes that right and wrong can have a content independent of culture. Rather, it is 'my culture provides the measure of what it right for me, and yours does the same for you'. In that sense, each culture is a 'moral monad'. This is nothing but the pluralization of the romantic nationalist idea of the incommensurability of national moralities (1999b: 141).

The problem is further complicated by the discourse of the actual leaders of minority groups. Their discourse, Norman argues, does not mirror the Kymlickian appeal to the need for a healthy cultural context as a necessary condition for individual. They are more likely to speak like nationalists and appeal to national identity and sentiments. The question liberal theorists have to address is 'to what extent do they remain good liberals while talking like nationalists' (1999: 61).

However, this may well be a problem specific to 'liberal' models of multiculturalism. As I have already indicated at the beginning of this chapter, most of those who are in the business of reconciling liberalism and multiculturalism are also committed to the beleaguered cause of liberal nationalism. Accordingly, they want to have the best of both worlds, a society which is at one and the same time liberal nationalist and multiculturalist. The question that springs to mind in this context is: why should our models for a multicultural society take a liberal national form? More importantly, why should a society that contains a plurality of cultural communities subscribe to a particular worldview, be it liberalism or nationalism?

This question is most directly addressed by Parekh in his recent *Rethinking Multiculturalism* (2000). According to Parekh, a multicultural society, by definition, consists of several cultural communities with their own distinct systems of meaning and significance:

It cannot therefore be adequately theorized from within the conceptual framework of any particular political doctrine which, being embedded in, and structurally biased towards, a particular cultural perspective, cannot do justice to others. This is as true of liberalism as of any other political doctrine. (*ibid*.: 13)

Liberals, however, disregard this obvious fact and continue to absolutize liberalism – hence their persistent tendency to make it their central frame of reference, divide all ways of life into liberal and nonliberal and equate the latter with illiberal. The crudity of this distinction would become clear, Parekh argues, if we were to divide all religions into Christianity and non-Christianity and equate the latter with anti-Christianity. Hence liberals need to break away from this crude binary distinction if they are to do justice to alternative ways of life and thought. They cannot do so unless they stop absolutizing the liberal way of life:

> . . . that in turn requires them to accept the full force of moral and cultural pluralism and acknowledge that the good life can be lived in several different ways, some better than others in certain respects but none is the best . . . The spirit of critical self-understanding opens up a vitally necessary theoretical and moral space for a critical but sympathetic dialogue with other ways of life, now seen not as objects of willing or grudging tolerance but as conversational partners in a common search for a deeper understanding of the nature . . . of human life. (*ibid*.: 110–11)

Liberals might reply to this charge by arguing that since we live in a liberal society, we need to develop a liberal theory of multicultural society. This argument, Parekh notes, excludes non-Western societies, many of which are not liberal and some do not even aspire to be liberal. Even so far as western societies are concerned, they are multicultural and include cultures some of which are liberal and some others nonliberal:

> Since the latter contest liberal principles, neither the society nor a theory of it can be constructed on these principles alone. To do so is both unjust, because it denies the legitimate claims of nonliberal cultures to participate in decisions relating to the

political structure of the wider society, and risky because the resulting structure cannot count on their allegiance. (*ibid.*: 14)

The Promise of Dialogue

We have already touched upon some of the problems with liberal multiculturalism and its infatuation with nationalism. But the question with which we set out is still there: how can we cope with cultural diversity? Is there a form of multiculturalism that does not seek to theorize cultural diversity from within a particular political doctrine, say, liberalism, and which does not take the nation for granted? Equally importantly, what are the prospects for collective political action under conditions of cultural diversity?

For some, the prospects for such action are indeed dim. Miller, for instance, argues that multiculturalists portray a society that is fragmented in many crosscutting ways, aspiring at the same time to a politics that redresses the injustices done to previously oppressed groups. Since, however, the injustices will be group-specific, Miller asks, how will it be possible to build a majority coalition to remedy each of them? Given finite resources, why would gays support favourable treatment for Muslims, or Jews or Blacks? (1995: 139).

Ignatieff makes a similar point, claiming that the problem with multicultural politics is not fragmentation, but 'autism': 'groups so enclosed in their own circle of self-righteous victimhood, or so locked into their own myths or rituals of violence, that they can't listen, can't hear, can't learn from anybody outside themselves'. What is denied here, Ignatieff notes, is the possibility of empathy by special acts of imaginative projection (1999: 97).

What kind of multiculturalism can enable us to transcend these problems? Any answer to this question should involve acquiring knowledge of cultures and moral practices other than our own, with a view to eroding the boundaries separating different cultures. Key to this process is the concept of 'dialogue'.

Several writers have proposed models of multicultural politics which have dialogue as their central component. Yuval-Davis, for example, speaks of 'transversal politics' in the context of feminist struggle, a form of coalition politics in which the differences among different groups are recognized and given a voice in and outside the political units. The boundaries of this coalition are not set in terms of 'who we are' but in terms of 'what we want to achieve' (1997: 126). Transversal politics, Yuval-Davis explains, espouses a 'dialogical standpoint epistemology', which holds that 'from each positioning the world is seen differently, and thus any knowledge based on just one positioning is "unfinished"'. Dialogue is critical to the success of this approach since 'the only way to approach "the truth" is by a dialogue between people of differential positionings, and the wider the better'. Transversal politics thus assumes *a priori* respect for others' positionings, rejecting any notion of hierarchy between differences. It also differentiates between positioning, identity and values; people who identify themselves as belonging to the same collectivity can actually be positioned very differently in terms of various social locations – their gender, class, sexuality, stage in the life cycle and so on. At the same time, people with similar identities and/or positionings can have very different values. This has two implications. First, community activists cannot and should not see themselves as 'representatives' of their constituencies; rather, they are 'advocates' working to promote the group's cause. More importantly, they do not have to be members of the group they advocate for: 'it is the message, not the messenger that counts'. This, in turn, avoids the necessity of constructing fixed and reified boundaries for social groups (this section is based on Yuval-Davis, forthcoming).

Miščević, on the other hand, proposes a model of 'interactive multiculturalism', enriched with a cosmopolitan perspective, which relies upon the existence of some sort of understanding between ethnically and culturally diverse groups. In this model, classical states are seen as only one kind of political organization among many – macro-regional, micro-regional and global, to mention some. And the ethnonational criterion of belonging is certainly not the most important criterion of political organization. States are typically multi-ethnic, with ethnic belonging most often cutting across state boundaries. Macro-regions are pivotal to this model, as they encompass sufficient cultural similarities to ground a macro-regional culture, half-way between a purely cosmopolitan and a purely ethnonational one (2001: 129, 285–90).

The centrality of dialogue and intercultural understanding are also emphasized by Benhabib who maintains that the emergence of international markets of labour, capital and finance, and the subsequent world-wide development of means of transportation and communication have produced a 'community of interdependence'. In this context, Benhabib argues, the articulation of 'a pluralistically enlightened ethical universalism' on a global scale emerges as a possibility and, in fact, as a necessity (1999: 51). This in turn requires us to understand each other, and to enter into a cross-cultural dialogue in which all are participants – 'all' referring to all of humanity. On the other hand, all dialogue, if it is to be distinguished from 'cajoling, propaganda, brainwashing, strategic bargaining and the like', presupposes certain normative rules:

> Minimally formulated these normative rules entail that we recognize the right to equal participation among conversation partners; the right to suggest topics of conversation, to introduce new points of view, questions and criticism into the conversation; and the right to challenge the rules of the conversation insofar as these seem to exclude the voice of some and privilege those of others. These rules of conversation can be summed up with the norms of 'universal respect' and 'egalitarian reciprocity'. (*ibid.*: 52)

The most elaborate model of a 'dialogical multiculturalism', however, comes from Parekh. For Parekh, a dialectical and pluralist form of universalism offers the most appropriate response to moral and cultural diversity. Parekh continues to have faith in the existence of universal moral values, but he argues that the best way of arriving at these values is through a universal or cross-cultural dialogue (2000: 127–8). According to Parekh, political dialogue has a distinct structure and is not as inconclusive and open-ended as some people suggest. 'Commitment to it implies a willingness both to accept certain norms, modes of deliberation, procedures, and so on and to live with and act on such consensus as the subject in question allows' (*ibid.*: 15).

Parekh argues that we need the dialogue to counter our tendency to universalize our own values. The dialogue brings together different historical experiences and cultural sensibilities, and ensures that the values we arrive at are genuinely universal. 'It subjects our reasons for holding them to a cross-cultural test and requires us to ensure that they are accessible and acceptable to members of very different cultures'. It thus provides those involved a motive to comply with the outcome (*ibid.*: 128).

From a more practical point of view, a multicultural society should foster a strong sense of unity and common belonging among its citizens; otherwise it cannot act as a united community able to take and enforce collectively-binding decisions. Yet it cannot ignore the demands of diversity either. Like any society, then, a multicultural society needs a broadly shared culture to sustain it. Since it involves a variety of cultures, this shared culture can only grow out of their interaction, and should both respect and cultivate their diversity, and unite them around a common way of life. At this point, Parekh notes that for those who are used to think of culture as a more or less homogeneous and coherent whole, the idea of a 'multiculturally constituted culture' might appear incoherent, even bizarre. In fact, Parekh argues, such a culture is a fairly common phenomenon in every culturally diverse society (*ibid.*: 196, 220).

How does such a culture look like? Parekh kicks off with a fairly common observation. In any multicultural society, cultures constantly encounter one another both formally and informally, and in private and public spaces.

> Guided by curiosity, incomprehension or admiration, they interrogate each other, challenge each other's assumptions, consciously or unconsciously borrow from each other, widen their horizons and undergo small and large changes . . . Over time they tend to throw up a new composite culture based on their respective contributions and insights and possessing a somewhat fuzzy but recognizable identity of its own. It is neither their lowest common denominator nor a mere collection of their arbitrarily selected beliefs and practices, but a more or less distinct culture in which these are all redefined, brought into a new relationship and compose a loosely-knit whole. Once developed, it forms the basis of their interaction, helps create a common ethical life, and throws up a body of common principles that inform public policies and structure political discourse. (*ibid.*: 220–1)

Parekh notes that like all cultures, the 'interculturally created' and 'multiculturally constituted' culture is an unplanned growth:

Its contents are broadly but not universally agreed, and remain subject to dispute. It is relatively open-ended, multistranded, pulls in different directions, and is constantly in the making. Since it grows out of the interaction between different cultures, it is internally plural and both unites them and respects their diversity. Not all members of society approve of all aspects equally, but they all find enough in it to own it as theirs and give it different degrees of allegiance. (*ibid.*: 221)

A multiculturally constituted common culture can only emerge and enjoy legitimacy if the constituent cultures participate in its creation in a climate of equality. They should enjoy equal respect, equal opportunities for self-expression, equal access to private and public spaces, equal ability to interrogate each other, in short more or less equal power and resources. 'Once these and other equalities necessary for a fair and effective interaction are ensured, the dialogue follows its own logic and its outcome cannot be predetermined' (*ibid.*).

Parekh concludes by stressing that from a multicultural perspective, no political doctrine or ideology can represent the full truth of human life. Each of them, be it liberalism, conservatism, socialism or nationalism, is embedded in a particular culture, thus necessarily narrow and partial (*ibid.*: 338). A truly multicultural society accepts the reality and desirability of cultural diversity and structures its political life accordingly. It is dialogically constituted, but the dialogue requires certain institutional preconditions such as 'freedom of expression, agreed procedures and basic ethical norms, participatory public spaces, equal rights, a responsive and popularly accountable structure of authority, and empowerment of citizens' (*ibid.*: 340).

It goes without saying that dialogical models are not completely problem-free. Thus one problem with intercultural dialogue, suggested by Young, is the question of who will speak for the differing cultural groups in the dialogue. In most situations of intercultural political dispute, Young argues, there are differences 'within' as well as 'between' the relevant cultural groups, and dynamics of power allow only some of the voices within the groups to be heard. According to Young, the genuine inclusion of all those affected by political decisions must involve the political process taking special measures to ensure that the members of more marginalized or less powerful social segments have an equal voice and equal influence (2001: 120–1). We should note in passing that the model of 'transversal politics' seems to be better equipped to cope with this problem as it insists on seeing 'community leaders' as advocates of particular causes, not as representatives (unless they are democratically elected), and urges them to be reflective of the multiplexity of their specific positionings in relation to other members of their collectivities. Yet political realities do not always keep pace with our theoretical models. Thus it may not be as easy to implement dialogical models under conditions of tense intercultural conflict as their protagonists would have us believe. This being said, models based on intercultural dialogue seem to be immune to the many ills with which liberal nationalist models of multiculturalism are inflicted and constitute a better response to the predicament of the global age we live in.

6

Nationalism and Globalization

Globalization and the 'Crisis' of Nationalism

The 'crisis' of the nation-state is one of the most worn-out clichés of the last decade, and the future of nations and nationalism appears to many to be more uncertain than ever under the twin pressures of globalization and identity politics. The nation-state is besieged from on top, says Hall, by the growing interdependence of the planet. The enormous changes brought by globalization are increasingly undermining the stability of any national formation. At the same time, however, there is a movement down below. Peoples and groups who were previously harnessed together in nation-states begin to rediscover identities they have long forgotten. 'So at one and the same time people feel part of the world and part of their village' (1996a: 343).

I have already addressed the question of identity politics in the previous chapter. The aim of the present chapter is to engage with the second threat, the threat from above, and explore the implications of globalization for the future of nations and nationalism. Some of the questions I shall discuss in this context are: Does globalization herald the end of the nation-state, or is it leading to the emergence of new forms of state? How does it affect the traditional concept of sovereignty? What does globalization entail for nationalism? Does it engender new forms of belonging above or beyond the nation?

126

Debates on Globalization

Globalization is one of the academic buzzwords of the last few decades, and there has been a veritable deluge of publications exploring various aspects of this phenomenon. Needless to say, it is impossible to do justice to all these debates within the limited compass of a single chapter. In any case, a detailed discussion of the causes, history and the normative status of globalization would deflect attention from the chapter's main purpose, the description and evaluation of the relationship between globalization and nationalism. Still, this problem cannot be tackled properly without some understanding of what exactly we mean by globalization.

Perhaps the most common definition of globalization equates it with 'increasing interdependence'. It is often argued that the fate of all parts of the globe is bound together more intensely than before through the interpenetration of economic, political and cultural relationships across existing borders and boundaries. Underlying this definition is the idea of 'global village', in which all local, regional and national elements are tied together in one interdependent whole (Holton 1998: 1–2).

There are three basic problems with this definition. First, it does not tell us what is new and distinctive about contemporary globalization. As a number of commentators remind us, interconnections between countries have intensified at various junctures during the 500-year history of the modern states-system (see for example Scholte 2000). What makes the cross-border transactions and interlinkages of the last few decades different? Why do we introduce a new term to describe these interlinkages, instead of using the old ones – such as 'internationalization'? Second, this definition is not sensitive to the uneven impact of globalization across different parts of the world. And third, it does not say enough about the extent to which this interdependence has captured people's imagination.

A second definition sees globalization in a more negative light, and identifies it with 'homogenization' and 'Westernization'. As Waters observes, globalization is an obvious candidate for ideological suspicion, because it appears to justify the expansion of Western culture and capitalism by implying that the forces that are transforming the world are beyond human control (1995: 3). Hence globalization is perceived as the domination of Western economic and cultural interests over the rest of the world – a tool that facilitates the perpetuation of inequality between rich and poor countries. A specific version of the homogenization argument lays emphasis on the 'Americanization' of global culture. The Americanization thesis points to the predominant American ownership of key resources for the production and dissemination of culture. It emphasizes the US's role in constructing a regulatory framework within culture and information industries that favours US interests. Finally, it draws our attention to the diffusion of cultural practices across a wider number of settings, influencing the very characteristics of modern social life. This was in many ways what Ritzer meant when he coined the term 'McDonaldization of Society', referring to 'the process by which the principles of the fast-food restaurant are coming to dominate more and more sectors of American society as well as of the rest of the world' (Ritzer 1993: 1; Holton 1998: 2–3, 166–8).

The homogenization/Westernization thesis does not provide an adequate account of globalization either. Globalization is not a single all-conquering and homogenizing force, driven by the logic of capitalism or Western cultural imperialism. As Pietersee notes, cultural experiences have not been simply moving in the direction of cultural uniformity and standardization. Such a conception overlooks the impact non-Western cultures have been making on the West:

> It downplays the ambivalence of the globalizing momentum and ignores the role of local reception of Western culture – for example the indigenization of Western elements. It fails to see the influence non-Western cultures have been exercising on one another. It has no room for crossover culture – as in the development of 'third cultures' such as world music. It overrates the homogeneity of Western culture and overlooks the fact that many of the standards exported by the West and its cultural industries themselves turn out to be of culturally mixed character if we examine their cultural lineages. (1995: 53)

In short, while the activities of many global businesses as well as international organizations do point in the direction of homogenization and standardization, there is still room for the reproduction of considerable social and cultural diversity within the interconnected global structure. What is more, some groups tend to react to increasing interconnectedness by demarcating their own boundaries more sharply, both socially and symbolically (Goldmann *et al.* 2000: 10–11).

A third definition of globalization emphasizes the diminishing significance of time and space as the world becomes more interconnected. This conception of globalization owes a lot to the work of David Harvey (1990) and Anthony Giddens (1990). Harvey, for instance, argues that we have been experiencing an intense phase of 'time–space compression' in the last two decades, which had a disorienting and disruptive impact upon political-economic practices, the balance of class power, as well as upon cultural and social life. What has happened, according to Harvey, is the 'annihilation of space through time'. Key to this was the deployment of new organizational forms and new technologies in production, and parallel accelerations in exchange and consumption (1990: 284–307).

For Giddens, too, globalization implies changes in the problematic of 'time–space distanciation', that is, how social life is ordered across time and space. Giddens notes that the conceptual framework of time–space distanciation directs our attention to the complex relations between local involvements and interaction across distance. In the modern era, Giddens argues, the level of time–space distanciation is much higher than in any previous period, and the relations between local and distant social forms and events become correspondingly 'stretched'. Globalization refers to that stretching process. It can thus be defined as 'the intensification of worldwide social relations which link distant localities in such a way that local happenings are shaped by events occurring many miles away and vice versa' (1990: 64).

Such a definition of globalization is more helpful than the previous two as it helps us distinguish the contemporary phase of globalization from earlier phases and as it alerts us to the pivotal role of the rise of a global consciousness. For some writers, these two insights are in fact closely related. Waters, for example, argues that what separates contemporary globalization from its earlier manifestations is its 'reflexivity', as his definition of globalization as 'a social process in which the constraints of geography on social and cultural arrangements recede and in which *people become increasingly aware that they are receding*' underlines (1995: 3, 45, emphasis mine).

In his recent overview of the globalization debate, Scholte makes a similar point, identifying globalization with changing conceptions of space. He argues that the proliferation and spread of supraterritorial connections – such as telephone calls, electronic finance and the depletion of stratospheric ozone – brings an end to what could be called 'territorialism', that is, a situation where social geography is entirely territorial. Although territory still matters very much in our globalizing world, Scholte remarks, it no longer constitutes the whole of our geography (2000: 42–8). Social space has this supraterritorial dimension partly because we often think globally: 'we conceive of the world not only as a patchwork of territorial realms, but also as a single place where territorial distance and borders are (at least in certain respects) irrelevant' (*ibid.*: 54).

Still, this definition does not say much about the uneven impact of globalization in different contexts and the thorny issue of the local–global dynamic. A more fruitful alternative is proposed by Robertson who has provided probably the most comprehensive account of the interplay between localizing and globalizing trends. Robertson begins by noting the extent to which much of the talk about globalization has tended to see it as a process that overrides locality. This widespread tendency takes on its most acute form in the claim that we live in a world of local assertions against globalizing trends, a world in which the idea of locality is sometimes construed as a form of opposition or resistance to the hegemonically global (1995: 26–9). In contrast, Robertson maintains that globalization has involved the reconstruction, in a sense the production, of 'home', 'community' and 'locality'. To that extent the local should not be seen as a counterpoint to the global. Instead it should be regarded, subject to some qualifications, as an 'aspect' of globalization. Thus Robertson coins the term 'glocalization' to emphasize that globalization has involved the simultaneity and the interpenetration of what are conventionally called the global and the local, or – in more abstract vein – the universal and the particular (*ibid.*: 30).

According to Robertson, the view that contemporary conceptions of locality are largely produced in global terms does not mean that all forms of locality are thus substantively homogenized. Robertson remains implacably opposed to the view that globalization implies a homogenization of local cultures. First, there is virtually overwhelming evidence that cultural messages emanating from 'the USA' are differentially received and interpreted; that local groups absorb communication from the 'center' in a great variety of ways. Second, the major alleged producers of 'global culture' – such as those in Atlanta (CNN) and Los Angeles (Hollywood) – increasingly tailor their products to a differentiated global market they partly construct. Third, seemingly 'national' symbolic resources are in fact increasingly available for differentiated global interpretation and consumption. And fourth, there is a substantial flow of ideas and practices from the so-called Third World to the seemingly dominant societies and regions of the world (*ibid.*: 38–9). In short, Robertson concludes, it makes no sense to define the global as if the global excludes the local. 'The global is not in and of itself counterposed to the local. Rather, what is often referred to as the local is essentially included within the global' (*ibid.*: 34–5).

The conception of globalization that informs my analysis thus emphasizes the diminishing significance of time and space in the organization of social and political life and the emergence of a global consciousness. It sees globalization as a segmented, uneven and in some cases localizing process (see also Hannerz 1996 and Appadurai 1996). In that sense, following Robertson, I shall reject the idea of a polarity between the local and the global, and assume that globalization involves the reproduction, and in some cases the production, of locality.

The Challenge of Globalization

Does globalization herald the end of the national era? This question cannot be answered properly without distinguishing between nation and state, and assessing the implications of globalization for each separately. In the case of the state, the question is whether states can preserve their sovereignty intact in an age of increasing cross-border economic activity and regulation, and where politics is conducted more and more at a supranational and subnational level. In the case of the nation, on the other hand, the question is whether there are forms of community that offer alternative foci of belonging.

Many commentators argue that the state is fast becoming outmoded by economic globalization. The story, by now a familiar one, is appositely summed up by Holton:

The global economy is characterized by massive flows of money and capital across political boundaries. Integrated global finance markets shift billions of dollars around the world daily in a manner that influences national economies through its impact on foreign exchanges, interest rates, the stock market, employment levels, and government tax revenues . . . Global business strategies are themselves enhanced by radical changes in information technology and telecommunications. These flows of investment, technology, communications, and profit across national boundaries are often seen as the most striking symptom of global challenge to the nation-state. (1998: 80–1)

The challenge to the state is not only economic, however. It is also argued that the state is superseded as a locus of political decision-making by regional and supranational bodies. Today the nation-state system is faced with an expanding web of intergovernmental organizations, supranational agencies and institutions, as well as nonstate actors and transnational bodies including multinational corporations, pressure groups and various nongovernmental organizations (NGOs) (Guibernau 2001).

On the other hand, the spread of supraterritoriality has facilitated the growth of nonterritorial identities and cosmopolitan solidarities. Increasing levels of mass migration, the impact of consumerism and mass communications have given rise to global hybrid cultures, which attract more and more people each day. In short, the nation is no longer the only form of community that counts for many people (Scholte 2000; Cheah 1998).

There is some truth in these arguments but the picture they give is at best a partial one. As Billig rightly remarks, there is a sense of 'as-if' in some versions of 'the crisis of the nation-state' thesis:

It is as if the nation-state had already withered away; as if people's national commitments have been flattened to the level of a consumer choice; as if millions of children in the world's most powerful nation do not daily salute one, and only one, style of flag; as if, at this moment around the globe, vast armies are not practising their battle manoeuvres beneath national colours. (1995: 139)

To begin with, we should note that economic globalization has not yet overrun the state. National borders still matter because most global economic actors feel the need for some kind of stabilizing framework of rules and support structures beyond the networks generated through the market (Holton 1998: 108). The global economy, in other words, is something that has to be actively implemented, reproduced, serviced, and financed. 'It requires that a vast array of highly specialized functions be carried out, that infrastructures be secured, that legislative environments be made and kept hospitable' (Sassen 2000: 217). This is true even in the case of multinational corporations, the paradigmatic actors of global scenarios. As Holton indicates, whether in the advanced economic nations or in the developing world, the model of multinational corporation dominance over nations is too simplistic. Multinational corporations do not operate outside national jurisdictions, whether at home or abroad. On the contrary, they depend on the state for stable property rights, for infrastructural support and favourable fiscal treatment. Hence the nation-state 'is not coming apart at the seams, but it is becoming increasingly implicated in wider sets of relationships with other nations, multinational corporations and global NGOs operating across political boundaries' (1998: 82–3, 108).

On the other hand, the nation continues to be an important source of political and cultural identity for many people around the world. We know well that close encounter with 'alien' cultures through global networks often leads to increased awareness of and determination to preserve national distinctiveness, and not vice versa. More generally, the daunting prospect of job loss as a result of global economic restructuring, the shrinking of national sovereignty, increasing levels of mass migration, and the dizzying pace of technological change, all combine to create an atmosphere in which security and identity are felt by many to be under threat. Not surprisingly, nationalism becomes the fundamental means to counter that threat (Scholte 2000: 163–4; Holton 1998: 156–7).

Given this, it is not surprising that the recent revival of ethnicity and nationalism are interpreted by many as resistance to the disruptive impact of globalization. In fact, as a number of scholars have noted, we may even talk about a rise in the incidence of nationalism under conditions of globalization. We have already seen how 'portable nationality', read under the sign of identity politics, is on the rapid rise everywhere in the world (Anderson 1996: 9). On the other hand, migration movements that are a product of demographic globalization do not only give rise to hybrid cultures, but also to 'absentee patriotism' or 'long-distance nationalism', as the political affinities of various diasporas around the world amply demonstrate (Pietersee 1995: 49; for 'long-distance nationalism', see Anderson 1998). Globalization does not only cause more nationalism in a reactive sense. There are two other ways in which globalization has encouraged the growth of national formations. First, globalization has reduced the relative power of the states, making it more difficult for them to counter the rise of minority nationalisms within their borders effectively. Second, ethnic and national movements have sometimes exploited transnational networks to advance their causes (Scholte 2000: 168).

In short, it is too premature to consider nationalism as an outmoded form of consciousness. As Cheah rightly argues, 'an existing global condition ought not to be mistaken for an existing mass-based feeling of belonging to a world community (cosmopolitanism) because the globality of the everyday does not necessarily engender an existing popular global political consciousness' (1998: 31). The spread of supraterritorial relations does not signal the end of territorially constructed solidarities that continue to thrive in a globalizing world. In fact, the central paradox of ethnic politics in today's world is that primordial loyalties have themselves become globalized. Such loyalties may indeed be the product of invented traditions or retrospective affiliations, but

. . . because of the disjunctive and unstable interplay of commerce, media, national policies, and consumer fantasies, ethnicity, once a genie contained in the bottle of some sort of locality . . . has now become a global force, forever slipping in and through the cracks between states and borders. (Appadurai 1996: 41; see also Scholte 2000: 160–1)

So far as politics is concerned, we see that as state power is transferred or withers away in one sphere, it is strengthened in another. Nation-states continue to be the only officially recognized actors in institutions such as the UN, NATO or ASEAN. In fact, nation-states are the main architects of these institutions, deciding on their functioning, structure and conditions of entry, and sustaining them financially. In many ways, then, the nation-state system is still very much alive and kicking (Guibernau 2001: 250–1; Anderson and Goodman 1999: 27).

Yet it is also the case the world inhabited by nation-states is changing and that globalization is a major source of this change. Hence contemporary nation-states are confronted with an increasing number of problems that cannot be resolved on a national basis. Individual nations either lack the technical or financial resources to tackle problems such as poverty or economic modernization, or they face common problems, such as security or environmental protection, that require the joint action of all to produce effective results (Holton 1998: 121). Moreover, the spread of global relations has given rise to a number of substate, suprastate and nonstate agencies, which has led some to talk about an era of post-sovereign governance. Others have suggested abandoning the traditional concept of sovereignty, which interprets it as an illimitable and indivisible form of public power. Sovereignty, they have argued, has to be conceived today as divided among a number of agencies, and limited by the very nature of this plurality (Held 1996: 415).

The resultant picture of the global polity is a rather complex one. First, there are multiple actors, and not only nation-states, involved. Second, national sovereignty is increasingly conditional upon compliance with a range of transnational regulatory regimes. This reflects increased international interdependency and the growth of problems that can only be effectively addressed through international cooperation and transnational agreement (Holton 1998: 123).

In sum, what we face under conditions of globalization is not the transcendence of the state as such, but a transformation of the functions of the state. Thus it is sometimes argued that the state is no longer exclusively a provider state, but is becoming more and more a regulatory state (Delanty and O'Mahony 2002: 170–1). This is a direct consequence of the nature of contemporary interdependence characterized by a relative shift over time from issues of military control, territoriality and legitimacy, to a range of social, economic and environmental issues in which all nations have a stake and must cooperate to find solutions. Such problems include the pollution of the natural environment, demographic pressures on resources, and growing economic inequalities (Holton 1998: 114).

When we turn to the other side of the hyphen, that is, the nation, we see that it is losing its grip on collective identification, with the rise of nonnational frameworks of belonging along the lines of class, gender, race, religion and sexual orientation. Here some commentators stress the crucial role of mass media, which connect people across great distances by converting the contents of human relationships into symbols or tokens. 'So effective can this process become that communities of interest or value-commitment can develop between people who have never met, much less joined together in a political event' (Waters 1995: 150). Moreover, the accelerated spread of supraterritoriality since the 1960s has promoted the rise of global consciousness and some increase in cosmopolitan attachments to a universal human community. On the other hand, globalization has also increased the range of cultural opportunities available at any particular locality, thereby undermining the state's ability to impose a single culture upon its population.

A direct result of the proliferation of cultural opportunities is an increase in cultural 'hybridization' or what some have called 'creolization'. Globalization intensifies intercultural relations and pluralizes cultural options, in the process blurring distinctions between nations (Scholte 2000: 23–4). Notions about forms of 'national genius', the indivisibility of the nation and its authenticity are now more difficult to hold as nations become more complex, mobile and culturally hybrid (Edensor 2002: 9).

Finally, globalization loosens the link between nation and state, and leads to the formation of deterritorialized identities. The possibility arises therefore of an increased measure of ethnic pluralism, in which ethnicities are not tied to any specific territory or polity (Waters 1995: 136).

The changes wrought by processes of globalization are skilfully summarized by Hannerz who begins by conceding that even in the Occidental heartlands, the idea of the nation is still largely in place for a great many people:

> Yet interspersed among those committed nationals, in patterns not always equally transparent, are a growing number of people of more varying experiences and connections. Some of them may wish to redefine the nation; place the emphasis, for example, more on the future and less on the past of which they happen not to have been a part . . . Others again are in the

nation but not of it. They may be the real cosmopolitans, or they are people whose nations are actually elsewhere, objects of exile or diaspora nostalgia . . . Or they may indeed owe a stronger allegiance to some other kind of imagined transnational community – an occupational community, a community of believers in a new faith, of adherents to a youth style. There may be divided communities, ambiguities, and conflicting resonances as well. (1996: 90)

Can we talk about the existence of a global culture in this context? For Featherstone, if by a global culture we mean something similar to the culture of the nation-state writ large, the answer is clearly negative. On this comparison the concept of a global culture fails, because the image of the culture of a nation-state is one which typically emphasizes cultural homogeneity and integration. According to this line of reasoning, it would be impossible to identify a global culture without the formation of a world state. However, if we try to employ a broader definition of culture and think more in terms of processes, it might be possible to refer to the globalization of culture and to point to transsocietal cultural processes (1990: 1).

Such a broader conception, Featherstone continues, may also enable us to appreciate emerging sets of 'third cultures', which are vessels for all sorts of cultural flows that cannot be merely understood as the product of bilateral exchanges between nation-states. It is thus misleading to conceive a global culture as necessarily entailing a weakening of the sovereignty of nation-states. It is also misleading to regard the emergence of third cultures as a slippery slope to homogenization. We should thus conceptualize global culture less in terms of alleged homogenizing processes and 'more in terms of the diversity, variety and richness of popular and local discourses, codes and practices which resist and play-back systemicity and order' (*ibid.*: 1–2).

Featherstone argues that while particular television programmes, sport spectacles, music concerts, advertisements may rapidly transit the globe, this is not to say that the response of those viewing and listening in different cultural contexts will be uniform. In the words of Friedman,

It is true that Coke, tourist T-shirts and transistors have become universal, that is, the things and symbols of Western culture have diffused into the daily lives of many of the world's peoples, even if they are made in Hong Kong. Yet still their mode of appropriating these things is vastly different from our own. (1994: 100)

What does this culture look like? According to Hannerz, the global culture is marked by 'an organization of diversity rather than by a replication of uniformity'. No total homogenization of systems of meaning and expression has taken place, nor is it likely that there will be one any time soon. But the world has become one network of social relationships, and between its different regions there is a flow of meanings as well as of people and goods. 'The world culture is created through the increasing interconnectedness of varied local cultures, as well as through the development of cultures without a clear anchorage in any one territory' (1990: 237).

Hannerz also claims that the real significance of the growth of transnational cultures is often not the new cultural experience that they themselves offer people, but their mediating possibilities:

The transnational cultures are bridgeheads for entry into other territorial cultures. Instead of remaining within them, one can use the mobility connected with them to make contact with the meanings of other rounds of life, and gradually incorporate this experience into one's personal perspective. (*ibid.*: 245)

We can now turn to the question of whether the processes of globalization, particularly the growth of transnational cultures, have led to a parallel rise in global political consciousness.

The Cosmopolitan Alternative

The transformations associated with globalization have given a new lease of life to the project of cosmopolitanism. For some commentators, the recent outburst of nationalism is merely the manifestation of an anarchic situation of extreme social fragmentation, which can also be described as one offering new opportunities for cosmopolitan community (Delanty and O'Mahony 2002: 171). For others, cosmopolitanism is no longer merely an ideal project but a variety of actually existing practical stances. Whatever reservations we may have about contemporary forms of transnationalism, we may see it as providing the material conditions for new radical cosmopolitanisms from below (see the examples in Cheah 1998: 21). In that sense, the term 'cosmopolitan' packs into itself not only 'the voluntary adventures of liberal self-invention and global travel, but also those less benignly configured mixtures of migration, nomadism, diaspora, tourism, and refugee flight' (Wilson 1998: 352).

The aim of this section is to outline the recent debates on cosmopolitanism, laying special emphasis on whether cosmopolitanism constitutes a more realistic option in today's globalized world. Let me begin with the basic doctrine of cosmopolitanism.

Which Cosmopolitanism?

Cosmopolitanism asserts that 'all individuals are ultimately of equal moral worth and have an equal right to lead a worthwhile and satisfying life' (Poole 1999: 158). According to Freeman, the fundamental principle of cosmopolitan ethics can be found in Article 1 of the Universal Declaration of Human Rights: 'All human beings are born free and equal in dignity and rights'. For cosmopolitans, this suggests that national identities and state borders are, in principle, irrelevant to any individual's entitlement to the necessary conditions of a good life. Following Barry, Freeman maintains that cosmopolitanism is 'a moral outlook, not an institutional prescription'. Thus it is not necessarily opposed to either nations or states, or to the right to national self-determination. 'It does, however, deny to state and national institutions primary ethical value' (1999: 60).

Other commentators note that cosmopolitanism is a flexible term, whose forms of detachment and multiple affiliation can be variously articulated and variously motivated. Thus for Anderson, cosmopolitanism espouses 'reflective distance from one's cultural affiliations, a broad understanding of other cultures and customs, and a belief in universal humanity' (1998: 267). Brennan, on the other hand, argues that cosmopolitanism does not only designate an enthusiasm for customary differences, but projects a theory of world government and corresponding citizenship (2001: 76). This last issue is far from settled however. Freeman, for example, plays down the issue of world government, and contends that since cosmopolitanism values the well-being of human beings before any institutions, it is not necessarily committed to world government (1999: 61). In what follows, I shall focus on cosmopolitanism as a state of mind, or a moral outlook, not as a theory of world government. Perhaps the best-known analyses of cosmopolitanism of this kind are provided by Nussbaum and Hannerz.

Nussbaum begins her famous essay on cosmopolitanism by noting that emphasis on patriotic pride is morally dangerous, and ultimately, subversive of some of the righteous goals patriotism sets out to serve. These goals, Nussbaum argues, would be better served by the old ideal of the cosmopolitan, 'the person whose allegiance is to the worldwide community of human beings', which is in any case more suited to our situation in the contemporary world (1996a: 4).

According to Nussbaum, we should regard our deliberations as, above all, deliberations about problems of people in particular concrete situations, not problems growing out of a unique national identity. The accident of where one is born, says Nussbaum, is just that, an accident: 'any human being might have been born in any nation'. Recognizing this, we should not let differences of nationality, class, ethnic membership or even gender erect barriers between us and our fellow human beings. 'We should recognize humanity wherever it occurs, and give its fundamental ingredients, reason and moral capacity, our first allegiance and respect'. We should always treat with equal respect the dignity of reason and moral choice in every human being (*ibid.*: 7–8).

Drawing on the Stoics, Nussbaum argues that we do not need to give up our local identifications to be a citizen of the world. We may thus think of ourselves not as devoid of local affiliations, but as surrounded by a series of concentric circles. The first one encircles the self, the next takes in the immediate family, then, in order, neighbours or local groups, fellow city-dwellers, and fellow countrymen. Outside all these circles is the largest one, that of humanity as a whole. Our task as citizens of the world, says Nussbaum, will be to 'draw the circles somehow toward the center', making all human beings more like our fellow city-dwellers, and so on.

> We need not give up our special affections and identifications, whether ethnic or gender-based or religious. We need not think of them as superficial, and we may think of our identity as con-

stituted partly by them. We may and should devote special attention to them in education. But we should also work to make all human beings part of our community of dialogue and concern, base our political deliberations on that interlocking commonality, and give the circle that defines our humanity special attention and respect. (*ibid.*: 9)

Nussbaum concludes her analysis by observing that to be a citizen of the world is often a lonely business. It is a kind of exile, 'from the comfort of local truths, from the warm, nestling feeling of patriotism, from the absorbing drama of pride in oneself and one's own'. Cosmopolitanism offers no such refuge; it offers only reason and the love of humanity, which may appear less colourful than other sources of belonging. Yet, she adds, the life of the cosmopolitan, who puts right before country and universal reason before the symbols of national belonging, need not be boring, or lacking in love (*ibid.*: 15–17). After all, 'many fine things can seem boring to those not brought up to appreciate them' (1996b: 139).

For Hannerz, on the other hand, the perspective of the cosmopolitan must entail relationships to a plurality of cultures – and the more the better. More importantly, cosmopolitanism includes a stance towards diversity itself, towards the coexistence of cultures in the individual experience. A genuine cosmopolitanism, Hannerz argues, is first of all an orientation, a willingness to engage with the Other. 'It is an intellectual and aesthetic stance of openness toward divergent cultural experiences, a search for contrasts rather than uniformity' (1990: 239).

At the same time, however, cosmopolitanism is a matter of competence:

> There is the aspect of a state of readiness, a personal ability to make one's way into other cultures, through listening, looking, intuiting and reflecting. And there is cultural competence in the stricter sense of the term, a built-up skill in manoeuvring more or less expertly with a particular system of meanings and meaningful forms. (*ibid.*)

According to Hannerz, being on the move is not enough to turn one into a cosmopolitan, and we must not confuse the latter with other kinds of travellers, such as tourists, exiles, labour migrants and expatriates. Cosmopolitans seek to immerse themselves in other cultures; they want to be participants, or at least do not want to be spotted within a crowd of participants, that is, of locals in their home territory. Tourists, by contrast, are not participants, but spectators. People engage in tourism specifically to go to another place.

The exile is not a real cosmopolitan either, for her involvement with a different culture is something that has been imposed on her. She is surrounded by the foreign culture but does not immerse herself in it. Sometimes her imperfections as a cosmopolitan may be the opposite of those of the tourist: she may build up a competence, but she does not enjoy it.

The same goes for most ordinary labour migrants for whom going away means higher income; 'often the involvement with another culture is not a fringe benefit but a necessary cost, to be kept as low as possible'. A surrogate home is created with the help of compatriots, in whose circle one becomes confined.

The concept of the expatriate, on the other hand, may be that which could be most readily associated with cosmopolitanism. Expatriates are people who have voluntarily chosen to live abroad for some period, and who know that they can go back whenever it suits them. This does not mean that all expatriates are cosmopolitan, but these are people who can afford to experiment. We often think of them as people of independent means, for whom openness to new experiences is a vocation, or people who can take along their work more or less where it pleases them (*ibid.*: 241–3).

This suggests that cosmopolitans do not always 'travel', that, most of the time, they are actually at home. Yet this has a completely different meaning in their case. Real cosmopolitans, Hannerz argues, are never quite at home again, in the way real locals can be:

> Home is taken-for-grantedness, but after their perspectives have been irreversibly affected by the experience of the alien and the distant, cosmopolitans may not view either the seasons of the year or the minor rituals of everyday life as absolutely natural, obvious and necessary. There may be a feeling of detachment, perhaps irritation with those committed to the local common sense and unaware of its arbitrariness. Or perhaps the cosmopolitan makes 'home' as well one of his several sources of

personal meaning . . . Or home is really home, but in a special way; a constant reminder of a pre-cosmopolitan past, a privileged site of nostalgia. (*ibid.*: 247–8)

Why, then, do we need cosmopolitanism? Several answers have been proposed by the proponents of the cosmopolitan ideal. The first answer is that the hybrid lifestyle of the cosmopolitan is in fact the only appropriate response to the modern world in which we live. We live in a world marked by technology and trade, by mass migration and the dispersion of cultural influences. In this context, to immerse oneself in the traditional practices of a particular culture involves an artificial dislocation from what actually is going on in the world (Rushdie 1991, cited in Waldron 1995: 100).

Waldron, on the other hand, draws our attention to the extent to which we owe in history and heritage to the international communities that have existed among merchants, clerics, lawyers, agitators, scholars, scientists, writers and diplomats. It is true that we are not the self-made atoms of liberal fantasy, but neither are we exclusively products of single national or ethnic communities. 'We are made by our languages, our literature, our cultures, our science, our religions, our civilization – and these are human entities that go far beyond national boundaries'. If we owe a debt of provenance to the social structures that have formed us, then we owe a debt to the global community and civilization, as well as whatever we owe to any particular region, country, nation or tribe (1995: 103).

Waldron reminds us at this point that our lives, whether individual or communal, are no longer self-sufficient. In that sense, no account of our being will be complete without acknowledging our dependence on larger social and political structures that go far beyond the particular community with which we identify ourselves (*ibid.*: 104).

Two other reasons have been adduced by Nussbaum. She argues first that through cosmopolitan education, we learn more about ourselves. For her, one of the greatest barriers to rational deliberation in politics is the unexamined feeling that one's own way of life is neutral and natural. By looking at ourselves through the eyes of others, we come to realize what is local and nonessential in our practices, and what is more broadly and deeply shared. Secondly, a cosmopolitan outlook enables us to solve problems that require international cooperation: after all, 'the air does not obey national boundaries'. To conduct this sort of global dialogue, we need knowledge not only of the geography and ecology of other nations, but also a great deal about their people, to be able to respect their traditions and commitments (1996a: 11–14).

Finally, Robbins reminds us that the technologies and institutions that have produced national feeling now exist massively and increasingly on a transnational scale. If people can get as emotional as Benedict Anderson (1991) says they do about their relations with fellow nationals they never see face-to-face, then now that print-capitalism has become electronic- and digital-capitalism, and now that this system is so clearly transnational, it would be strange if people did not get emotional in much the same way about others who are not fellow nationals, people bound to them by some transnational sort of fellowship (Robbins 1998a: 6).

No matter how desirable a cosmopolitan world is, however, it needs to be pointed out that the world outside academia is a long way from such realization (Hann 1995: 125). As Billig rightly reminds us, 'one can eat Chinese tomorrow and Turkish the day after; one can even dress in Chinese and Turkish styles. But being Chinese or Turkish are not commercially available options'. Cosmopolitans too are constrained by the permanence of national identity (1995: 139). This inevitably leads us to question the viability of the cosmopolitan project.

Critiques of Cosmopolitanism

The cosmopolitan project has been severely criticized by several writers for entailing uniformity, for being elitist, inauthentic, detached, and thus, utopian.

To begin with, it is argued that cosmopolitanism is only a viable option for a privileged subset of citizens of wealthy industrial societies, those who have the resources necessary to travel, learn other languages, and absorb other cultures (Yack 1999: 104; Poole 1999: 162). Accordingly, Glazer argues that cosmopolitan values have made considerable headway in the more developed part of the world, where, for example, European loyalty slowly gains on national loyalty. But in the developing world, he notes, resistance to cosmopolitan values is strong. 'The advocacy of cosmopolitan values is often viewed suspiciously as an arrogant insistence by formerly colonial powers that their values, Western values, be adopted' (1996: 64).

Robbins makes a similar point, noting that beyond the adjectival sense of 'belonging to all parts of the world; not restricted to any one country or its inhabitants', the word 'cosmopolitan' immediately evokes the image of a privileged person: 'someone who can claim to be a "citizen of the world" by virtue of independent means, expensive tastes, and a globe-trotting lifestyle'. The association of cosmopolitanism with privilege is unattractive to us, says Robbins, because deep down we tend to admit that intellectuals (particularly those in the academia) are a 'special interest' group representing nothing but themselves (1998b: 248).

In this context, Falk contends that to conceive of cosmopolitanism as an alternative to nationalism without addressing the subversive challenge of neoliberal globalism promoted by transnational corporations and banks is 'to risk indulging a contemporary form of fuzzy innocence'. In order to be credible, says Falk, 'cosmopolitanism has to be combined with a critique of the ethically deficient globalism embodied in neoliberal modes of thought' (1996: 57).

A second criticism blames cosmopolitanism for entailing uniformity and standardization. According to Tamir, for example, a postnational age in which national differences are obliterated and all share in one shallow universal culture, watch soap operas and CNN, eat McDonalds and drink Coca-Cola is more a nightmare than a utopian vision. The way to confront ethnocentric nationalism, Tamir argues, is not to suggest that national interests should be denied altogether, but to offer an alternative national view (1993: 166–7).

This is directly related to the third charge levelled against cosmopolitanism, namely the charge of inauthenticity or rootlessness. The cosmopolitan ideal, critics argue, embodies all the worst aspects of classical liberalism – 'atomism, abstraction, alienation from one's roots, vacuity of commitment, indeterminacy of character, and ambivalence towards the good'. As Waldron observes, the accusation is implicit in the undertones of words like 'deracinated', 'alienated'; it is no accident that these terms often carry negative and cautionary connotations (1995: 102).

For the critics, then, cosmopolitanism must come to terms with difference. According to Barber, for example, our attachments start parochially and only then grow outward. 'To bypass them in favor of an immediate cosmopolitanism is to risk ending up nowhere – feeling at home neither at home nor in the world' (1996: 34). Himmelfarb, on the other hand, aims directly at Nussbaum's theory, and asks where can we find the substantive, universal, common values cosmopolitanism is supposed to be based on? What are they, specifically and concretely? To answer those questions, Himmelfarb argues, is to enter the world of reality, which is the world of nations, countries and peoples (1996: 74). According to Himmelfarb, cosmopolitanism turns a blind eye to the givens of life: parents, ancestors, family, race, religion, heritage, history, culture, tradition, community and nationality. These are, however, essential attributes of the individual. To pledge one's 'fundamental allegiance' to cosmopolitanism is to try to transcend not only nationality but all the particularities and realities of life that shape one's natural identity. Cosmopolitanism, Himmelfarb concludes, has a nice, high-minded ring to it, but it is an illusion, and, like all illusions, perilous (*ibid.*: 77).

It is also argued in this context that we cannot properly appreciate the primary attachments of others unless we have our own primary attachments (Poole 1999). Thus McConnell argues that human affections begin close to home; 'wider circles of affection grow out of, and are dependent upon, the closer and more natural ties'. In that sense, effective cosmopolitanism is only a by-product of moral education in a great tradition. A student who does not care about her own culture's accomplishments, McConnell concludes, is unlikely to find much value in the accomplishments of others (1996: 78–80). Bok agrees, claiming that there is nothing wrong with encouraging children to explore their local existence in order to reach beyond it by degrees. Acknowledging particular bonds, communities and cultures need not blind one to problems within any of the circles of allegiance 'nor involve exceptionalism or disparagement or dismissal of others' (1996: 44).

A final point is brought forward by Putnam who argues that there is no such thing as a universal conception of 'the good life'. First, there is not just one form of 'good life'. The life of a spiritual religious community, the life of a group of bohemian artists, the life of a creative group of computer programmers, and many other lives can all be good in their own (utterly incompatible) ways. And second, good lives do not just spring from rational insights. Ways of life require centuries of experimentation and innovation to develop. In the absence of such concrete ways of life, universal principles of justice are empty, just as in the absence of critical reason, inherited forms of life degenerate into tenacity and blind allegiance to authority. 'Tradition without reason is blind; reason without tradition is empty' (1996: 94).

The fourth objection to cosmopolitanism concerns its 'abstract' or 'thin' nature. According to McConnell, what we share with other humans is too abstract to be a strong focus for affections. Since 'the world' has never been the locus of citizenship, McConnell notes, a child who is taught to be a 'citizen of the world' is taught to be a citizen of an abstraction. 'Abstract cosmopolitanism may well succeed in introducing skepticism and cynicism regarding the loyalties that now exist, but it is unlikely to create a substitute moral community' (1996: 81). Barber makes the same point, arguing that the idea of cosmopolitanism, like such kindred ideas as legal personhood, contract society, and the economic market, offers little or nothing for the human psyche to fasten on (1996: 33).

As a result, and this is the fifth objection, the cosmopolitan ideal is utopian. This point is made most forcefully by Cheah who begins by conceding that the world today is more interconnected than before, and that transnational mobility is clearly on the rise. But, Cheah warns, one should not automatically take this to imply that popular forms of cosmopolitanism already exist. Even if a popular global consciousness exists, is it (or can it ever be) sufficiently institutionalized to become a viable alternative to the nation-state? Or is it merely a cultural consciousness without political clout (1998: 36)?

According to Cheah, it is questionable whether existing forms of cosmopolitanism are mass-based, even though they initiate or participate in grassroots activities. Even grassroots feminist NGOs do not speak for 'all women'. Moreover, it is not clear how these cosmopolitan activities are related to transnational underclass migrant communities. Thus Cheah asks:

. . . over and above interventions on behalf of underprivileged migrant minority groups on an ad hoc basis, to what extent can activist cosmopolitanisms take root in the latter in a consistent manner to generate a genuinely pluralized mass-based global political community within the Northern constitutional nation-state as distinguished from the defensive identity politics of ethnic, religious, or hybrid minority constituencies? (*ibid.*: 37)

For Cheah, it is doubtful whether transnational migrant communities can be described as examples of cosmopolitanism. After all, how many of these migrants feel that they are citizens of the world? More importantly, it is unclear whether in the current interstate system, the so-called international public sphere or global civil society can achieve social redistribution on a global scale if it does not go through the institutional agency of the nation-state (*ibid.*).

Kymlicka expresses a similar concern in an exchange with Waldron on the desirability of 'a cosmopolitan alternative'. For Kymlicka, the fact some Québécois now eat Mexican food and practice Zen Buddhism does not mean that they cease to form a distinct culture, living and working in French-language institutions. 'It simply means that the societal culture they belong to is an open and pluralistic one, which borrows whatever it finds worthwhile in other cultures, integrates it into its own, and passes it on to subsequent generations' (2001: 211). In other words, these groups wish to be cosmopolitan, and embrace the cultural exchange Waldron emphasizes, without accepting Waldron's own 'cosmopolitan alternative', which denies that people are deeply attached to their own languages and cultural community. What they want is to preserve their existence as a culturally distinct group (*ibid.*: 212).

In fairness to what we may call, for want of a better term, 'classical cosmopolitans', it needs to be pointed out that not everybody agrees with these criticisms. Thus in his defense of Nussbaum's cosmopolitan alternative, Amartya Sen asks: 'Why should a belief that one's "fundamental allegiance" is as a citizen of the world deny all sensitivity to *other* identities'? According to Sen, the cosmopolitan ideal need not dispute the fact we have other, more particular, identities. What matters in this context is the need to accept that we all have a multiplicity of loyalties. As long as plural concerns are admitted, Sen notes, it does not matter where our primary allegiance lies (1996: 112–13). Sen believes that Nussbaum's focus on world citizenship corrects a serious neglect, that of the interest of people who are not related to us through, say, kinship or community or nationality. 'The assertion that one's fundamental allegiance is to humanity at large brings every other person into the domain of concern, without eliminating anyone' (*ibid.*: 114). Jonathan Rée, on the other hand, wonders how it is possible to annex local attachments to the principle of nationality. After all, part of the meaning of nationality is the obliteration of local particularity in favor of national uniformity. Moreover,

> . . . as soon as you begin to analyze the substance of local sentiments – memories of songs, poems, or stories, or of honey for tea, or getting your shoes yellow with buttercup pollen, smelling the smoke of Gauloises, or hearing the crackling flames as you fall asleep in front of a fire – it becomes evident that they all define different localities, different communities, different networks of social sympathy. It is fantastic to suppose that they could all extend precisely to the edges of a single nation and there come abruptly to a halt. (1998: 82)

Rée notes that it is in the nature of our local loyalties that they will be plural and out of alignment with each other, and that they will change over a lifetime. Nationalities, however, are categorically different: 'as a rule, you only have one of them and, normally, you have to keep it for life'. It is essential to the principle of nationality that it present itself as the embodiment of intimate local feelings – it would lose most of its popular attraction otherwise – but the claim is essentially false (*ibid.*: 82–3).

This brings us to the recent attempts to reconfigure cosmopolitanism in response to the criticisms we have reviewed above.

Cosmopolitanism Reconfigured

According to Hollinger, the most prominent feature of recent attempts to reconfigure cosmopolitanism is the reticence of its protagonists about the label 'cosmopolitanism'. This reticence, Hollinger argues, is most clearly displayed in their effort to modify the label in question with a string of adjectives – vernacular cosmopolitanism, rooted cosmopolitanism, critical cosmopolitanism, comparative cosmopolitanism, national cosmopolitanism, discrepant cosmopolitanism, situated cosmopolitanism, and actually existing cosmopolitanism, and so on. The different adjectives do not designate different schools, but different attempts to say pretty much the same thing in relation to the one, huge shadow that continues to haunt the new cosmopolitanism: the image of old cosmopolitanism, the cosmopolitanism associated with the Enlightenment (2001: 237).

The old cosmopolitanism, as we have seen, was accused of being insufficiently responsive to diversity, particularity, the realities of power and the need for politically viable solidarities. It is in response to these criticisms that attempts to rethink the cosmopolitan ideal came to the fore: the point, Hollinger argues, is to bring cosmopolitanism down to earth, to indicate that cosmopolitanism can deliver at least some of the goods provided by local (above all national) affiliations (*ibid.*).

Hollinger seems to be right about his observations, although it is not clear whether all the protagonists of the so-called 'new cosmopolitanism' would agree with him, particularly with regard to the need to bring cosmopolitanism down to earth by offering a precise definition of it. Thus for Pollock *et al.*, cosmopolitanism should instead be viewed as 'a project whose conceptual content and pragmatic character are not only as yet unspecified but also must always escape positive and definite specification, precisely because specifying cosmopolitanism positively and definitively is an uncosmopolitan thing to do' (2000: 577–8). These conceptual disagreements notwithstanding, models of reconfigured cosmopolitanism seem to share three important features: they all define cosmopolitanism as rooted, as involving multiple affiliations and as anti-elitist.

As we have seen earlier, classical cosmopolitanism has often been described – rightly or wrongly – as a form of detachment from the bonds, commitments, and affiliations that constrain ordinary citizens' lives. 'It has seemed to be a luxuriously free-floating view from above' (Robbins 1998a: 1). Yet today the term is extended to transnational experiences that are particular and unprivileged, even coerced. In such a context, the commonsensical opposition between cosmopolitanism and nationalism is no longer self-evident. Like nations, says Robbins, cosmopolitanisms are now plural and particular. And like nations, they are both European and non-European, and they are weak and underdeveloped as well as strong and privileged:

. . . like the nation, cosmopolitanism is there – not merely as an abstract ideal, like loving one's neighbor as oneself, but habits of thought and feeling that have already shaped and been shaped by particular collectivities, that are socially and geographically situated, hence both limited and empowered. Like nations, worlds too are 'imagined' . . . It is thus less clear what cosmopolitanism is opposed to, or what its value is supposed to be. (*ibid.*: 2)

Today's cosmopolitanism, then, is located and embodied. It is built out of the imperfect historical materials – religious loyalties, commercial interests, diasporas and the like – that are already at hand. Large-scale loyalties that underpin the new cosmopolitanisms 'do not stand outside history like an ultimate court of appeal' (*ibid.*: 6).

In any case, Robbins argues, absolute homelessness is a myth: no one actually is or can ever be a cosmopolitan in the sense of belonging nowhere. Nor can anyone be a cosmopolitan in the sense of belonging everywhere:

The interest of the term cosmopolitanism is located, then, not in its full theoretical extension where it becomes a paranoid fantasy of ubiquity and omniscience, but rather (paradoxically) in its local applications, where the unrealizable ideal produces normative pressure against such alternatives as, say, the fashionable *hybridization.* (1998b: 260)

Robbins's sketch is given a concrete form by Appiah, who calls himself a 'rooted cosmopolitan' or a 'cosmopolitan patriot'. Cosmopolitan patriots, claims Appiah, can entertain the possibility of a world in which everyone is a rooted cosmopolitan, attached to a home of her own, but taking pleasure from the presence of other, different, places that are home to other, different, people. They can also accept that in such a world not everyone will find it best to stay in their country of origin; hence the circulation of people between different localities will involve not only cultural tourism, but migration, nomadism, diaspora (1996: 22). In short, cosmopolitan patriots value the variety of human forms of social and cultural life, and they do not want everybody to become part of a homogeneous global culture. They acknowledge the existence of local differences (both within and between states) in moral climate. And so long as these differences meet certain general ethical constraints, they are happy to let them be (*ibid.*: 26).

The second distinguishing feature of new cosmopolitanisms is their acceptance of the fact that each individual happens to belong – simultaneously – to groups and communities of various sizes and kinds; that there are no privileged, natural units as nationalists would have us believe (Miščević 2001: 25). Waldron argues that if we live a cosmopolitan life, we draw our allegiances from here, there, and everywhere. Fragments of culture come into our lives from different sources, and there is no guarantee that they will all fit together: 'the self constituted under the auspices of a multiplicity of cultures might strike us as chaotic, confused, even schizophrenic' (1995: 110).

According to Waldron, the cosmopolitan does not dispute that people are formed by special attachments and involvements, by culture and community. Instead, she shows how each person has a multiplicity of different and perhaps disparate communal allegiances. 'Such integrity as the cosmopolitan individual has therefore requires management' (*ibid.*).

Robbins makes the same point by arguing that instead of being an ideal of detachment, actually existing cosmopolitanism is a reality of '(re)attachment, multiple attachment, or attachment at a distance'. We are connected to all sorts of places, consciously or unconsciously, including places that we have never travelled to, that we have perhaps only seen on television (1998a: 3). Pollock *et al.* concur, and claim that cosmopolitanism should be conceptualized as 'ways of inhabiting multiple places at once, of being different beings simultaneously, of seeing the larger picture stereoscopically with the smaller' (2000: 587).

The final distinctive characteristic of new cosmopolitans is their insistence on liberating cosmopolitanism from its historical association with elitism. Robbins, for example, admits that cosmopolitanism is an outgrowth or ideological reflection of global capitalism; yet, he believes, following Rabinow, that it remains possible to speak of '*critical* cosmopolitanism'. 'Capital may be cosmopolitan, but that does not make cosmopolitanism into an apology for capitalism' (1998a: 8). Cheah, too, argues that although capitalism is the condition of possibility of both nationalism and cosmopolitanism, neither discourse can be reduced to its ideological instrument or regarded as its simple reflection (1998: 31).

Falk, on the other hand, distinguishes what he calls 'neo-cosmopolitanism' from older forms of cosmopolitanism, and contends that the former is characterized by either the Greenpeace efforts to prevent Shell Oil from sinking an oil rig with toxic properties in the North Sea, or by the world-wide campaign in 1995 to protest the resumption of French nuclear weapons tests. This form of cosmopolitanism is a type of 'globalization-from-below that is people- and nature-oriented and contrasts with globalization-from-above that is capital-driven and ethically neutral' (1996: 58).

The advocates of the new cosmopolitanism are fully aware that 'there is no inherent virtue in transnationality' (Robbins 1998a: 11). However, even if cosmopolitanism cannot deliver an explicitly and directly political programme, understood as an ethos, or a 'receptive attitude towards otherness', it can at least lead us in the direction of internationalist political education.

> By suggesting that there is no right place to stand, it can take some of the moralism out of politics. Better still, by doing so it can liberate us to pursue a long-term process of translocal connecting that is both political and educational at once. (Robbins 1998b: 261)

Clifford, on the other hand, notes that 'whatever the ultimate value of the term cosmopolitan, pluralized to account for a range of uneven affiliations, it points, at least, toward alternative notions of "cultural identity"' (1998: 365). Clifford, too, is aware that cosmopolitanisms guarantee nothing politically:

> They offer no release from mixed feelings, from utopic/dystopic tensions. They do, however, name and make more visible a complex range of intercultural experiences, sites of appropriation and exchange. These cosmopolitical contact zones are traversed by new social movements and global corporations, tribal activists and cultural tourists, migrant worker remittances and e-mail. Nothing is guaranteed, except contamination, messy politics and more translation. (*ibid.*: 369)

Globalization as Opportunity

If globalization is a segmented, uneven and localizing process, and not an all-conquering and homogenizing force, then it makes no sense to ask whether it is good or bad. Its effects are largely determined by our ability to navigate through the multiple processes it sets in motion – hence difficult to predict and subject to change. In other words, globalization is very much what we make of it (see also Scholte 2000).

Building on that, I shall propose an alternative conceptualization of globalization in this section and discuss its implications for nations and nationalism. More specifically, I shall argue that we should conceptualize globalization as an opportunity to conjure up postnational forms of community and belonging. The crux of the argument is the belief that with increased rates and intensity of crossborder exchanges and mobility, globalization has increased people's reflexiveness with regard to their identity and facilitated the emergence of alternatives to the nation-state. However, it is important to stress at the outset that the proliferation of forms of community and belonging does not signify a move beyond the nation as such, but beyond treating the nation as the main or dominant structure of political identity – towards seeing it as one frame of reference among many.

How does globalization promote the formation of alternative networks of identity then? To start with, the increasing rate and intensity of global interactions advances our ability to establish connections across national borders. As Nussbaum remarks, there are today more practical opportunities for world citizenship than before. Nongovernmental organizations of many kinds are mobilizing to influence government action on various issues ranging from ecology to domestic violence. Through such groups, Nussbaum points out, it is possible to exert pressure on national governments to take action toward certain global aims (1996b: 134–5).

On the other hand, as the flow of information and images becomes increasingly dominated by electronic media (and thus detached from the capacity to read and write), and as such media increasingly link producers and audiences across national boundaries, we witness the emergence of what Appadurai calls a 'community of sentiment', a group that begins to imagine and feel things together. Collective experience of the mass media, Appadurai notes, can create fellowships of 'worship' and 'charisma'. These fellowships are often transnational, even postnational, and they frequently operate beyond the boundaries of the nation (1996: 8, 22). These crossborder exchanges are complemented by increasing levels of mobility, both geographical and social. As Malkki argues, there has emerged a new awareness of the global social fact that, now more than perhaps ever before, people are chronically mobile and routinely displaced, and invent homes and homelands in the absence of territorial, national bases (1996: 434). Some people, like exiles or migrant workers, are indeed taken away from the territorial bases of their local culture, but still try to surround themselves with some approximation of it. There is also 'a greater number who, even staying home, find their local cultures less pervasive, less to be taken for granted, less clearly bounded toward the outside' (Hannerz 1990: 249).

Combined, increased levels of crossborder exchanges and mobility lead to new forms of reflexivity and questioning. An implication of greater interconnectedness is that most of us now have the experience of personally running into a larger share of it in our own lives:

> If it used to be the case that we could live in ignorance of most of the combined cultural inventory of the world, in the global ecumene each one of us now, somehow, has access to more of it – or, conversely, more of it has access to us, making claims on our senses and minds. (Hannerz 1996: 25)

Globalization thus increases the sense of a fluid and fragmented self, particularly for people who can afford to spend large proportions of their time in transnational spaces, where multiple identities readily converge. Under conditions of globalization, identity is less easily taken for granted. Some commentators believe that the new visions of identity, nation and displacement challenge the commonsense views, not by refuting the national order of things, but, rather, by constructing an alternative, competing nationalist metaphysic. It is increasingly claimed that state and territory are no longer sufficient to make a nation (Malkki 1996: 446).

The extension of the level of global cultural interrelatedness has also led some to talk of the emergence of a 'global ecumene', defined as a 'region of persistent culture interaction and exchange' (Hannerz 1996). According to Featherstone, this is a process whereby a series of cultural flows produce:

> firstly, cultural homogeneity and cultural disorder, in linking together previously isolated pockets of relatively homogeneous culture which in turn produces more complex images of the other as well as generating identity-reinforcing reactions; and also secondly, transnational cultures, which can be understood as genuine 'third cultures' which are orientated beyond national boundaries. (1990: 6)

A similar point is made by Appadurai who argues that 'the era in which we could assume that viable public spheres were typically, exclusively, or necessarily national could be at an end'. In this context, Appadurai continues, we need to pay special attention to the relation between mass mediation and migration, the two facts that underpin the cultural politics of globalization. In particular, we need to take a closer look at the variety of what have emerged as diasporic public spheres (1996: 21–2).

For Appadurai, 'the nationalist genie', never perfectly contained in the bottle of the territorial state, is now itself diasporic:

> Carried in the repertoires of increasingly mobile populations of refugees, tourists, guest workers, transnational intellectuals, scientists and illegal aliens, it is increasingly unrestrained by ideas of spatial boundary and territorial sovereignty. This revolution in the foundations of nationalism has crept up on us virtually unnoticed. Where soil and place were once the key to the linkage of territorial affiliation with state monopoly of the means of violence, key identities and identifications now only partially revolve around the realities and images of place. (*ibid.*: 160–1)

Appadurai notes that the movements we see today in various parts of the world – in Serbia and Sri Lanka, Mountain Karabakh and Namibia, Punjab and Québec – are what might be called 'trojan nationalisms'. Such nationalisms actually contain transnational, subnational links and, more generally, nonnational identities and aspirations.

Because they are so often the product of forced as well as voluntary diasporas, of mobile intellectuals as well as manual workers, of dialogues with hostile as well as hospitable states, very few of the nationalisms can be separated from the anguish of displacement, the nostalgia of exile, the repatriation of funds, or the brutalities of asylum seeking. (*ibid.*: 165)

Three keywords can be invoked to describe the new forms of community and belonging which threaten the primacy of the nation-state – though not the nation-state itself: *deterritorialization*, *pluralization* and *hybridization*. First, most of the available alternatives to the nation-form are, by and large, nonterritorial. In fact, identity-building has itself been 'deterritorialized' and assumed a symbolic character. In fact, some writers go so far as to proclaim the end of 'methodological territorialism' which was prompted by the growth of mercantile and industrial capitalism, and the rise of the nation-state system several centuries ago (Scholte 2000: 57). Others remind us that mapping requires agreement on coordinates; yet what we see in the contemporary world is the progressive loss of agreement as to what these coordinates should be. 'This is a world in which both points of departure and points of arrival are in cultural flux, and thus the search for steady points of reference, as critical life choices are made, can be very difficult' (Appadurai 1996: 44; Poole 1999: 165).

This is also because we live (and have always lived) in a world of overlapping identities and affinities. The nation is only one of the competing structures of identity in our lives, and not necessarily the most important one. Today a good many of our relationships to people and places cross boundaries. As Hannerz points out, intimate circles and small networks can also be involved here; the transnational is not always enormous in scale. These relationships do not always correspond to established ideas of nationhood, and in this way the latter becomes less pervasive, and even compromised. The sense of historical rootedness may be replaced by an intense experience of discontinuity and rupture, as in the case of the transnational migrant; 'the fraternity of the present . . . is in opposition to the sedimented differences of history' (1996: 89).

Hannerz is keen to stress that such personal experiences do not come in only a few varieties. An important characteristic of the present phase of globalization is the proliferation of kinds of ties that can be transnational. In all that variety, such ties may entail a weakened personal involvement with the nation and national culture, a shift from the tendency to take it for granted, perhaps a critical distance to it. In such ways, the nation may become more hollow than it was (*ibid.*).

On the other hand, in their great diversity, these outside linkages do not coalesce into any single conspicuous alternative to the nation:

> The people involved are not all 'cosmopolitans' in the same sense; most of them are probably not cosmopolitans in any precise sense at all. It is also in the nature of things that we are not always sure who is affected by these linkages. Some may be of a more dramatic and conspicuous kind, others apparently mundane and hardly noticeable to anyone not in the know, not intimately familiar with the other's network and biography. Globalization of this kind, diffused within social life, is opaque. (*ibid.*)

A corollary of the processes of deterritorialization and pluralization is hybridization which entails increasing levels of cultural mixing. According to Pietersee, structural hybridization, or the increase in the range of organizational options, and cultural hybridization are in fact signs of an age of boundary crossing – but not of the erasure of boundaries. Thus, state power remains extremely strategic, but it is no longer the only game in town. 'The tide of globalization reduces the room of manoeuvre for states, while international institutions, transnational transactions, regional cooperation, subnational dynamics and non-governmental organizations expand in impact and scope' (1995: 63).

We can make better sense of hybridization in historical terms, Pietersee argues, by writing diaspora histories of global culture. Owing to nationalism being the dominant paradigm since the nineteenth century, cultural achievements have been routinely claimed for 'nations' – that is, culture has been 'nationalized', or territorialized. A different historical record can be constructed on the basis of the contributions of diasporas, migrations, strangers, brokers to culture formation and diffusion (*ibid.*: 63–4).

The hybridization perspective also increases our sensitivity to essentialism. It unsettles the holistic concept of culture which underpins nationalism, racism, ethnicism, religious fundamental-ism, civilizational chauvinism and, we might add, most forms of liberal multiculturalism. It shows us that 'the kaleidoscope of col-lective experience is in motion', has been in motion all along and 'the fixities of nation, community, ethnicity and class have been grids superimposed upon experiences more complex and subtle than reflexivity and organization could accommodate' (*ibid.*: 64). Not everybody agrees with this account, however. According to Friedman, probably the most trenchant critic of the hybridization perspective, the whole debate on globalization as increasing plu-ralization and hybridization is a symptom of the general fragmen-tation process of the world system as well as the intellectual cosmopolitan reaction to that process, one that displays a highly ambivalent attitude to the ethnification process itself and the desire for something broader and more global (1997: 75). For Friedman, this is 'the hyphenated reality of the postmodern cos-mopolitan', a reality that is defined by the plurality of knowledges, of cultures and of their continuous fusion:

> The metaphor for this position is expressed in the concepts of ecumene, the global village. This is the forging not of a new unity but of a collection of disparate entities under the political umbrella of a super-state, a cultural elite, a council of leaders. The model is not the macro-nation but the medieval Church, the great encompasser. (*ibid.*)

Friedman notes that the internal and external threats to the nation lead to increasing racism and a general ethnification of the nation-state. The intellectual elite positioned above this fragmentation must somehow confront this reality, and define its own existence, its own world. Hybridization seems to be a politically correct solu-tion for this group (*ibid.*). This entails the construction of a world in which the homogenizing tendencies of all identification are eliminated by a postmodernist fusion of all cultures into a new het-erogeneous homogeneity of the 'third space', which, Friedman contends, must have boundaries of its own if it is to be a space, and thus be based on oppositions to its own others. Not surprisingly, the champions of the 'third space' identify themselves against redneck nationalists, ethnics and indigenes of the world. 'It is pre-cisely in the metaphor of border-crossing that the notion of homogeneous identity is carried and reinforced, since it is a prerequisite of such transgression'. But for whom, Friedman asks, is such cultural transmigration a reality?

> In the works of the postcolonial border-crossers, it is always the poet, the artist, the intellectual, who sustains this displacement and objectifies it in the printed word. But who reads the poetry, and what are the other kinds of identification occurring in the lower reaches of social reality? (*ibid.*: 79)

In short, hybridization theorists are a group that self-identifies and/or identifies the world in such terms, 'not as a result of ethnographic understanding, but as an act of self-definition', which in turn becomes definition for others via processes of socialization inherent in the structures of power that these groups occupy: intellectuals close to the media and the media intelligentsia itself; in a certain sense, all those who can afford a cosmopolitan identity. Friedman notes that the old cosmopolitan was a modernist who identified above and beyond ethnicity and particular cultures. He was a progressive intellectual, a believer in rationality. The new cosmopolitans, on the other hand, are 'ecumenical collectors of culture'. They represent nothing but a gathering of differences, often in their own self-identifications (*ibid.*: 81–3).

Friedman argues that his criticisms make empirical sense as well. He claims that the realities of underclass neighbourhoods are different than those of the highly educated world travellers of the culture industries. The urban poor, ethnically mixed ghetto is an arena that does not automatically breed hybrid identities. In periods of global expansion, survival depends on creating secure life spaces:

> Class identity, local ghetto identity, tend to prevail, just as the local arena may itself be divided into gang territories. The shift from the mid-1970s to today has been towards an increasing ethnification of such public social arenas, a generalized increase in identity politics. (*ibid.*: 83–4)

In such a process, Friedman concludes, there is little room for the hybrid identification pleaded for by cultural elites. 'Even hybridity tends to become ethnic, that is, bounded and oppositional' (*ibid.*).

So far I have been engaging critically with contemporary theoretical and normative debates on nationalism. It is now time, however, to go one step further and sketch the outline of an alternative approach to nationalism. This is the task of the following two chapters.

7

Rethinking Nationalism: a Social Constructionist Approach

We often take our nationalities for granted now, notes Spillman in her recent study of national commemorations in the United States and Australia, pointedly capturing what we may call the 'idiosyncrasy' of our times. The nation-state is the guiding principle of social and political organization, and nationhood the paramount frame of reference; 'national identity flavors everyday life in familiar ways, and a commonsense rhetoric of nationality makes an unnoticed backdrop to public life. We hardly question the grounding of common appeals to national identity' (1997: 2). Yet this is precisely what we need to do, that is, to resist the clamour of nationalist talk and to question appeals to national identity. In what follows, I shall argue that a social constructionist perspective provides the fulcrum of such a critical inquiry.

The term 'social construction' first appeared in the title of Peter Berger and Thomas Luckmann's 1966 treatise in the sociology of knowledge, *The Social Construction of Reality*. Since then, it has been widely adopted in a variety of disciplines, whether as an epistemological position or a social theory. I shall use the term here as the view that 'all knowledge, and therefore all meaningful reality as such, is contingent upon human practices, being constructed in and out of interaction between human beings and their world, and developed and transmitted within an essentially social context' (Crotty 1998: 42). Constructionism claims that meanings are constructed by human beings as they engage with the world they are interpreting. This mode of meaning generation is 'social', however, in the sense that it is shaped by the conventions of language and other social processes. In other words, while humans may be described as engaging with their world and making sense of it, such a description will be misleading if it is not set in a genuinely historical and social perspective (*ibid.*: 54–5; see also Burr 1995; Gergen 1994, 1999). It needs to be noted in passing that the terms 'constructionism' and 'constructivism' are sometimes used interchangeably. I shall use the term 'social constructionism' throughout to stress the social dimension of meaning construction and to avoid possible confusions – as the term 'constructivism' was initially used in developmental psychology, to refer to Swiss biologist and psychologist Jean Piaget's (1896–1980) theory of cognitive development.

The aim of this chapter is to provide the outline of a social constructionist approach to nationalism. This involves three steps. The first step is to conceptualize nationalism as a form of discourse, a task I have already undertaken in Chapter 2. To recapitulate, I have argued that nations cannot be defined effectively in terms of objective markers or subjective feelings alone. There is no perfect list of characteristics that would make a nation. On the other hand, subjective feelings of identification are not sufficient to differentiate nations from other groupings for which similar feelings exist, such as families or religious groups. I have also claimed that attempts to define nationalism in terms either of culture or politics are futile. Nationalism brings the cultural and the political together: it involves the 'culturalization' of politics and the 'politicization' of culture. This is exactly why the project of distinguishing between different types of nationalism, depending on whether they are based on cultural or political criteria, does not work. Such an attempt conceals what is common to all nationalisms, that they are both cultural and political phenomena. We thus need an alternative conceptualization of nationalism, one that carries us beyond the objective/subjective and culture/politics dichotomies while at the same time enabling us to capture what is common to all nationalisms. Both of these goals can be achieved if we see nationalism as a form of 'discourse', or as *a particular way of seeing and interpreting the world, a frame of reference that helps us make sense of and structure the reality that surrounds us.* This conceptualization reveals that nationalism is more than a political doctrine, that is, a more basic way of thinking that impinges upon our entire view of the world. It also shows that all manifestations of nationalism are shaped by the common discourse of nationalism.

The discourse of nationalism, like similar identity discourses, operates by dividing the world into 'us' and 'them' and by presenting particular formulations of the nation as the natural and authentic version, thereby obscuring the divisions and differences of opinion that exist within the nation. The nationalist discourse does not arise in a social vacuum, but makes ample use of state and civil society institutions to sustain and reproduce itself.

In this chapter, I shall build on the first step and further elaborate the nature of the nationalist discourse, in order to clarify what distinguishes the nationalist discourse from other, similar, discourses. Before that, however, I shall identify the premises upon which a social constructionist analysis is based. Thus the second step of my approach consists in discussing the epistemological contentions of social constructionism. The third and final step, on the other hand, involves the mapping out of the dimensions of the nationalist discourse.

Before moving on, let me stress that what follows is not an attempt to advance a 'universal' theory of nationalism. As I have pointed out in Chapter 3, I believe that no such theory is possible. My aim is much more modest: I intend to formulate an approach that would enable us to identify and make sense of what is common to all nationalisms, namely the discourse of nationalism. What lurks behind this project is an urge to question what we often take for granted, that is, the claims of the nationalist discourse, and reveal their contingent and heterogeneous nature.

The Elements of a Social Constructionist Approach

To gain a fuller understanding of what social constructionism entails for the study of nationalism, it may be helpful to clear away two misconceptions that plague all such analyses.

The first misconception is the widespread belief that social constructionism is tantamount to some form of instrumentalism. Hence for Motyl, the theoretical contribution of constructivism (which he uses interchangeably with social constructionism) will be trivial if it does not argue that elites create national identity consciously (1999: 70). His conclusion seems to be confirmed by Eriksen's observation that '[p]eople are loyal to ethnic, national, or other imagined communities not because they were born into them, but because such foci of loyalty promise to offer something deemed meaningful, valuable or useful' (1999: 55). Yet this is not the whole story. As Eriksen continues to show, what is deemed valuable is culturally determined; it is defined from within. And the individual who perceives alternatives and chooses between them does not choose her own cognitive matrix, that is, her cultural context. In short, 'individuals choose their allegiances, but not under circumstances of their own choice' (*ibid.*: 55–6). Motyl seems to be aware of this when he observes that many established elites construct – and here we might add, 'reproduce' – identity simply by 'doing their job', by unmindfully following the rules, patterns, habits and procedures prescribed by institutions. In that sense, it is possible for national self-awareness to be generated unconsciously, 'by the force of numerous cumulative acts with unintended consequences'. After all, what is 'functional' or 'instrumental' may appear 'natural, meaningful, symbolically inevitable and profoundly national' in a given context. And 'other ways of doing things may appear to be materially dysfunctional but can make perfect sense within a cultural matrix that demands such traditions for the sake of internal consistency and coherence' (1999: 75–6).

In short, social constructionism does not amount to instrumentalism. As Brubaker notes, that this is a false opposition becomes clear when we think of the cognitive dimension of nationalism. Considered from a cognitive point of view, Brubaker argues, nationalism is

a way of identifying interests, or more precisely, a way of specifying interest-bearing units, of identifying the relevant units in terms of which interests are conceived. It furnishes a mode of vision and division of the world, to use Pierre Bourdieu's phrase, a mode of social counting and accounting. Thus it inherently links identity and interest – by identifying how we are to calculate our interests. (1998: 291–2)

The second misconception concerns the ontological status of our social constructions. What do we mean when we say that nations and nationalism are socially constructed? For the critics of social constructionism, this suggests that they have no basis in 'reality', that they are 'false' or 'artificial'. But once again, this is a spurious opposition. It is absurd to suggest that nations or nationalisms are not real for those who believe in them, that therefore they should be dismissed or trivialized. Nationhood may exist in people's minds, but this does not make it ephemeral; 'on the contrary, it is all the more real and powerful as a result' (Geary 2002: 40). This is so for at least two reasons. First, whatever their origins and the extent of mythologizing that go into their making, nations assume a life of their own in time. They are home to the manifold social ties their members develop and the locus of their hopes and dreams. Second, they are very real as aspects of lived experience and bases for action. In fact, as Calhoun notes, people often endorse narratives they know to be problematic, gaining an identification with these as 'our stories', and a recognition of them as background conditions of everyday life (1997: 34).

In short, nations and nationalisms may be socially constructed, but they are not easily deconstructed. Social constructionism does not dispute the reality of nationhood, minimize its power or discount its significance; it simply construes its reality, power and significance in a different way (Brubaker 2002: 168). It warns us against the dangers of taking it for granted, or treating it as a given. It encourages us to inquire into the processes through which it becomes a significant site of identification, to raise questions about why it gets defined as 'real' or 'natural', who stands to gain from maintaining national identities or from mobilizing them under particular circumstances (Norval 1999; Goldmann *et al.* 2000).

Having dismissed two common misconceptions that afflict social constructionist analyses, we may now turn to the premises upon which such analyses are based.

Contingency

Nationalists tend to present the nation as the natural or logical outcome of a series of readily identifiable features, such as common territory, language, religion or a sense of belonging together. For them, the emergence of the nation is inevitable: things could not have been otherwise.

However, the existence of cultural commonalities or affective ties does not guarantee that any particular collectivity will develop a sense of identity and claim a national status. Rather, national identities are the product of social and economic changes that render pre-existing commonalities as both politically important, and ones with which people identify (Moore 2001: 12–13; Calhoun 1997: 32). One implication of this view, according to Moore, is that

> if history had been different, Serbs and Croats needn't have thought of themselves as Serbs and Croats; they could have believed that they were all Serbs or all Croats or all Yugoslavs. Many different kinds of identities were (historically) a possibility, but failed, for various reasons, to be compelling. (*ibid.*)

Thus national identities, like all other social identities, are constructed out of characteristics that can become the basis of quite different kinds of social identities in altered circumstances (Hechter 2000: 96; see also Halliday 2000b: chapters 2 and 3).

The fact that national identities are contingent does not imply that they are interchangeable or infinitely malleable however. Finlayson, drawing on Laclau, shows us that when a particular identity is successfully instituted, a 'forgetting of the origins' tends to occur; the system of possible alternatives vanishes and the traces of the original contingency fade away:

> 'In this way, the instituted tends to assume the form of a mere objective presence. This is the moment of sedimentation'. In other words, through repetition, with attendant concealment and forgetting, otherwise contingent practices become sedimented and appear as objective or natural. (1998: 115)

Given this, what we should do is to examine the mechanisms whereby these identities present themselves as 'natural' and 'inevitable'. One way of doing this might be to undertake what Brubaker calls an 'eventful analysis' of nationness and nationalism. According to Brubaker, we are all used to thinking of nationhood as something that develops. Hence we have no dearth of studies tracing the long-term political, economic and cultural changes that led to the gradual emergence of nations over centuries. What we need instead, he contends, is sustained analytical discussions of nationness as an event, 'as something that suddenly crystallizes rather than gradually develops, as a contingent, conjuncturally fluctuating, and precarious frame of vision and basis for individual and collective action' (1996: 20–1).

Heterogeneity and Plurality

Nationalist rhetoric presents the nation as a unified, homogeneous, seamless whole, without reference to its internal diversity. Even when such diversity is acknowledged, nationalism is considered to override other forms of identification within a society or to encompass these differences in a larger identity. According to Duara, this argument is characteristic to many analyses of nationalism which, ever since Karl Deutsch, emphasize the role of the proliferating mass media in facilitating nation-building projects in different parts of the world. What this account tends to overlook is that this same technology also enables rivals of the nascent nation-state to construct alternative forms of political and even national identity. The state is never able to eliminate alternative constructions of the nation among its constituent communities. As a result:

> . . . the way in which the nation is imagined, viewed and voiced by different self-conscious groups can indeed be very different. Indeed we may speak of different 'nation-views' as we do 'world-views', which are not overriden by the nation, but actually define or constitute it. In place of the harmonized, monologic voice of the Nation, we find a polyphony of voices, overlapping and criss-crossing; contradictory and ambiguous; opposing, affirming and negotiating their views of the nation. (1996: 161–2)

The nationalist claim to homogeneity is not plain rhetoric however. As Appadurai points out, 'most modern nations achieve their sense of their cultural homogeneity in the face of remarkable and known diversities and fierce micro-attachments that have to be erased, marginalized or transformed' (2000: 132). Thus apparent unity and homogeneity is often constituted by repression. The repressed elements are either silenced or explicitly denigrated and relegated to the margins.

The same applies to the claims of 'authenticity', a natural corollary of the project of homogenization. These claims, Tamir argues, are used to imply that there is a single genuine interpretation of a national culture, whereas all the others are factitious and invalid. 'Agents of revision are therefore likely to be called disloyal and their products inauthentic'. Thus, like homogeneity, the term authenticity could serve as an instrument of conservatism and social oppression (1993: 50–1). Parekh affirms Tamir's conclusion, reminding us that every long-established political community includes several different strands of thought and visions of the good life. 'Since every definition of national identity is necessarily selective and must be relatively simple to achieve its intended purposes, it stresses one of the strands and visions and delegitimizes or marginalizes others'. A definition of national identity can thus become a vehicle of silencing dissident voices and moulding the entire society in a particular image with all its authoritarian and repressive implications (2000: 231).

Given these complications, what are the theoretical options available to analysts of nationalism? One option, suggested by Verdery, is to treat the 'nation as a symbol and any given nationalism as having multiple meanings, offered as alternatives and competed over by different groups manoeuvring to capture the symbol's definition and its legitimating effects' (1993: 39). Groups orienting to the nation all take it to be the paramount symbol, Verdery argues, but they have different intentions for it. Treating the nation as a symbol increases our sensitivity to the social tensions and struggles within which it has become a significant idiom – 'a form of currency, used to trade on issues that may not be about the nation at all' (*ibid.*: 41–2).

The second option is to remind ourselves constantly that people are members of different collectivities at any one time. This alternative view of social identification may enable us to see a person's identities in terms of a set of partly overlapping group allegiances. This means that a person's sense of 'national' identity may have to compete with other sources of identity derived from class, gender, age, religion or ethnicity.

Finally, given the existence of multiple competing definitions of national identity, we should be able to ask which version will be victorious and why. In other words, we should investigate the process through which a successful version presents itself as authentic, camouflaging all traces of construction and competition (see also Reicher and Hopkins 2001).

Change

As we have seen, there is no single narrative of the nation, and no nation is ever free of ambiguity and contestation. Thus neither the boundaries nor the content of national cultures can ever be fixed once and for all. In the words of Parekh:

> Culture . . . is not a passive inheritance but an active process of creating meaning, not given but constantly redefined and reconstituted. It does have a structure which directs and delimits the range of new meanings, but the structure is relatively loose and alterable. Even as a culture shapes its adherents' forms of consciousness, they in turn redefine and reconstitute it and expand its cognitive and evaluative resources. (2000: 152–3)

The same goes for national identities, which are constructed through a multiplicity of relations. These relations reflect existing social hierarchies, hence particular structures of power and control. As the configuration of power in a given society changes, so do the identities. Two things flow from these observations. First, 'however institutionalised nations become, and however well established the symbolism that denotes them, nations remain elusive and indeterminate, perpetually open to context, to elaboration and to imaginative reconstruction' (Cubitt 1998, cited in Edensor 2002: vii). We should thus ask how ideas about nation and identity are produced and reproduced as central elements in a political struggle. We should see the 'nation as a construct, whose meaning is never stable but shifts with the changing balance of social forces' and ask what kind of leverage this construct has afforded certain groups – and why those groups rather than others (Verdery 1993: 41).

Second, we should remind ourselves that the process of nation formation has not come to an end. As Geary notes in his study of the origins of European nations:

> Ethnogenesis is a process of the present and the future as much as it is of the past. No efforts of romantics, politicians or social scientists can preserve once and for all some essential soul of a people or a nation. Nor can any effort ensure that nations, ethnic groups and communities of today will not vanish utterly in the future. The past may have set the parameters within which one can build the future, but it cannot determine what the future must be. (2002: 174)

The Problem of Reification

Reification is about 'representing a transitory, historical state of affairs as if it were permanent, natural, outside of time'. Reification portrays processes as things or events of a quasi-natural kind, in such a way that their social and historical character is eclipsed (Thompson 1990: 65). There have been very few attempts to get to grips with the question of reification despite the fact that it constitutes a serious epistemological problem so far as the study of nations and nationalism is concerned. A notable exception in this regard is Brubaker who has provided the most elaborate analysis of the problem to date.

According to Brubaker, most discussions of nationhood are discussions of nations: 'nations are understood as real entities, as communities, as substantial, enduring collectivities'. This realist, substantialist understanding of nations informs not only the view of nationalism held by nationalists themselves, but also much of the scholarship on nationalism. Thus most discussions of nationhood and nationalism begin with the question 'what is a nation?' This question, Brubaker argues, is not as theoretically innocent as it seems: 'the very terms in which it is framed presuppose the existence of the entity that is to be defined' (1996: 13–14). Accordingly, we casually reify ethnic and national groups in our everyday talk and writing, speaking of 'the Serbs', 'the Croats', 'the Russians' and so on as if they were internally homogeneous, externally bounded groups, even unitary collective actors with common purposes (1998: 293).

Brubaker introduces the term 'groupism' to refer to 'the social ontology that leads us to talk and write about ethnic groups and nations as real entities, as communities, as substantial, enduring, internally homogeneous and externally bounded collectivities' (1998: 292). The problem with the treatment of nations as real entities, according to Brubaker, is that it adopts categories of practice as categories of analysis. It takes a conception inherent in the practice of nationalism and makes it central to the theory of nationalism (1996: 15). Yet the problem is not only intellectual. Reification, Brubaker notes, is also a social process. As such, it is central to the practice of ethnic politics. Reifying groups is precisely what ethnopolitical entrepreneurs, who may live 'off' as well as 'for' ethnicity, are in the business of doing. By invoking groups, these entrepreneurs seek to evoke them, summon them, call them into being:

> When they are successful, the political fiction of the unified group can be momentarily yet powerfully realized in practice. As analysts, we should certainly try to account for the ways in which – and conditions under which – this practice of reification, this powerful crystallization of group feeling, can work . . . But we should avoid unintentionally doubling or reinforcing the reification of ethnic groups in ethnopolitical practice with a reification of such groups in social analysis. (2002: 166–7)

This last point is crucial, says Brubaker, and needs to be emphasized more than ever, at a time when groupist language prevails in everyday life, journalism, politics and much of social research. We should treat 'groupness' as variable, 'as emergent properties of particular structural or conjunctural settings' (1998: 298):

> We should not ask 'what is a nation' but rather: how is nationhood as a political and cultural form institutionalized within and among states? How does nation work as practical category, as classificatory scheme, as cognitive frame? What makes the use of that category by or against states more or less resonant and effective? What makes the nation-evoking, nation-invoking efforts of political entrepreneurs more or less likely to succeed? (1996: 16)

Brubaker issues a word of caution at this stage, noting that to argue against the realist and substantialist way of thinking about nations is not to dispute the reality of nationhood. Rather, it is to reconceptualize that reality. 'It is to decouple the study of nationhood and nationness from the study of nations as substantial entities, collectivities or communities'. In other words, 'it is to treat nation not as substance but as institutionalized form; not as collectivity but as practical category; not as entity but as contingent event' (*ibid.*).

Reification is problematic from an empirical point of view as well. As Brubaker and Laitin note, ethnic and national groups are not 'given' entities with unambiguous rules of membership. In most cases, membership is fluid and context-dependent. High rates of intermarriage mean that many people are not sure where they belong when they are faced with interethnic violence. There is rarely a single leader authorized to speak in the name of the group. On the other hand, it is difficult to know whether, when, where, to what extent, and in what manner the posited beliefs and fears are actually held by members of such groups (1998: 438–43). What is more, as I have argued in preceding sections, ethnic and national identities are constituted in social processes that involve diverse intentions, constructions of meaning, and conflicts. 'Not only are there claims from competing possible collective allegiances, there are competing claims as to just what any particular ethnic or other identity means' (Calhoun 1997: 36). In short, as analysts, we should not take these identities for granted, but always investigate them empirically.

By way of conclusion, we should concede, following Handler, that 'reification is an epistemological problem not easily vanquished, for it pervades the rhetorical and conceptual apparatus of our scientific worldview'. Hence we may succeed in disposing of one set of reifying concepts from our scholarly analyses, only to find ourselves employing others in their place (1994: 27). On the other hand, we should not forget that 'the tendency to partition the social world into putatively deeply constituted, quasi-natural intrinsic kinds' is mere common sense for many people. As analysts, we should be able to take account of such common sense primordialism. However, this does not mean we should replicate it in our scholarly analyses or policy assesments: 'as "analysts of naturalizers", we need not be "analytic naturalizers". Instead, we need to break with vernacular categories and common sense understandings' (Brubaker 2002: 166).

Reproduction, Agency and Resistance

If nations are contingent, heterogeneous and subject to change, how could they implant themselves in the hearts and minds of millions of people all around the world? In other words, how do people become national?

The answer lies in the reproduction of national identities through the institutions of the state and in everyday life. The nation, as we have seen, tends to present itself as a homogeneous, organic whole within which there is unity of outlook and purpose. However, the nation is something that must be constructed in the face of serious resistance even among supposed 'insiders' (Kaiser 2001: 329). Moreover, this process does not end once the nation-state is established. Magic wears out, as Durkheim told us a long time ago, and the nation must constitute itself again and again (Marvin and Ingle 1999: 248). Thus, in the words of Balibar:

A social formation only reproduces itself as a nation to the extent that, through a network of apparatuses and daily practices, the individual is instituted as *homo nationalis* from cradle to grave, at the same time as he/she is instituted as *homo economicus, politicus, religious* . . . (1990: 345)

There are two forms of reproduction: institutional and informal. In that regard, reproduction can be seen as the outcome of an interaction between agency and structure, or between individual paths and collective-institutional projects (see also Kaiser 2001). As Appadurai puts it, 'the nation-state creates a vast network of formal and informal techniques for the nationalization of all space considered to be under its sovereign authority', through apparatuses as diverse as museums and village dispensaries, post offices and police stations, tollbooths and telephone booths (1996: 189).

The institutions (private or public) through which the nation-state reproduces itself include the family, schools, the workplace, the media and the army. According to Balibar, the family–school couple is particularly important in this context as they together constitute the dominant ideological apparatus in today's societies, which is reflected in their growing interdependence and in their tendency to divide up the time devoted to the training of individuals between them. In this context, Balibar notes, that the school is also the main site of the inculcation of nationalist ideology is a secondary phenomenon. The importance of schooling lies in its role in the production of the nation as a linguistic community. What is decisive here 'is not only that the national language should be recognized as the official language, but, much more fundamentally, that it should be able to appear as the very element of the life of a people' (1990: 351–7).

Reproduction is not limited to the institutions of the state however. The national is also constituted and reproduced in the volatile settings of everyday life. As Billig reminds us in his ground-breaking study of 'banal nationalism', the symbols of nationhood do not disappear from sight once the nation-state is established, but become absorbed into the environment of the newly created homeland. They provide a continual background for political discourses, for cultural products, and even for the structuring of newspapers. 'In so many little ways, the citizenry are daily reminded of their national place in a world of nations. However, this reminding is so familiar, so continual, that it is not consciously registered as reminding'. In this way, what is 'ours' is presented as if it were the objective world. 'The homeland is made both present and unnoticeable by being presented as *the* context' (1995: 8, 41, 109).

We only become aware of the process of reproduction when we are torn apart from our habitual environment. Reflexive awareness, in other words, results from disruption. A confrontation with different cultural codes can reveal that others act differently, 'inducing a heightened sense of awareness towards what seemed common-sense enactions' (Edensor 2002: 89). As many authors have pointed out, the experience of exile is crucial in this context as it has the ability to transform one's relationship to one's place of birth and help develop a critical reflexivity. In the words of Benedict Anderson, the 'nationalizing' moment comes when one is torn out of the quotidian and finds oneself in fearful exile (1998: 61; see also Smith and West 2001).

The discussion so far seems to portray reproduction as an all-powerful, irreversible process, with no room for individual agency or resistance. This picture, however, is at best a partial one, for nationalism, like all institutional projects, has room for resistance. The 'weak' can fight back by recasting the original ascriptions that relegate them to the margins; they can challenge the prevalent interpretations of key symbols. Consequently, these small acts of resistance can lead, at least incrementally, to some degree of change in the larger distribution of power (Herzfeld 1997: 30).

Taking the possibility of resistance into account, Roseberry proposes us to use the Gramscian concept of 'hegemony', not to understand the complex unity of coercion and consent in situations of domination, as Gramsci originally intended, but to understand struggle, or the ways in which the words, images, symbols, organizations and institutions of the subordinate populations to talk about or resist their domination are shaped by the process of domination itself:

What hegemony constructs, then, is not a shared ideology but a common material and meaningful framework for living through, talking about, and acting about social orders characterized by domination . . . The common material and meaningful framework is, in part, discursive, a common language or way of talking about social relationships that sets out the central terms around which and in terms of which contestation and struggle can occur. (1996: 80)

The image of 'hegemony' Roseberry portrays fits in perfectly with the way nationalism is conceptualized in this book, and enables us to understand both the process of reproduction of nationalism and how (and the extent to which) it can be resisted. When a common discursive framework achieves hegemony, certain forms of activity are given official approval, while others are declared offensive and inadmissible. In such a context, even 'forms and languages of protest or resistance must adopt the forms and languages of domination in order to be registered or heard' (*ibid.*: 81). The merit of this conception of hegemony, Roseberry argues, is that it helps us draw a more complex map of a field of force over which a particular discourse reigns. 'By drawing our attention to points of rupture, areas where a common discursive framework cannot be achieved, it serves as a point of entry into the analysis of processes of domination'. Applied to the discourse of nationalism, it allows us to see it as a 'project', rather than an 'achievement' (*ibid.*: 82–3).

This shows us the importance of micro-level analyses for a fuller understanding of nationalism. People are often the main actors in history. Hence our macro stories must be complemented with parallel stories on a micro level (Laitin 1998: 139). We need to inquire into the actual lived experiences of people in local communities – 'not as "hypothetical isolates" cut off from larger historical and institutional forces, but as sites where the global and the local are intertwined in the production of material conditions and the ideologies that make sense of, sometimes resist, the forces of change' (Willford 2001: 23).

Theoretical Implications

Having discussed the premises upon which a social constructionist approach is based and some of the questions they raise, I would now like to pull the threads together and highlight the theoretical implications of such an analysis. Before starting, however, a word of caution is in order. What I have said so far on the socially constructed nature of national phenomena does not imply that a simple exposure of the processes by which nations and nationalisms constitute themselves will shake the nationalists' belief in them, 'show them the light' so to speak. As Suny remarks, 'primordial identity construction cannot be reduced to a mistake, a self-deception, or false consciousness'. Rather we need to appreciate the work primordialism and essentialism perform for those who are caught in their net (2001b: 892).

Building on my discussion of social constructionism so far, I shall suggest that there are four basic ways of doing this, all related to one or more of the premises I have identified above.

First, we need to take a critical stance towards all that we take as simply 'given'. As I have noted in my discussion of contingency, 'objectivity is nothing but that which is socially constituted, and which has become *sedimented* over time' (Norval 1999: 84, original emphasis). Positing objectivity in this manner opens up the space for the thought of *desedimentation*: any sedimented practice may be contested politically, and 'once its historically constituted character is revealed, it loses its naturalised status as "objectively given"'. This in turn enables us to develop a theoretical account of national identification; in other words, of the historical, social, and political processes through which images for identification are constructed and sustained, contested and negotiated (*ibid.*: 84–6).

Second, we need to discover which political interests are secured in and by particular constructions of nationhood. If nations do not have essential identities and if they all contain groups that have different constructions of the nation, then every identity conceals a particular relationship of power. Thus we need to decode the relationships that create and sustain national identities. We need to explore how a particular representation of the nation comes to dominate others, who stands to gain by it and which other projects are marginalized or eliminated in the process.

Third, we need to distinguish consistently between categories and groups, and problematize, rather than presume, the relationship between them. As Brubaker reminds us, not all group-making projects succeed. We can thus ask about the degree of groupness a particular category attains in a particular setting, and about the political, social, cultural and psychological processes through which categories get invested with groupness.

> We can study the politics of categories both from above and from below. From above, we can focus on the ways in which categories are proposed, propagated, imposed, institutionalized, discursively articulated, organizationally entrenched, and generally embedded in multifarious forms of 'govermentality'. From below, we can study the 'micropolitics' of categories, the ways in which the categorized appropriate, internalize, subvert, evade, or transform the categories that are imposed on them. (2002: 169–70)

This distinction between groups and categories also allows us to steer clear from the trap of reification. When we start our analysis with 'the Romanians' and 'the Hungarians' as groups, we are almost automatically led to attribute identity, agency, interests and will to groups. When we begin with 'Romanian' and 'Hungarian' as categories, however, we can avoid reification and focus on processes and relations, rather than substances (*ibid.*: 183).

Finally, Brubaker contends that sensitivity to the variable and contingent nature of groupness, and to the fact that high levels of groupness may be more the result of conflict than its underlying cause, can draw our analytical attention to the processes through which groupness may subside:

> Declining curves of groupness have not been studied systematically, although they are just as important, theoretically and practically. Once ratcheted up to a high level, groupness does not remain there out of inertia. If not sustained at high levels through specific social and cognitive mechanisms, it will tend to decline, as everyday interests reassert themselves, through a process of what Weber called 'routinization'. (*ibid.*: 177)

This last point brings us to the fourth implication of social constructionism, namely the need to study the processes of reproduction that sustain groups. We thus need to commit ourselves to exploring the institutional and discursive mechanisms under which nationalisms are maintained and, just as importantly, can be resisted or challenged.

Mapping the Discourse of Nationalism

It is now time to introduce the third and final step of a social constructionist approach. As I have argued earlier, beyond the specific
narratives of nations, there is the metanarrative or discourse of the
nation, 'the cluster of ideas and understandings that came to surround the signifier "nation" in modern times' (Suny 2001b: 870).
This cluster of ideas has several dimensions which differentiate
it from other, nonnationalist, forms of discourse. The aim of the
following sections is to identify and explore these dimensions in
an attempt to show what distinguishes nationalism from other
political discourses. I shall identify four such dimensions below:
the spatial, the temporal, the symbolic and the everyday. Before
moving on, however, two qualifications should be made. First, the
labels I have chosen for my categories are quite generic, and some
of them can easily be used to analyse other discourses as well. Thus
I do not argue that, say, the symbolic dimension is specific to the
discourse of nationalism. What differentiates nationalism from
other discourses is the 'combination' of all four dimensions, and,
of course, the thematic content of a particular dimension. It is true
for example that religion too has its own symbolism. Yet it has other
dimensions as well, which nationalism will not have, and the symbolism of religion will be different than the symbolism of nationalism. Second, and this further reinforces my first point, the
dimensions I identify are not mutually exclusive; rather they
overlap and intersect to a significant degree – hence the need to
take their combination into account.

The Spatial Dimension

It is difficult to think of a nation without a particular territory, an
actual or imagined homeland. In that sense, territory is central to
the construction of ethnic and national identities. It may be used
as an instrument of classification to differentiate what is ours from
theirs; as a means of communication with culturally meaningful
landmarks and boundaries; or as a container shaping group imagination (Yiftachel 2001: 364). Not surprisingly, geography attained
the status of an academic discipline at a time and in those countries caught up in the process of nation-building. Kaiser, drawing

on MacLaughlin, argues that this state-centered political geography took the nation-state for granted, and regarded it as the optimum unit for social advancement. In this way, academic geography unintentionally contributed to the process of nation-building, 'provided rational justifications for a capitalist-dominated nation-state, and aided the destruction of movements emphasizing the importance of regional social and political autonomy' (MacLaughlin 1986, cited in Kaiser 2001: 321).

The reconstruction of social space as national territory is then an essential component of the project of nation-building. Various terms have been proposed to cover this process, such as 'territorial socialization' or 'territorial institutionalization'. I shall adopt Kaiser's term here and refer to this process as 'national territorialization of space'. As Kaiser notes, nationalists employ a variety of techniques to increase territorial consciousness. Chief among these is map-making. Maps delimiting the boundaries of historic homelands and the geographic extent of the future community, with sites of symbolic significance well marked, and frequently with text in national language, all combine to create a powerful tool for imagining states. Beyond this, the boundaries of the historic homeland have been logo-ized and reproduced on stamps, flags, and posters and in textbooks to inculcate the image of the homeland in the minds of the population to be nationalized, as well as to the outside world. 'Along with cartographic representations, those engaged in national territorialization projects also frequently personified the homeland with the invention of stereotypical masculine or feminine characters' (Kaiser 2001: 324). Kaiser also draws our attention to the role of poets, writers, and artists who have always been significant agents in national territorialization projects through works paying homage to the homelands being constructed. In such works, 'it is frequently the case that a particular landscape – one likely to evoke nostalgic feelings about the land and the past – is chosen as the symbolic representation of the homeland in its entirety'. Finally,

national territorialization . . . involves the selection and commemoration of particular historic figures, events, and sites, which helps to ground the fiction of the nation and homeland in specific places and times. Monuments in the landscape help to project an image of permanence onto the nation and its relationship to the land, and thus reinforce the imagery of primordialism and 'rootedness'. (*ibid.*)

The state plays a pivotal role in all this. It uses the various institutions at its disposal to instill the notion of 'one nation, one territory'. Such policies are implemented mainly through national education, where children are taught the history and geography of the nation in a way that demonstrates the 'eternal' and 'immutable' existence of a homeland. Other government programmes, such as the establishment of museums, the construction of roads, the naming of places and regions, and the production of maps and plans, all help the people to 'imagine' and 'construct' the state as their natural homeland (Yiftachel 2001: 368–9).

It would not be an overstatement to say that the project of national territorialization has been a huge success. In today's 'national order of things', the link between identity and place is largely 'naturalized'. A person going into exile often takes a handful of the native soil with her; a returning national hero or politician kisses the ground upon setting foot once again on the 'national soil'. Similarly, the ashes or bodies of persons who have died on foreign soil are transported back to their 'homelands': 'in death, too, native or national soils are important' (Malkki 1996: 437).

In her compelling essay on the territorialization of national identity, Malkki also draws our attention to the extent to which the links between people and place are conceived in specifically botanical metaphors. Thus people are often thought of, and tend to think of themselves, as being rooted in place and as deriving their identity from that rootedness. The roots in question, Malkki adds, are not just any kind of roots; very often they are arborescent in form. Not surprisingly, nations and national identities too are conceptualized in terms of roots, trees, origins, ancestries, racial lines, evolutions, developments, or other familiar, essentializing images. What they all share, Malkki argues, is a genealogical form of thought, which is peculiarly arborescent (*ibid.*: 437–8).

According to Malkki, this fascination with roots leads to a peculiar sedentarism in our thinking. This sedentarism is almost invisible for it is largely taken for granted. Moreover, this sedentarism is not inert: 'it actively territorializes our identities, whether cultural or national . . . It also directly enables a vision of territorial

displacement as pathological – the pathologization of uprooted-
ness in the national order of things' (*ibid.*: 441–2).
The spatial dimension is crucial to the functioning of the
nationalist discourse in two respects. The first is symbolic. Particular sites are selected by the nationalist discourse either to provide
evidence of a glorious past, or a 'golden age' or to commemorate
significant episodes in the nation's history (Edensor 2002: 45).
These sacred national sites often correspond to the values and histories of the dominant group and are thus imbued with symbolism
which reproduces the identity and the privileged position of the
dominant ethnic culture (Yiftachel 2001: 370). There are also
nationally popular sites of assembly and congregation. These are
places where large numbers of people gather to carry out communal activities like demonstrations, festivals and so on – like the
Times Square in New York and Trafalgar Square in London. 'In
contrast to the rather purified, single-purpose spaces of state
power, they are more inclusive realms which allow for the play of
cultural diversity' (Edensor 2002: 48).
It needs to be noted at this point that the selection of a symbolic
landscape and the choice of historic figures, events, and sites to
commemorate are rarely uncontested. In the words of Kaiser:

. . . the national construction of social space is a conflict-ridden
process as various nationalist voices compete to have their image
of homeland and nation attain dominance . . . This contestation
does not end with the creation of a commemorative site or the
selection of a symbolic landscape, since each is reinterpreted to
suit competing nationalist interests and perceived needs at different points in time . . . Viewed in this way, national territorialization must be seen as a dynamic, contingent, and contentious
process, rather than as an internally harmonious project that
puts into place a universally accepted set of images and perceptions about the nation and homeland being made. (2001: 325)

The second way in which the spatial dimension contributes to the
functioning of the nationalist discourse is more mundane, hence
less visible. This concerns the absorption of familiar localities into
the nation. The semiotic imprint of familiar features constitutes a
sense of being in place, or at home, in most locations within the
nation (Edensor 2002: 51). According to Edensor, these fixtures

are not only read as signs, but are felt and sensed in an unreflexive fashion – the plethora of everyday, mundane signifiers which
are not present when we go abroad. These vernacular features are
embedded in local contexts but recur throughout the nation as
serial features. The most important point about these features,
Edensor argues, is that they stitch the local and the national
together through their serial reproduction across the nation. Some
of these features, on the other hand, are more overtly celebrated
as everyday symbols of national identity – for example, pubs as
national icons (*ibid.*: 51–2).

In short, territory plays a vital role in distinguishing the modern
nation-state from prior forms of collective social life and governance. Everything else that is invoked as vital to the nation-state,
Appadurai rightly reminds us, is a principle of attachment that the
nation-state shares with other sociopolitical forms. Blood, race,
language, history, culture, 'all have prenational expressions and
nonnational applications. They can be used to justify, extend or
inculcate love of the nation but they are not distinctive of the
national form'. Without some idea of territorial sovereignty – and
here one might add the idea of a 'homeland' – the modern nation-
state loses all coherence (2000: 135).

The Temporal Dimension

As Hobsbawm once observed, nations without a past are contradictions in terms. 'What makes a nation is the past; what justifies
one nation against others is the past and historians are the people
who produce it' (1996: 255). Yet there is something peculiar about
this past. So far as nationalism is concerned, the question of a true
history is beside the point. National histories sanctify as real not
what is veridical, but what is felt to unify the community. Thus whatever works for the community are selected from the past and presented as 'facts' outside of relations of time and space. In Marvin
and Ingle's words, this is the process of reframing, or 'tinkering
strategically with the past' (Marvin and Ingle 1999: 155; see also
Allan and Thompson 1999).

On the other hand, there is an intricate relationship between
the past and the present. The construction of national history generally reflects present concerns and beliefs about the past. In that

sense, the selection process is echoic, not linear: 'the present must hear itself in what is selected from the past' (Marvin and Ingle 1999: 152). Thus:

[f]ar from being somehow 'behind' the present, the past exists as an accomplished presence in public understanding. In this sense it is written into present social reality, not just implicitly as a residue, precedent or custom and practice, but explicitly as itself – as History, National Heritage and tradition. Any attempt to develop and assert a critical historical consciousness will find itself in negotiation if not open conflict with this established public understanding of the 'past'. It is therefore important to understand what it is that functions as the 'past' and to distinguish it from history. (Wright 1984, cited in Allan and Thompson 1999: 39)

This is where the question of 'authenticity' comes in. The public understanding of the past that Wright talks about presents it as 'authentic', that is, the only true version. This is not surprising since nationalists are inclined to produce Whig histories, that is, favourable accounts of 'how we came to be who we are'. As Calhoun indicates, the point is not just that such a history is not neutral. By its nature, nationalist historiography – that which tells the story of the nation – embeds actors and events in the history of the nation whether or not they had any conception of that nation (1997: 51). We can easily unmask these claims once we see the past as providing a legacy of traditions and symbols for individuals and groups, and not as a fixed inheritance. The meanings of events may be reconfirmed or reinterpreted. 'The timing of incidents or other elements of former times may be altered or given a new significance; even the ordering of the chronology of parts of an individual's or group's past may be rescheduled' (Roberts 1999: 201). In short, nations do not have a single history: there are competing narratives to be told. Different factions, classes, religions, regions, genders or ethnicities always struggle for the power to speak for the nation, and to present their particular voice as the voice of the whole nation, defining the history of other subsections accordingly. In other words, 'the voice of the nation' is a fiction. 'National histories are continually being re-written, and the re-writing reflects current balances of hegemony' (Billig 1995: 71).

Once we accept this, we can start questioning how particular conceptions of the past come to be accepted as authentic, how certain customs, symbols or rituals are being invoked to 'rule out' alternative configurations of the past. This in turn increases our sensitivity to the fact that 'what is selected to be remembered is partially determined by what is chosen to be forgotten, that which is to be dismissed as being "inappropriate"' (Allan and Thompson 1999: 42).

Remembering is then key to a nation's identity. The meaning of any group identity, that is, a sense of sameness over time and space, is sustained by remembering (Gillis 1994: 3). According to Gillis, popular memory differs from elite memory in important ways. While elite memory attempts to create a consecutive account of all that happened from a particular point in the past, popular memory makes no effort to fill in all the blanks.

If elite time marched in a more or less linear manner, popular time danced and leaped. Elite time colonized and helped construct the boundaries of territories that we have come to call nations. But popular time was more local as well as episodic . . . This was not a time that could be contained within fixed boundaries. It was measured not from beginnings but from centers . . . Content to live in a present that contained both the past and the future, ordinary people did not feel compelled to invest in archives, monuments, and other permanent sites of memory, but rather they relied on living memory. (*ibid.*: 6)

Gillis argues that the recent proliferation of anniversaries, memorial services, and ethnic celebrations suggests that remembering has become more democratic. Today, we are more likely to do our 'memory work' at times and places of our choosing. Everyone is now her own historian, which in turn means that life can no longer be lived sequentially along a single time line. In short, even though ordinary people are more interested in and know more about their pasts than ever before, their knowledge is no longer confined to compulsory time frames and spaces of the old national historiography (*ibid.*: 14–17).

The temporal dimension also plays itself out in the intricate link between the dead, the living and the unborn. This link is pivotal to nationalism's claim to continuity and regeneration. The message that national myths convey is simple: nations are immortal; they transcend contingency. The celebration of death for the nation and the commemoration and veneration of the dead assume critical importance in this context (Tamir 1997).

Tamir, focusing on the former aspect, notes how the nation is endowed with a religious content, which makes dying in its protection a holy obligation, a desirable end, which would allow a person to enter into the *patria eterna*, into a better, heavenly world. This religious dimension also turns the death in war of a loved one into a gain that outweighs the personal loss (*ibid.*: 230).

On the other hand, the state tries to overcome the fear of death by portraying the deaths of patriots as instantaneous, gracious and painless rather than as brutal and painful, through memorial rites and patriotic literature. The state also offers those who are ready to sacrifice their lives in its defense a series of benefits, ranging from material goods, social status and mobility to more abstract awards such as glory, respect and public idolization. In any case, when enlisting, many people hope that they will never need to face danger and that, if they do, 'the state will fulfill its promise to do its best to lessen the risks involved, come to their rescue, never leave them behind if wounded, and make an exchange for them if they are ever captured by the enemy'. On the other hand, there are costs to be incurred for refusing to fight, ranging from social exclusion to the restriction of working opportunities and career development (*ibid.*: 235–9).

The second mechanism through which the nation secures its continuity is the commemoration and veneration of the dead. National monuments, memorial services, funerals and rites of commemoration constitute sites of collective memory. In performing them, the nation asserts that as long as it exists, it will show gratitude to all those who struggle and sacrifice their lives for its survival:

> It will turn them into heroes, perhaps even canonize them. The military cemeteries, the memorial days, are all ways of living up to this solemn oath: the fallen shall not be forgotten; they will go on living in the memory of the nation. We live because of them, and in living we save their memory and imbue their death with meaning. (*ibid.*: 236)

Benedict Anderson, on the other hand, draws our attention to the ethical implications of death for the nation. The tombs of unknown soldiers treat all the dead as absolutely equivalent. The names are stripped of all substantive sociological significance. No class, no religion, no age, and no politics is indicated. 'No priorities either: hence the usual telephone-book alphabetic sequence' (1998: 363). It does not make any difference whether they met their ends on a glorious or a shameful battlefield:

> The sacrifice of their lives is thus radically separated from historical Right or Wrong. This separation is elegantly achieved by positioning them all as sacrificial victims. National Death has, so to speak, paid their bills and cleared their moral books. The National Dead are never killers. (*ibid.*)

The same applies to the unborn members of the nation. It is in the name of the unborn that we are asked to work hard, pay our taxes, and make other sacrifices – in order to preserve heritages, reduce national debts, protect environments, defend frontiers. The unborn too have no social lineaments at all, and it is exactly this purity that guarantees their goodness, and that allows them to impose on us obligations. In this way, Anderson concludes, 'we can observe how the national dead and the national unborn, in their uncountable billions, mirror each other, and provide the best sureties of the ineradicable Goodness of the nation' (*ibid.*: 362–4).

The Symbolic Dimension

Nationalism, says McClintock, is a theatrical performance of invented community. Its power lies in its capacity to organize a sense of collective unity through the management of mass national commodity spectacle. In this respect, nationalism inhabits the realm of fetishism:

> More often than not, nationalism takes shape through the visible, ritual organization of fetish objects – flags, uniforms, airplane logos, maps, anthems, national flowers, national cuisines and architectures as well as through the organization of collective fetish spectacle – in team sports, military displays, mass

rallies, the myriad forms of popular culture and so on. (1996: 274)

Symbols are those images, objects and activities that are utilized by individuals and groups in social intercourse to achieve objectives through influencing and controlling behaviour (Smith 2001: 521). Above all, symbols are used to induce action by forming and maintaining a belief system. The meanings associated with a symbol need not have a substantial relationship to it to be effective. 'Indeed most symbols, even when sanctioned by tradition, are intrinsically arbitrary. Moreover, meanings assigned to symbols may subsequently be altered, forgotten, or elaborated upon'. As a result, symbolic meanings are often subject to misinterpretation, multiple meanings, and degradation (*ibid.*).

As Smith points out, no known society has operated without the use of symbols:

Collectively, they constitute an important force for social solidarity, transformation, and renewal. Symbols indeed appear to be necessary for the establishment of social cohesion, the legitimization of institutions and of political authority, and the inculcation of beliefs and conventions of behavior. (*ibid.*: 522)

It is therefore not surprising that the nationalist discourse makes ample use of symbols to define and justify its social norms and values, to create 'maps' for social actors. This last point is crucial because ideologies not only reflect a particular historical consciousness of specific social actors (a model 'of'), they provide a 'template' for the creation of that reality (a model 'for') (Willford 2001: 3). Thus when a state achieves independence through war or when an existing regime is overthrown, old symbols are often ritually destroyed, ridiculed, and outlawed; a new set of symbols arise in their place, especially a flag, national anthem, 'sacred texts', and an image of the true patriot. New nations also create new capital cities and new names for the country, and sometimes even a new calendar or alphabet (Smith 2001: 527).

It needs to be noted at this stage that the construction of national symbols, as in the case of territory or a suitable past, is rarely uncontested. As a result, the meaning of symbols is never fixed or static. In fact, as some writers have argued, they need to be flexible in order to retain their relevance over time and to appeal to diverse groups. On this account, the symbols that are the most effective are those that carry the most meanings (Donnan and Wilson 1999: 75; Edensor 2002: 5).

Among the various national symbols, flags are perhaps the most pervasive. There is in fact a quasi-religious aura surrounding the flags, reflected in the words and ceremonies associated with their use in the modern era, which is strictly regulated by law and enforced by severe penalties for 'desecration' (Smith 2001: 528; see also Marvin and Ingle 1999: 30–1). The flag is the ultimate symbol of nationhood; hence it is present in all circumstances where the nation is implicated – elections, inaugurations, court hearings, public gatherings, legislatures, on vehicles of all kinds, in schools and churches, in funerals and at sports events and holiday festivities, in international conferences and competitions, and of course, in every form of military activity. According to Smith, 'flags are a particularly useful form of symbol because of their adaptability, the appeal of their colors and emblems, their relative inexpensiveness and ease of manufacture, their hypnotic motion when flying and their long-distance visibility' (2001: 529). As the exact origin of most flags is either unknown to the general public or relatively obscure, they are particularly well-suited to myth-building. Their age, creation, involvement in historic events, and similar characteristics can easily be manipulated without the likelihood that most people will be aware of the deception. Thus flags represent the presumed distingushing characteristics of the nation, such as its struggle for existence, its natural resources, its ethnic or religious composition. Those meanings are communicated to citizens by formal schooling and through their association with specific experiences and situations which reinforce the desired interpretation of the symbol (*ibid.*).

The symbolic dimension of the nationalist discourse is also visible in rituals, which we might define, following Kertzer, 'as symbolic behaviour that is socially standardized and repetitive' (1988, cited in Donnan and Wilson 1999: 66). Rituals play a crucial role in collective identity formation in any society. Marvin and Ingle argue that in the best rituals, members feel group survival is at stake. In such cases, the need for ritual is never in doubt. 'The more uncertain its outcome . . . the greater the ritual magic that will be deployed and the more transformative will be the result' (1999: 91).

On the other hand, failed rituals produce disunity, and the greater the failure, the larger the division (*ibid.*: 93). Rituals may fail because, no matter how clear and concrete they may appear in form and structure, they also have a timeless, abstract and multidimensional quality:

> Each of the symbols of a ritual may serve to condense many meanings into one object, such as a nation's flag, or one symbol can be multivocal, in that many different messages are received by the ritual's participants . . . Mystification, then, is a part of many rituals. Some rites may even have as a principal aim the disorientation of their participants. Such rituals entail participants entering a liminal state, a transitional condition which is confusing, sometimes polluting and almost always transformative . . . During these rituals the participants, and their relationships within their culture, are ambiguous and in flux. (Donnan and Wilson 1999: 66)

To sum up, the symbolic dimension of the nationalist discourse aims to provide an alphabet for a collective consciousness or national subjectivity, through its traditional icons, its metaphors, its heroes, its rituals, and its narratives (Berlant 1991: 20). Through the symbolic dimension, or what Berlant aptly calls the 'National Symbolic', the nation aspires to achieve the inevitability of the status of natural law, a birthright. This communally held collection of images and narratives makes the national subject or citizen at home in the nation. Yet, Berlant reminds us, this domestic political comfort leads to a kind of amnesia, as events and signs that disrupt the nation's official-historical meaning are excluded from its public version. 'The National Symbolic thus seeks to produce a fantasy of national integration, although the content of this fantasy is a matter of cultural debate and historical transformation (*ibid.*: 22, 57).

The Everyday Dimension

The national cannot be subsumed by that which is consciously wielded as symbolic, 'for it is ingrained in unreflexive patterns of social life, stitched into the experience and the assumptions of the everyday' (Edensor 2002: 10). National culture, in other words, is also rooted in the 'trivial'. Yet this crucial insight was neglected until recently, and much of the literature on nationalism preferred to focus on the symbolic dimension of nationalism at the expense of the routine habits of everyday life. The balance is relatively redressed in the last decade with the publication of a spate of studies that addressed the more mundane, 'banal' aspects of national identity (see for example Billig 1995; Edensor 2002; Linde-Laursen 1993).

These studies show us that the top-down view of culture, or the idea of culture constructed purposefully by national elites and imposed on a relatively passive population, is seriously misleading. National identity is produced, reproduced and contested in the taken-for-granted details of social interaction, the habits and routines of everyday life. As Berlant notes, the nation's presence in the generic citizen's daily life is more latent and unconscious than it is in her incidental, occasional relation to national symbols, spaces, narratives, and rituals (1991: 4). Everyday forms of knowledge are rarely the subject of conscious reflection, because they constitute part of the arsenal of skills required to sustain social life. According to Löfgren, this is precisely why the strongest influences of 'the national' are found on the level of everyday practice rather than in rhetoric or ideological statements. This ongoing homogenization, he argues, tends to produce a strong feeling of what he calls 'hominess'. Crossing the border, we feel at home among bureaucratic procedures, consumer habits, road signs and inside jokes. What we have here is a 'territorialization of familiarity', which often does not have to be the result of ideological campaigns, and this is what gives national belonging such a strong platform (1993: 190).

There are a number of ways in which the national is instantiated in everyday life. Nationalism leaves its imprint on a host of popular cultural practices including sports, common pastimes and holidaying. It informs the shared norms that determine the 'appropriate' ways of behaving – of dressing, talking, eating, and so on. Hence there are proper ways to behave in public spaces such as cafés, gardens, parks and bars, and domestic spaces like kitchens, meeting rooms and bedrooms:

There are, of course, national stereotypes which are formed around these spaces and activities – Italians are 'good lovers',

French are 'excellent cooks' and English have a skill in garden-
ing . . . Such cultural codes not only reconstruct these sites as
theatres for specified forms of behaviour but also train bodies
to adopt dispositions and actions 'in keeping' with these venues.
(Edensor 2002: 95)

These cultural codes are conveyed through popular representations of everyday life, in soap operas, magazines and other forms
of popular fiction. According to Edensor, these familiar worlds
entrench such codes and routines in national worlds. Moreover,
'so dense are these intertextual references to habitual, everyday
performances in the fictional worlds of television and media, and
so repetitive are their enactions by one's intimates, that they
acquire a force which militates against deconstruction' (*ibid.*: 92).
    Even the familiar objects of everyday life bear the mark of
nationalism. This is most evident in such obvious markers as
stamps, coins, flags, coats of arms, costumes or car stickers. Then
there are souvenirs and other popular artefacts which are collected
as symbols of other nations by tourists.
    In passing, we should also note the interplay between the terri-
torial and everyday dimension, whereby the familiar sites of everyday life such as the pub, the beach, and even the home, can be
coded and read in terms of the national themes they instantiate.
Hence Fiske, Hodge and Turner demonstrate how the pub, for
example, exemplifies traditional Australian values of egalitarian
mateship, and the beach the idea of being an outdoor, fun-loving
country (1987, cited in Smith and West 2001: 94).
    How does the state relate to the everyday dimension? States gen-
erally have policies and programmes that seek to regulate, define
and shape every facet of social life. However when we see daily practices that match official pronouncements of policy, we should
not rush to the conclusion that state nationalism dominates. As
Wilk notes, often the state's policies merely rationalize what has
happened after the fact, or hijack or appropriate an ongoing development. In that sense, we can perhaps talk about the competing
presence of official, planned policies of nationalism and unofficial,
unplanned ideas and practices of nationalism, which are outside
the purview of the state (1993: 296, 313–14). Eriksen's vivid account
of formal and informal nationalisms in Trinidad and Tobago, and
Mauritius provides a good illustration of this last point.

Eriksen's point of departure is that nationalism is essentially a dual phenomenon with its loci in the formal state organization and in the informal civil society (1993: 1–2). State nationalism, Eriksen argues, is only successful when it is acknowledged in civil society. Yet the identity presented by the institutions of the state does not always fit with the experiences of the people to whom it is directed. The ideology does not, in these cases, communicate with the needs and aspirations of part of the population, and its symbolism is therefore ultimately impotent. This gives rise to another form of nationalism quite different from the formal, bureacratic nationalist ethos which is characteristic of the modern nation-state, but which does not necessarily contradict it. Unlike state nationalism, this form of nationalism has firm roots in the immediate experiences of people, and can therefore more easily contribute to the production of shared meanings (*ibid.*: 6–11).

Eriksen makes two further observations on formal and informal nationalisms. First, he notes that the contradictions between the two value-systems sometimes create practical dilemmas for the individuals who lead their lives between the poles. But these dilemmas, which seem unresolvable intellectually, are not necessarily seen as inherently destructive; people tend to shrug and identify them as natural (*ibid.*: 11–12). Second, he warns us that the distinction between formal and informal nationalism cannot be reduced to a distinction between 'inauthentic' and 'authentic' symbolisms. Formal nationalism is no less authentic than informal nationalism, nor is it less efficient in mobilizing or integrating individuals ideologically. 'It must, however, attach itself to effective rules of transformation in order that in its abstract symbolism – the flag, to mention but one example – is made relevant in the informal structuring of daily experiences' (*ibid.*: 18).

The distinction Eriksen develops is crucial in understanding the interplay between the symbolic and the everyday dimension of the nationalist discourse, and the ambivalent role of the state. As he asserts in the case of formal and informal nationalisms, everyday enactments of the national do not necessarily subvert the symbolism propagated by the state and its various institutions. These should better be regarded as complementary aspects of every national identity, at times overlapping, at other times diverging or contradicting.

In short, we are 'national' not only when we salute our flag or sing our national anthem, but also when we vote, watch the six o'clock news, follow sports competitions, observe (while barely noticing) the repeated iconographies of landscape and history in TV commercials, and imbibe the visual archive of reference and citation in movies (Eley and Suny 1996: 29).

This chapter has tried to explore the contribution social constructionism can make to our understanding of nationalism and to map the dimensions of the nationalist discourse. There are two lessons to be gleaned from all this. First, we should not take nations and nationalism for granted or as 'given'; instead, we should explore the historical and social conditions under which they come to be perceived as the natural condition of our times. Second, we should never forget that the sheer force of argument will not make nations and nationalism go away. We must always remind ourselves that simply because something is socially constructed does not mean it can be deconstructed at will. Yet, as Glover rightly observes, the spread of a more sophisticated understanding of the way national self-images and narratives are constructed could slowly erode uncritical nationalism (1997: 28). The challenge ahead of us is to write a history from outside the ideology of the nation-state. The challenge is enormous as it requires historians to come to grips with their own ethical values, and the enormity of it derives from the fact that these values have themselves been intimately shaped by the nation-state (Duara 1996: 172).

8
Conclusion: Postnational Futures

'We need to think ourselves beyond the nation', says Arjun Appadurai, the leading proponent of postnational social formations in discussions of globalization and the future of nationalism. This is not to suggest, he hastens to add, that imagination alone will carry us beyond the nation, or that the nation is simply a thought or an imagined thing. 'Rather, it is to suggest that the role of intellectual practices is to identify the current crisis of the nation and in identifying it to provide part of the apparatus of recognition for postnational social forms' (1996: 158).

Needless to say, Appadurai is neither the first, nor the only to call for a postnational world. The hope for broader frameworks of political cooperation than that of the nation-state, or indeed, for the creation of a single world community, has inspired politicians and thinkers of all stripes for centuries, from the Stoics to Montesquieu, Rousseau and Kant, from Marx to Lenin and Rosa Luxemburg. In fact, 'internationalism', be it in the form of transnational political and religious loyalties, Enlightenment universalism or simply trading links, has preceded and for a long time coexisted with nationalism (Halliday 1988, 2001). This is largely forgotten today owing to the success of the nationalist discourse in suppressing alternative discourses and political languages, thereby presenting itself as the natural framework for all political interaction. This also impairs our ability to make sense of nationalism by blinding us to the fact that the latter is at the same time an international discourse, envisioning a world system of putative nation-states and making nationhood a condition of entry to this system and its representative institutions (Calhoun 1995).

It should thus come as no surprise that many of the debates on the possibility of transcending nations have historical antecedents. The period of the Second International (1889–1914) is particularly noteworthy in this respect. As Nimni argues in his Introduction to the English translation of Otto Bauer's classic *The Question of Nationalities and Social Democracy* (2000 [1924]), a re-examination of the debates in this period reveals striking similarities to contemporary debates on multiculturalism and, I would add, cosmopolitanism. The Second International is not only important because it represents, in many ways, the apogee of the international labour movement. It also offered a forum for the discussion of the so-called 'nationalities question', enabling thinkers and politicians on the revolutionary left to grapple with the thorny issue of national rights and national self-determination. It is possible to identify three positions with regard to these issues in the context of the Second International: national-cultural autonomy espoused by Bauer and Renner, the radical internationalism of Luxemburg and the strategic defense of the right to self-determination by Lenin (for this classification, see Forman 1998). The first two of these positions merit further attention in this context as the views of Bauer, Renner and Luxemburg are extremely pertinent to contemporary discussions of multiculturalism and cosmopolitanism.

Bauer and Renner's ideas on the nationalities question arose in a specific historical and political context, with the specific aim of bringing the dissolution of the multinational Austria-Hungarian Empire to a halt by granting its constituent nationalities 'national-cultural autonomy'. This would enable national communities to be organized as autonomous units or sovereign collectives, whatever their residential location within the empire (Nimni 2000; Löwy 1998). The model proposed by Bauer and Renner stressed the need to separate the nation and the state, thus challenged the intuitive assumption that national self-determination required the establishment of independent nation-states. According to this model, all citizens would declare their nationality when they reach voting age; members of each national community would thus form a single public body that is sovereign and has the authority to deal with all national-cultural affairs (Nimni 2000: xvii–xviii). The model also stipulates that national functions would be restricted to education and culture, while the federal state would deal with social and economic issues as well as joint finances, justice, defense and foreign policy (Stargardt 1995: 90).

Their concern for national differences has not led Bauer and Renner to abandon their commitment to internationalism however. For Bauer, the attempt to impose one species of socialism, 'which is itself the product of a particular national history, of particular national characteristics', on workers' movements 'with entirely different histories, entirely different characteristics', was utopian. Rather, the international socialist movement must take the national differentiation of methods of struggle and ideologies within its ranks into account and teach its nationally differentiated troops to mobilize their efforts in the service of common goals. After all, 'it is not the leveling of national differences, but the promoting of international unity within national diversity that can and must be the task of the International' (2000 [1924]: 18).

Rosa Luxemburg's views on the national question were also shaped under particular circumstances, more specifically, in the context of the political conflict between the Polish Socialist Party (PPS) and the Social Democratic Party of the Kingdom of Poland (SDKP) – which she founded – on the issue of the independence of Poland. Describing the PPS's pro-independence position as 'social patriotic', Luxemburg opposed the liberation of Poland on the grounds that the future of Polish economic development lay within Russia (Munck 1986; Löwy 1998). The industrialization of Poland thanks to the protectionist policies of the Czarist Empire led not only to the strengthening of bourgeoisie but also created a growing proletariat. The independence of Poland would be a retrograde step from the viewpoint of socialism as it would impede the development of capitalism in Poland (Nimni 1991: 50–4). More generally, Luxemburg believed that 'the nation as a homogenous sociopolitical entity does not exist. Rather, there exist within each nation, classes with antagonistic interests and rights'. The national state is a specifically bourgeois formation, a necessary tool and condition of its growth (Luxemburg 1908–09, cited in Forman 1998: 89). Given this, to talk about a theoretical 'right of nations' valid for all nations at all times is nothing but a metaphysical cliché, just like the so-called 'right to work' advocated by the nineteenth-century Utopians or the 'right of every man to eat from gold plates' proclaimed by the writer Chernishevsky (*ibid.*, cited in Löwy 1998: 32). According to Luxemburg, only socialism can bring about self-determination of peoples. 'So long as capitalist states exist . . . there can be no "national self-determination", either in war or peace' (Luxemburg 1967 [1915]: 61).

This does not mean that Rosa Luxemburg condoned national oppression. Rather, for her, national oppression is only one form of the process of oppression in general, which is a product of the division of societies into antagonistic classes. The task of the proletariat is to abolish the very root of the system of oppression, namely the class society. 'Since all forms of oppression are derived from the need to sustain class divisions, the emancipation from class societies will necessarily bring about the end of oppression of nations' (Nimni 1991: 53).

Hence Luxemburg's position was antinationalist, and not antinationality. She drew a clear line between opposition to persecution and oppression, and support for nationalism. In any case, it was not possible to decide which people suffered the greater injustice (Forman 1998: 84). In a letter to her friend Mathilde Wurm, who expressed particular concern for the torment of the Jews, she asked:

What do you want with this particular suffering of the Jews? The poor victims on the rubber plantations in Putuyamo, the Negroes in Africa with whose bodies the Europeans play a game of catch, are just as near to me . . . I have no special corner of my heart reserved for the ghetto: I am at home wherever in the world there are clouds, birds and human tears . . . . (Luxemburg 1978: 179–80)

This brief historical digression may appear to be out of place at first blush, perhaps an oddity given the book's focus on contemporary debates. It may even be received with a mocking smile, as a pointless attempt to flog a long-dead horse. Yet my aim is completely different. My exegesis into the ideas of Bauer, Renner and Luxemburg are intended to show that there was a lively debate at the beginning of the twentieth century on the conceptual and political problems posed by nationalism and on ways of transcending the nation-state which they saw as the source of most problems. In other words, this historical digression was meant to be a 'reminder' – a very important one, indeed, considering the left's change of heart with regard to nationalism in later decades. The historical conditions – the most important being the rise of a string of national liberation movements in much of the Third World against Western imperialism – that led to this change of heart are well-known, and need not be repeated here (see also my discussion of 'the liberation argument' in Chapter 4). What is clear is that the assertion of national self-determination gradually came to be regarded as a progressive development by many on the left. The internationalism of the pre-1914 period has been replaced 'by indulgence of every particularism and nastiness, provided it comes from an oppressed people' (Halliday 1992: 488).

Today, the situation is even more bizarre. Those who consider themselves on the left, whether of the New Left, the liberal left, or social democratic left, are at the forefront of the project of resuscitating nationalism. The list is long and includes such names as Benedict Anderson (1998, 2003) who eulogizes the inherent 'goodness' of nations in these 'straitened millennial times', Tom Nairn (1997) who never hides his sympathy for the Scottish national cause, David Miller (1996, 2000) who is prepared to allow for 'a certain amount of mythologizing' if this is the price we must pay to sustain national identities, and Kai Nielsen (1999a) who believes that even cosmopolitans should be liberal nationalists and goes so far as to proclaim himself a 'social liberal cosmopolitan nationalist', regardless of how oxymoronic this may sound – among many others. In this context, it seems difficult not to agree with Fred Halliday's observation that the debate on the left, of nationalism, far from having progressed, has gone backwards over the last decades, and the firm and critical stance of socialists – of all hues – in the pre-1914 period has all but disappeared (1992: 487).

This seems rather awkward considering that many of the problems that have led the revolutionary left to 'think beyond nations' are still there, be they economic inequalities between the North and the South (which are in fact exacerbated by rampant neoliberal globalization), the political and cultural arrogance of prosperous countries and the sense of unease this creates in the rest of the world. It is possible to identify two sets of reasons for transcending the existing system of nation-states in this broader context.

First, the world we live in is neither the best of all possible worlds nor a historical inevitability. I have already exposed the moral and political dangers of taking nationhood for granted in Chapters 4 and 7. I have thus identified 'complacency' with the existing order as the most serious problem of the normative literature on nationalism. Against this, I have called attention to the failure of most political theorists to come to terms with the intricacies of identification processes, or their tendency to turn a blind eye to the shifting and fragmentary nature of national attachments. I have tried to highlight the problem of scale, the inability of normative justifications of nationalism to explain what makes nations 'the contours of our ethical landscape' at the expense of other communities to which we belong. Finally, I have drawn attention to the historical record of nationalism – 'not just the wars, the massacres, the intolerance, but the everyday nastiness of much nationalism, its pretty-mindedness, its meanspiritedness, the endless self-serving arguments, the vast culture of moaning, whingeing, kvetching, self-pity, special pleading' (Halliday 2000a: 158–9) – which gives little relief to those who wish to uphold moral values. I have shown how the philosophical defenses of nationalism always work with abstract and highly benign forms of nationalism, with no counterparts in the real world. I have argued that such political naïveté is dangerous since the benefits that may flow from nationhood may be bought at too high a price to those trapped on the wrong side of the border. Given that, what we need is a critical perspective, a standpoint from which to observe the actual practices of nations. A postnational/internationalist perspective might provide us with such a critical edge, propelling us to think over better alternatives to the existing order (Forman 1998; Halliday 1988).

There is also a second reason for considering a move beyond nations. As I have tried to show in Chapter 6, most problems that continue to plague the world today are of an international character. There is, in that sense, more need for greater international cooperation. At the same time, we see the emergence of new forms transnational linkages, between social movements, NGOs and other elements of civil society. Increasing opportunities for travel and communication enable many people to establish links (and mobilize) across national frontiers. In fact, some commentators believe that a new internationalism is in the making, as demonstrated by protest actions in Seattle, London and Prague which targeted international trade and finance institutions (Myers 2002). This transnational resistance is different from its predecessors in that it brings together a large number of highly diverse groups and movements, from labour unions, peasant organizations, indigenous people's organizations, to women's movements, NGOs and social and youth organizations, which are only united in their opposition to neoliberal globalization (Seoane and Taddei 2002: 99). Others are more cautious about the future success of these movements. Thus for Halliday, 'the diverse anti-capitalist and protest movements of the 1990s and beyond, from radical ecologists, anti-capitalists and Chiapas guerillas lack an organizational cohesion that would challenge the powers of states and corporations that they denounce' (2001: 128).

Yet one thing remains true in the current geopolitical context, and that is the steady erosion of the sovereignty of nation-states – which was, it needs to be noted, never absolute anyway. According to Appadurai, the sovereignty deficit threatens not just individual nation-states, but the very system of nation-states. What we need, in this context, is a line of thinking that repudiates the conceptual framework of the modern nation-form. It is this framework, in particular the idea that identity and politics need to be contained in formally equal, spatially distinct envelopes, which leads to so many complications. The reason for this is not hard to guess:

. . . the world in which we live is formed of forms of consociation, identification, interaction and aspiration which regularly cross national boundaries. Refugees, global laborers, scientists, technicians, soldiers, entrepreneurs and many other social categories of persons constitute large blocks of meaningful association that do not depend on the isomorphism of citizenship with cultural identity, of work with kinship, of territory with soil, or of residence with national identification. It is these delinkages which might best capture what is distinctive about *this* era of globalization. (2000: 141)

The crucial question here is whether these 'delinkages' might become sources for new forms of attachment that are politically effective. The crucial question, in other words, is: will anyone be prepared to die for the cause of internationalism?

The short answer to this question is, yes. One need only recall the International Brigades, nearly 30 000 people from 53 different countries, who fought against fascism in Spain. And, of course, not

a few people from the UN, Red Cross and other humanitarian
NGOs have given their lives for universalist causes in recent years.
Yet one needs to be cautious. There are a number of classical prob-
lems with internationalist projects that are aptly summarized by
Halliday:

> First, it is not often clear how far what is represented as an inter-
> national interest is in fact the interest of a particular state or
> group within the international system. Second, there endures a
> tension between the aspiration to a global culture or identity and
> the existence, and value, of diversity: a world in which everyone
> spoke the same language or ate the same food would be dull
> indeed . . . Third, the creation and sustaining of any interna-
> tional order involve resources and political will, something often
> lacking, not least as the challenges of globalization promote
> nationalist responses. Finally, while advocates of international-
> ism call for greater cooperation to realize common goals, it is
> not always evident that an 'international interest' can be identi-
> fied, in the sense of a course of action that will maximize benefit
> to all. (2001: 127–8)

However, it is not clear why these, 'classical', problems should
undermine the need to move beyond nations. I have already
pointed out some of the problems raised by attempts to uphold
diversity for its own sake. It is obvious that a diversity of authoritarian and fundamentalist cultures would not make much moral sense.
In any case, why would a postnational world be a world in which
'everyone spoke the same language and ate the same food'? As I
have tried to show in Chapter 6, the emerging global culture is not
necessarily something akin to the culture of the nation-state writ
large. Rather, it reflects the diversity, variety and richness of popular
and local discourses, codes and practices. In that sense, the global
culture is marked by 'an organization of diversity rather than by a
replication of uniformity' (Hannerz 1990: 237; Featherstone 1990).
    Then there is the question of universality. How do we know that
what is represented as an international interest is not in fact the
interest of a particular state within the international system? Is it
possible to identify an 'international interest' anyway? Most probably, not. As Butler, among others, reminds us, the meaning of
the 'universal' is usually culturally determined, and the specific

articulations of the universal work against its claim to a 'transcultural' status. However, the contingent and culturally variable character of universality does not undermine the usefulness or importance of the term 'universal':

> If standards of universality are historically articulated, then it would seem that exposing the parochial and exclusionary character of a given historical articulation of universality is part of the project of extending and rendering substantive the notion of universality itself . . . The universal begins to become articulated precisely through challenges to its existing formulation, and this challenge emerges from those who are not covered by it. (1996: 45–8)

One way of doing this is to set different conceptions of universality in dialogue with one another, in order to increase our awareness of cultural divergence and to expand our capacity for transformative intercultural encounters. Thus emerges the call for 'translation' (A. Anderson 1998: 281):

> . . . articulating universality through a difficult labor of translation, one in which the terms made to stand for one another are transformed in the process, and where the movement of that unanticipated transformation establishes the universal as that which is yet to be achieved, and which, in order to resist domestication, may never be fully or finally achievable. (Butler 1996: 52)

Finally, there is the charge of 'political naïveté', or utopianism. It is true that the resources and political will to create any form of internationalist or postnational order are lacking. It is also true that postnational forms of loyalty and belonging are far from representing the everyday reality for many people around the world and are unlikely to be so in the foreseeable future. Yet is this enough to turn a blind eye to the possibility of such forms taking over national ones altogether? As Tamir rightly asks in an essay on the prospects of a global state, 'why aren't discussions on issues of justice or equality considered naïve'?

> Why are the difficulties embodied in the construction of just institutions not used to deter theorists from developing theories

of justice, while the difficulties embodied in the formation of global institutions are used to trump the idea of a global state? More generally, why do discussions of normative issues within state boundaries bend in the idealistic direction, while discussions concerning normative international matters defer to realistic constraints? . . . Does the inability to realize an ideal in the foreseeable future undermine its importance? Must political theory restrict itself to offering only feasible reforms? (2000: 251–2)

The difficulty here, Tamir notes, is that our imagination is embedded in reality. In other words, it is easier for us to imagine what there is. What is more, social institutions make every effort to restrict our imagination, claiming that they are natural, unavoidable, and unchangeable. Fighting these images, Tamir concludes, is no easy matter. 'Nevertheless, neither political theory nor international relations can fall captive to the present' (*ibid.*: 253).

The same point is made by Wood who argues that we must not permit our hopes to be turned to despair by the failure of any single social movement or political experiment, 'nor may we abandon them simply because we have the misfortune to be living at a time when humanity's progress has been interrupted'. At this point, Wood reminds us how the Abbé de Saint-Pierre's project, which he named the European Union, was scoffed at by all but a few visionaries in its own century. Yet today there is a European Union that has not only realized, but utterly surpassed, all the Abbé's hopes that were dismissed as fantastic by his contemporaries. Wood then asks:

Do we really know that it will not someday be the same with other dreams and projects, such as Kant's own projects of an ideally just republican constitution and the necessary condition for it, a society free of the threat of war and the stifling burden of armaments? . . . Or the projects of abolishing racial, religious, and ethnic hate and oppression, or of dismantling the prison walls, both internal and external, of patriarchy and homophobia, or of ending the exploitation of those who labor by those who own, and with it the terrible gulf between rich and poor, both within society and between societies? (1998: 72–3)

Undoubtedly, none of these projects seems feasible in our life-times. In fact, there is not a vision today of how an alternative order might look like. In that sense, the cause of postnationalism is clearly utopian. Yet as Oscar Wilde remarked in his essay on 'The Soul of Man Under Socialism':

> A map of the world that does not include Utopia is not worth even glancing at, for it leaves out the one country at which Humanity is always landing. And when Humanity lands there, it looks out, and, seeing a better country, sets sail. Progress is the realization of Utopias. (2000 [1891]: 189)

No doubt, this will require a lot of creative imagining on the part of those who retain a certain dose of skepticism towards all forms of 'nationalist bickering', using Lenin's term. We should never forget that imagination has been central to agency for most of human history. It was the imagination, in its collective forms, that created the idea of nationhood; the seeds of a postnational order will also be sown by the imagination. In that sense, 'the imagination is today a staging ground for action, and not only for escape' (Appadurai 1996: 7, 31). As Appadurai notes, if such thought experiments can be constructed, we may be freed from the inexorable logic of nationalism. The new forms of community and attachment might not resemble nations at all. 'In that case, in pursuing the potential of these new forms, we have nothing to lose but our terms' (2000: 142).

Bibliography

Ali, Tariq (2002) *The Clash of Fundamentalisms: Crusades, Jihads and Modernity*, London: Verso.

Allan, S. and A. Thompson (1999) 'The Time-Space of National Memory', in K.J. Brehony and N. Rassool (eds), *Nationalisms Old and New*, Basingstoke: Macmillan, 35–50.

Alter, P. (1989) *Nationalism*, London: Edward Arnold.

Anderson, A. (1998) 'Cosmopolitanism, Universalism, and the Divided Legacies of Modernity', in P. Cheah and B. Robbins (eds), *Cosmopolitics: Thinking and Feeling Beyond the Nation*, Minneapolis: University of Minnesota Press, 265–89.

Anderson, B. (1991) *Imagined Communities: Reflections on the Origin and Spread of Nationalism*, 2nd edn, London: Verso.

Anderson, B. (1996) 'Introduction', in G. Balakrishnan (ed.), *Mapping the Nation*, London: Verso, 1–16.

Anderson, B. (1998) *Spectres of Comparison: Nationalism, Southeast Asia and the World*, London: Verso.

Anderson, B. (2003) 'Responses', in P. Cheah and J. Culler (eds), *Grounds of Comparison: Around the Work of Benedict Anderson*, New York and London: Routledge, 225–45.

Anderson, J. and J. Goodman (1999) 'Transnationalism, "Postmodern" Territorialities and Democracy in the European Union', in K.J. Brehony and N. Rassool (eds), *Nationalisms Old and New*, Basingstoke: Macmillan, 17–34.

Appadurai, A. (1996) *Modernity at Large: Cultural Dimensions of Globalization*, Minneapolis: University of Minnesota Press.

Appadurai, A. (2000) 'The Grounds of the Nation-State: Identity, Violence and Territory', in K. Goldmann, U. Hannerz and C. Westin (eds), *Nationalism and Internationalism in the Post-Cold War Era*, London: Routledge, 129–42.

Appiah, K.A. (1996) 'Cosmopolitan Patriots', in J. Cohen (ed.), *For Love of Country: Debating the Limits of Patriotism – Martha C. Nussbaum with Respondents*, Boston, Mass.: Beacon Press, 21–9.

Archard, D. (1999) 'The Ethical Status of Nationality', in D.M. Clarke and C. Jones (eds), *The Rights of Nations: Nations and Nationalism in a Changing World*, Cork: Cork University Press, 145–65.

Balibar, E. (1990) 'The Nation Form: History and Ideology', *New Left Review*, XIII (3), 329–61.

Barber, B. (1996) 'Constitutional Faith', in J. Cohen (ed.), *For Love of Country: Debating the Limits of Patriotism – Martha C. Nussbaum with Respondents*, Boston, Mass.: Beacon Press, 30–7.

Barry, B. (1996) 'Nationalism versus Liberalism?', in B. O'Leary (ed.), 'Symposium on David Miller's *On Nationality*', *Nations and Nationalism*, 2 (3), 430–5.

Barry, B. (1999a) 'Self-Government Revisited', in R. Beiner (ed.), *Theorizing Nationalism*, New York: State University of New York Press, 247–77.

Barry, B. (1999b) 'The Limits of Cultural Politics', in D.M. Clarke and C. Jones (eds), *The Rights of Nations: Nations and Nationalism in a Changing World*, Cork: Cork University Press, 127–44.

Barth, F. (1969) 'Introduction', in F. Barth (ed.), *Ethnic Groups and Boundaries*, Boston: Little, Brown, 9–38.

Bauer, O. (1996) [1924] 'The Nation', in G. Balakrishnan (ed.), *Mapping the Nation*, London: Verso, 39–77.

Bauer, O. (2000) [1924] *The Question of Nationalities and Social Democracy* (trans. by J. O'Donnell, ed. by E.J. Nimni), Minneapolis: University of Minnesota Press.

Bauman, Z. (1992) 'Soil, Blood and Identity', *The Sociological Review*, 40, 675–701.

Bauman, Z. (1998) *Globalization: The Human Consequences*, Cambridge: Polity.

Beiner, R. (1999) 'Introduction: Nationalism's Challenge to Political Philosophy', in R. Beiner (ed.), *Theorizing Nationalism*, New York: State University of New York Press, 1–25.

Benhabib, S. (1999) ' "Nous" et "les Autres": The Politics of Complex Cultural Dialogue in a Global Civilization', in C. Joppke and S. Lukes (eds), *Multicultural Questions*, Oxford: Oxford University Press, 44–62.

Benner, E. (1997) 'Nationality without Nationalism', *Journal of Political Ideologies*, 2 (2), 190–206.

Benner, E. (2001) 'Is There a Core National Doctrine?', *Nations and Nationalism*, 7 (2), 155–75.

Berger, P. and T. Luckmann (1967) [1966] *The Social Construction of Reality: A Treatise in the Sociology of Knowledge*, New York: Anchor Books.

Berlin, Isaiah (1991) 'The Bent Twig: On the Rise of Nationalism', in *The Crooked Timber of Humanity: Chapters in the History of Ideas* (ed. by H. Hardy), Princeton: Princeton University Press, 238–61.

Berlant, L. (1991) *The Anatomy of National Fantasy: Hawthorne, Utopia, and Everyday Life*, Chicago: University of Chicago Press.

Billig, M. (1995) *Banal Nationalism*, London: Sage.

Bok, S. (1996) 'From Part to Whole', in J. Cohen (ed.), *For Love of Country: Debating the Limits of Patriotism – Martha C. Nussbaum with Respondents*, Boston, Mass.: Beacon Press, 38–44.

Brennan, T. (2001) 'Cosmopolitanism and Internationalism', *New Left Review*, 7, 75–84.

Breuilly, J. (1996) 'Approaches to Nationalism', in G. Balakrishnan (ed.), *Mapping the Nation*, London: Verso, 146–75.

Brighouse, H. (1996) 'Against Nationalism', in J. Couture, K. Nielsen and M. Seymour (eds), *Rethinking Nationalism (Canadian Journal of Philosophy*, supplementary volume) Calgary, Alberta: University of Calgary Press, 365–405.

Brock, G. (1999) 'The New Nationalisms', *Monist*, 82 (3), 367–86.

Brown, D. (2000) *Contemporary Nationalism: Civic, Ethnocultural & Multicultural Politics*, London: Routledge.

Brubaker, R. (1996) *Nationalism Reframed: Nationhood and the National Question in the New Europe*, Cambridge: Cambridge University Press.

Brubaker, R. (1998) 'Myths and Misconceptions in the Study of Nationalism', in J.A. Hall (ed.), *The State of the Nation: Ernest Gellner and the Theory of Nationalism*, Cambridge: Cambridge University Press, 272–306.

Brubaker, R. (2002) 'Ethnicity without Groups', *Archives Européennes de Sociologie*, XLIII (2), 163–89.

Brubaker, R. (2004) *Ethnicity without Groups*, Cambridge, Mass.: Harvard University Press.

Brubaker, R. and D.D. Laitin (1998) 'Ethnic and Nationalist Violence', *Annual Review of Sociology*, 24, 423–52.

Brubaker, R. and F. Cooper (2000) 'Beyond "Identity"', *Theory and Society*, 29, 1–47.

Buchanan, A. (1995) 'The Morality of Secession', in W. Kymlicka (ed.), *The Rights of Minority Cultures*, Oxford: Oxford University Press, 350–74.

Burr, V. (1995) *An Introduction to Social Constructionism*, London and New York: Routledge.

Butler, J. (1996) 'Universality in Culture', in J. Cohen (ed.), *For Love of Country: Debating the Limits of Patriotism – Martha C. Nussbaum with Respondents*, Boston, Mass.: Beacon Press, 45–52.

Calhoun, C. (1993) 'Nationalism and Ethnicity', *Annual Review of Sociology*, 19, 211–39.

Calhoun, C. (1995) 'Foreword', in M.R. Ishay, *Internationalism and Its Betrayal*, Minneapolis: University of Minnesota Press, ix–xiv.

Calhoun, C. (1997) *Nationalism*, Buckingham: Open University Press.

Calhoun, C. (forthcoming) 'Introduction', in H. Kohn, *The Idea of Nationalism*, new edn, New Brunswick: Transaction Publishers.

Caney, S. (1996) 'Individuals, Nations and Obligations', in S. Caney, D. George and P. Jones (eds), *National Rights, International Obligations*, Boulder, Col.: Westview Press, 119–38.

Canovan, M. (1996) *Nationhood and Political Theory*, Cheltenham: Edward Elgar.

Canovan, M. (1998) 'Crusaders, Sceptics and the Nation', *Journal of Political Ideologies*, 3 (3), 237–53.

Chatterjee, P. (1990) 'The Nationalist Resolution of the Women's Question', in K. Sangari and S. Vaid (eds), *Recasting Women: Essays in Colonial History*, New Brunswick, NJ: Rutgers University Press, 233–53.

Cheah, P. (1998) 'Introduction Part II: The Cosmopolitical – Today', in P. Cheah and B. Robbins (eds), *Cosmopolitics: Thinking and Feeling Beyond the Nation*, Minneapolis: University of Minnesota Press, 20–41.

Cheah, P. and B. Robbins (eds) (1998) *Cosmopolitics: Thinking and Feeling Beyond the Nation*, Minneapolis: University of Minnesota Press.

Clifford, J. (1998) 'Mixed Feelings', in P. Cheah and B. Robbins (eds), *Cosmopolitics: Thinking and Feeling Beyond the Nation*, Minneapolis: University of Minnesota Press, 362–70.

Connor, W. (1994) *Ethnonationalism: The Quest for Understanding*, Princeton: Princeton University Press.

Crotty, M. (1998) *The Foundations of Social Research: Meaning and Perspective in the Research Process*, London: Sage.

Couture, J. and K. Nielsen, with M. Seymour (1996) 'Liberal Nationalism: Both Cosmopolitan and Rooted', in J. Couture, K. Nielsen and M. Seymour (eds), *Rethinking Nationalism* (*Canadian Journal of Philosophy*, supplementary volume) Calgary, Alberta: University of Calgary Press, 579–662.

Cullingford, C. (2000) *Prejudice: From Individual Identity to Nationalism in Young People*, London: Kogan Page.

Dahbour, O. (1996) 'The Nation-State as a Political Community: A Critique of the Communitarian Argument for National Self-Determination', in J. Couture, K. Nielsen and M. Seymour (eds), *Rethinking Nationalism* (*Canadian Journal of Philosophy*, supplementary volume) Calgary, Alberta: University of Calgary Press, 311–43.

Day, G. and A. Thompson (2004) *Theorizing Nationalism*, Basingstoke and New York: Palgrave Macmillan.

Delanty, G. and P. O'Mahony (2002) *Nationalism and Social Theory: Modernity and the Recalcitrance of the Nation*, London: Sage.

Donnan, H. and T.M. Wilson (1999) *Borders: Frontiers of Identity, Nation and State*, Oxford: Berg.

Duara, P. (1996) 'Historicizing National Identity, or Who Imagines What and When', in G. Eley and R.G. Suny (eds), *Becoming National*, Oxford and New York: Oxford University Press, 151–77.

Dunn, J. (ed.) (1995) *Contemporary Crisis of the Nation-State?*, Oxford: Blackwell.

Dunn, J. (1999) 'Nationalism', in R. Beiner (ed.), *Theorizing Nationalism*, New York: State University of New York Press, 27–50.

Edensor, T. (2002) *National Identity, Popular Culture and Everyday Life*, Oxford and New York: Berg.

Eley, G. and R.G. Suny (1996) 'Introduction: From the Moment of Social History to the Work of Cultural Representation', in G. Eley and R.G. Suny (eds), *Becoming National*, Oxford and New York: Oxford University Press, 3–38.

Elshtain, J.B. (1991) 'Sovereignty, Identity and Sacrifice', *Millenium: Journal of International Studies*, 20 (3), 395–406.

Enloe, C. (1989) *Bananas, Beaches & Bases: Making Feminist Sense of International Politics*, Berkeley and Los Angeles, Cal.: University of California Press.

Eriksen, T.H. (1993) 'Formal and Informal Nationalism', *Ethnic and Racial Studies*, 16 (1), 1–25.

Eriksen, T.H. (1999) 'A Non-Ethnic State for Africa? A Life-World Approach to the Imagining of Communities', in P. Yeros (ed.), *Ethnicity and Nationalism in Africa: Constructivist Reflections and Contemporary Politics*, Basingstoke and New York: Palgrave, 45–64.

Falk, R. (1996) 'Revisioning Cosmopolitanism', in J. Cohen (ed.), *For Love of Country: Debating the Limits of Patriotism – Martha C. Nussbaum with Respondents*, Boston, Mass.: Beacon Press, 53–60.

Featherstone, M. (1990) 'Global Culture: An Introduction', *Theory, Culture & Society*, 7, 1–14.

Finlayson, A. (1998) 'Ideology, Discourse and Nationalism', *Journal of Political Ideologies*, 3 (1), 99–118.

Forman, M. (1998) *Nationalism and the International Labor Movement: The Idea of the Nation in Socialist and Anarchist Theory*, University Park, Pennsylvania: Pennsylvania State University Press.

Foucault, M. (2002a) [1972] *The Archaeology of Knowledge*, London: Routledge.

Foucault, M. (2002b) [1994] *Power, Essential Works of Foucault 1954–1984*, vol. 3 (ed. by J.D. Faubion), London: Penguin.

Foucault, M. (1981) 'The Order of Discourse' (trans. by I. McLeod), in R. Young (ed.), *Untying the Text: A Poststructuralist Reader*, Boston and London: Routledge & Kegan Paul, 51–78.

Freeman, M. (1999) 'The Right to National Self-Determination: Ethical Problems and Practical Solutions', in D.M. Clarke and C. Jones (eds), *The Rights of Nations: Nations and Nationalism in a Changing World*, Cork: Cork University Press, 45–64.

Friedman, J. (1994) *Cultural Identity and Global Process*, London: Sage.

Friedman, J. (1997) 'Global Crises, the Struggle for Cultural Identity and Intellectual Porkbarrelling: Cosmopolitans versus Locals, Ethnics and Nationals in an Era of De-Hegemonisation', in P. Werbner and T. Modood (eds), *Debating Cultural Hybridity: Multi-Cultural Identities and the Politics of Anti-Racism*, London and New Jersey: Zed Books, 70–89.

Gans, C. (2003) *The Limits of Nationalism*, Cambridge: Cambridge University Press.

Geary, P.J. (2002) *The Myth of Nations: The Medieval Origins of Europe*, Princeton and Oxford: Princeton University Press.

Gellner, E. (1983) *Nations and Nationalism*, Oxford: Blackwell.

Gergen, K.J. (1994) *Realities and Relationships: Soundings in Social Construction*, Cambridge, Mass.: Harvard University Press.

Gergen, K.J. (1999) *An Invitation to Social Construction*, London: Sage.

Giddens, A. (1990) *The Consequences of Modernity*, Cambridge: Polity.

Gillis, J.R. (1994) 'Memory and Identity: The History of a Relationship', in J.R. Gillis (ed.), *Commemorations: The Politics of National Identity*, Princeton: Princeton University Press, 3–24.

Glazer, N. (1996) 'Limits of Loyalty', in J. Cohen (ed.), *For Love of Country: Debating the Limits of Patriotism – Martha C. Nussbaum with Respondents*, Boston, Mass.: Beacon Press, 61–5.

Glover, J. (1997) 'Nations, Identity, and Conflict', in R. McKim and J. McMahan (eds), *The Morality of Nationalism*, New York and Oxford: Oxford University Press, 11–30.

Goldmann, K., U. Hannerz and C. Westin (2000) 'Introduction: Nationalism and Internationalism in the post-Cold War Era', in K. Goldmann, U. Hannerz and C. Westin (eds), *Nationalism and Internationalism in the Post-Cold War Era*, London: Routledge, 1–21.

Goodin, R.E. (1988) 'What Is So Special about Our Fellow Countrymen?', *Ethics*, 98, 663–86.

Goodin, R.E. (1997) 'Conventions and Conversions, or, Why Is Nationalism so Nasty?', in R. McKim and J. McMahan (eds), *The Morality of Nationalism*, New York and Oxford: Oxford University Press, 88–104.

Greenfeld, L. (2000) 'Democracy, Ethnic Diversity and Nationalism', in K. Goldmann, U. Hannerz and C. Westin (eds), *Nationalism and Internationalism in the Post-Cold War Era*, London: Routledge, 25–36.

Greenfeld, L. (2001) 'Etymology, Definitions, Types', in A.J. Motyl (ed.), *Encyclopedia of Nationalism*, vol. 1, San Diego, Cal.: Academic Press, 251–65.

Guibernau, M. (2001) 'Globalization and the Nation-State', in M. Guibernau and J. Hutchinson (eds), *Understanding Nationalism*, Cambridge: Polity, 242–68.

Habermas, J. (1994) 'Struggles for Recognition in the Democratic Constitutional State', in A. Gutmann (ed.), *Multiculturalism: Examining the Politics of Recognition*, Princeton: Princeton University Press, 107–48.

Hall, J.A. (2003) 'Conditions for National Homogenizers', in U. Özkırımlı (ed.), *Nationalism and Its Futures*, Basingstoke and New York: Palgrave Macmillan, 15–31.

Hall, S. (1977) 'Culture, the Media, and the "Ideological Effect"', in J. Curran, M. Gurevitch and J. Woollacott (eds), *Mass Communication and Society*, London: Sage, 315–48.

Hall, S. (1996a) 'Ethnicity: Identity and Difference', in G. Eley and R.G. Suny (eds), *Becoming National*, Oxford and New York: Oxford University Press, 339–49.

Hall, S. (1996b) 'Introduction: Who Needs "Identity"?', in S. Hall and P. du Gay (eds), *Questions of Cultural Identity*, London: Sage, 1–17.

Hall, S. (1996c) 'The Problem of Ideology: Marxism without Guarantees', in D. Morley and K.H. Chen (eds), *Stuart Hall: Critical Dialogues in Cultural Studies*, London: Routledge, 25–46.

Halliday, F. (1988) 'Three Concepts of Internationalism', *International Affairs*, 64 (2), 187–98.

Halliday, F. (1992) 'Bringing the "Economic" Back In: The Case of Nationalism', *Economy and Society*, 21 (4), 483–90.

Halliday, F. (2000a) 'The Perils of Community: Reason and Unreason in Nationalist Ideology', *Nations and Nationalism*, 6 (2), 153–71.

Halliday, F. (2000b) *Nation and Religion in the Middle East*, London: Saqi Books.

Halliday, F. (2001) *The World at 2000: Perils and Promises*, Basingstoke and New York: Palgrave Macmillan.

Handler, R. (1994) 'Is "Identity" a Useful Concept?', in J.R. Gillis (ed.), *Commemorations: The Politics of National Identity*, Princeton: Princeton University Press, 27–40.

Hann, C. (1995) 'Intellectuals, Ethnic Groups and Nations: Two Late-Twentieth-Century Cases', in S. Periwal (ed.), *Notions of Nationalism*, Budapest: Central European University Press, 106–28.

Hannerz, U. (1990) 'Cosmopolitans and Locals in World Culture', *Theory, Culture & Society*, 7, 237–51.

Hannerz, U. (1996) *Transnational Connections: Culture, People, Places*, London and New York: Routledge.

Harvey, D. (1990) *The Condition of Postmodernity: An Enquiry into the Origins of Cultural Change*, Cambridge, Mass. and Oxford: Blackwell.

Hastings, A. (1997) *The Construction of Nationhood: Ethnicity, Religion and Nationalism*, Cambridge: Cambridge University Press.

Hechter, M. (2000) *Containing Nationalism*, Oxford: Oxford University Press.

Held, D. (1996) 'The Decline of the Nation-State', in G. Eley and R.G. Suny (eds), *Becoming National*, Oxford and New York: Oxford University Press, 407–416.

Held, D., A. McGrew, D. Goldblatt and J. Perraton (1999) *Global Transformations: Politics, Economics and Culture*, Cambridge: Polity.

Heng, G. and J. Devan (1992) 'State Fatherhood: The Politics of Nationalism, Sexuality and Race in Singapore', in A. Parker, M. Russo, D. Sommer and P. Yaeger (eds), *Nationalisms and Sexualities*, New York: Routledge, 343–64.

Herzfeld, M. (1997) *Cultural Intimacy: Social Poetics in the Nation-State*, New York and London: Routledge.

Himmelfarb, G. (1996) 'The Illusions of Cosmopolitanism', in J. Cohen (ed.), *For Love of Country: Debating the Limits of Patriotism – Martha C. Nussbaum with Respondents*, Boston, Mass.: Beacon Press, 72–7.

Hobsbawm, E.J. (1996) 'Ethnicity and Nationalism in Europe Today', in G. Balakrishnan (ed.), *Mapping the Nation*, London: Verso, 255–66.

Hollinger, D.A. (2001) 'Not Universalists, Not Pluralists: The New Cosmopolitans Find Their Own Way', *Constellations*, 8 (2), 236–48.

Holton, R.J. (1998) *Globalization and the Nation-State*, Basingstoke: Macmillan.

Hroch, M. (1985) *Social Preconditions of National Revival in Europe: A Comparative Analysis of the Social Composition of Patriotic Groups Among the Smaller European Nations*, Cambridge: Cambridge University Press.

Hroch, M. (1993) 'From National Movement to the Fully-Formed Nation: The Nation-Building Process in Europe', *New Left Review*, 198, 3–20.

Hroch, M. (1998) 'Real and Constructed: The Nature of the Nation', in J.A. Hall (ed.), *The State of the Nation: Ernest Gellner and the Theory of Nationalism*, Cambridge: Cambridge University Press, 91–106.

Hurka, T. (1997) 'The Justification of National Partiality', in R. McKim and J. McMahan (eds), *The Morality of Nationalism*, New York and Oxford: Oxford University Press, 139–57.

Hutchinson, J. (2003) 'Nationalism, Globalism, and the Conflict of Civilizations', in U. Özkırımlı (ed.), *Nationalism and Its Futures*, Basingstoke and New York: Palgrave Macmillan, 71–92.

Ignatieff, M. (1994) *Blood and Belonging: Journeys into the New Nationalism*, London: Vintage.

Ignatieff, M. (1999) 'Nationalism and the Narcissism of Minor Differences', in R. Beiner (ed.), *Theorizing Nationalism*, New York: State University of New York Press, 91–102.

Johnson, J. (2000) 'Why Respect Culture?', *American Journal of Political Science*, 44 (3), 405–18.

Joppke, C. and Steven Lukes (1999) 'Introduction: Multicultural Questions', in C. Joppke and S. Lukes (eds), *Multicultural Questions*, Oxford: Oxford University Press, 1–24.

Juergensmeyer, M. (2002) 'The Paradox of Nationalism in a Global World', in U. Hedetoft and M. Hjort (eds), *The Postnational Self: Belonging and Identity*, Minneapolis: University of Minnesota Press, 3–17.

Kaiser, R.J. (2001) 'Geography', in A.J. Motyl (ed.), *Encyclopedia of Nationalism*, vol. 1, San Diego, Cal.: Academic Press, 315–33.

Kirloskar-Steinbach, M. (2001) 'Liberal Nationalism – A Critique', *TRAMES: A Journal of the Humanities and Social Sciences*, 5 (2), 107–19.

Kohn, Hans (1958) [1944] *The Idea of Nationalism: A Study in Its Origins and Background*, New York: The Macmillan Company.

Kristeva, J. (1993) *Nations Without Nationalism* (trans. by L.S. Roudiez), New York: Columbia University Press.

Kukathas, C. (1992) 'Are There any Cultural Rights?' *Political Theory*, 20 (1), 105–39.

Kymlicka, W. (1995) *Multicultural Citizenship: A Liberal Theory of Minority Rights*, Oxford: Oxford University Press.

Kymlicka, W. (1997) 'The Sources of Nationalism: Commentary on Taylor', in R. McKim and J. McMahan (eds), *The Morality of Nationalism*, New York and Oxford: Oxford University Press, 56–65.

Kymlicka, W. (1999a) 'Misunderstanding Nationalism', in R. Beiner (ed.), *Theorizing Nationalism*, New York: State University of New York Press, 131–40.

Kymlicka, W. (1999b) 'Minority Nationalism within Liberal Democracies', in D.M. Clarke and C. Jones (eds), *The Rights of Nations: Nations and Nationalism in a Changing World*, Cork: Cork University Press, 100–26.

Kymlicka, W. (2001) *Politics in the Vernacular: Nationalism, Multiculturalism and Citizenship*, Oxford: Oxford University Press.

Kymlicka, W. and C. Straehle (1999) 'Cosmopolitanism, Nation-States, and Minority Nationalism: A Critical Review of Recent Literature', *European Journal of Philosophy*, 7 (1), 65–89.

Laitin, D.D. (1998) 'Nationalism and Language: A Post-Soviet Perspective', in J.A. Hall (ed.), *The State of the Nation: Ernest Gellner and the Theory of Nationalism*, Cambridge: Cambridge University Press, 135–57.

Laitin, D.D. (2001a) 'Political Science', in A.J. Motyl (ed.), *Encyclopedia of Nationalism*, vol. 1, San Diego, Cal.: Academic Press, 575–88.

Laitin, D.D. (2001b) 'Trapped in Assumptions', Review of Anthony D. Smith's *Myths and Memories of the Nation*, *Review of Politics*, 63 (1), 176–9.

Levy, J.T. (2000) *The Multiculturalism of Fear*, Oxford: Oxford University Press.

Lichtenberg, J. (1997) 'Nationalism, For and (Mainly) Against', in R. McKim and J. McMahan (eds), *The Morality of Nationalism*, New York and Oxford: Oxford University Press, 158–75.

Lichtenberg, J. (1999) 'How Liberal Can Nationalism Be?', in R. Beiner (ed.), *Theorizing Nationalism*, New York: State University of New York Press, 167–88.

Lieven, A. (2004) *America Right or Wrong: An Anatomy of American Nationalism*, London: Harper Collins.

Linde-Laursen, A. (1993) 'The Nationalization of Trivialities: How Cleaning Becomes an Identity Marker in the Encounter of Swedes and Danes', *Ethnos*, 58 (III–IV), 275–93.

Löfgren, O. (1993) 'Materializing the Nation in Sweden and America', *Ethnos*, 58 (III-IV), 161–96.

Löwy, M. (1998) *Fatherland or Mother Earth? Essays on the National Question*, London and Sterling, Virginia: Pluto Press.

Luxemburg, R. (1967) [1915] *The Junius Pamphlet: The Crisis in the German Social Democracy*, Colombo: A Young Socialist Publication.

Luxemburg, R. (1978) *The Letters of Rosa Luxemburg* (ed. by S.E. Bronner), Boulder, Col.: Westview Press.

MacCormick, N. (1999a) 'Nation and Nationalism', in R. Beiner (ed.), *Theorizing Nationalism*, New York: State University of New York Press, 189–204.

MacCormick, N. (1999b) 'Liberal Nationalism and Self-Determination', in D.M. Clarke and C. Jones (eds), *The Rights of Nations: Nations and Nationalism in a Changing World*, Cork: Cork University Press, 65–87.

Malkki, L. (1996) 'National Geographic: The Rooting of Peoples and the Territorialization of National Identity among Scholars and Refugees', in G. Eley and R.G. Suny (eds), *Becoming National*, Oxford and New York: Oxford University Press, 434–53.

Mann, M. (1995) 'A Political Theory of Nationalism and its Excesses', in S. Periwal (ed.), *Notions of Nationalism*, Budapest: Central European University Press, 44–64.

Margalit, A. and J. Raz (1990) 'National Self-Determination', *The Journal of Philosophy*, LXXXVII (9), 439–61.

Marshall, M.G. and T.R. Gurr (2003) *Peace and Conflict 2003: A Global Survey of Armed Conflicts, Self-Determination Movements, and Democracy*, College Park, MD: Center for International Development and Conflict Management, University of Maryland.

Marvin, C. and D.W. Ingle (1999) *Blood Sacrifice and the Nation*, Cambridge: Cambridge University Press.

Mayer, T. (2000) 'Gender Ironies of Nationalism: Setting the Stage', in T. Mayer (ed.), *Gender Ironies of Nationalism: Sexing the Nation*, London: Routledge, 1–22.

McClintock, A. (1996) ' "No Longer in a Future Heaven": National-ism, Gender and Race', in G. Eley and R.G. Suny (eds), *Becoming National*, Oxford and New York: Oxford University Press, 260–84.

McConnell, M. (1996) 'Don't Neglect the Little Platoons', in J. Cohen (ed.), *For Love of Country: Debating the Limits of Patriotism – Martha C. Nussbaum with Respondents*, Boston, Mass.: Beacon Press, 78–84.

McKim, R. and J. McMahan (1997) 'Introduction', in R. McKim and J. McMahan (eds), *The Morality of Nationalism*, New York and Oxford: Oxford University Press, 3–7.

McMahan, J. (1997) 'The Limits of National Partiality', in R. McKim and J. McMahan (eds), *The Morality of Nationalism*, New York and Oxford: Oxford University Press, 107–38.

Miller, D. (1995) *On Nationality*, Oxford: Oxford University Press.

Miller, D. (1996), 'On Nationality', in B. O'Leary (ed.), 'Symposium on David Miller's *On Nationality*', *Nations and Nationalism*, 2 (3), 409–21.

Miller, D. (2000) *Citizenship and National Identity*, Cambridge: Polity.

Mills, S. (2004) *Discourse*, 2nd edn, London and New York: Routledge.

Miščević, N. (2001) *Nationalism and Beyond: Introducing Moral Debate about Values*, Budapest: Central European University Press.

Moore, M. (2001) *The Ethics of Nationalism*, Oxford: Oxford University Press.

Motyl, A.J. (1999) *Revolutions, Nations, Empires: Conceptual Limits and Theoretical Possibilities*, New York: Columbia University Press.

Mouzelis, N. (1998) 'Ernest Gellner's Theory of Nationalism: Some Definitional and Methodological Issues', in J.A. Hall (ed.), *The State of the Nation: Ernest Gellner and the Theory of Nationalism*, Cambridge: Cambridge University Press, 158–65.

Munck, R. (1986) *The Difficult Dialogue: Marxism and Nationalism*, London: Zed Books.

Myers, J.C. (2002) 'Politics Without Borders: Internationalist Political Thought', *New Political Science*, 24 (3), 395–410.

Nairn, T. (1997) *Faces of Nationalism: Janus Revisited*, London: Verso.

Nathanson, S. (1997) 'Nationalism and the Limits of Global Humanism', in R. McKim and J. McMahan (eds), *The Morality of Nationalism*, New York and Oxford: Oxford University Press, 176–87.

Nielsen, K. (1999a) 'Cosmopolitan Nationalism', *Monist*, 82 (3), 446–69.

Nielsen, K. (1999b) 'Cultural Nationalism, Neither Ethnic nor Civic', in R. Beiner (ed.), *Theorizing Nationalism*, New York: State University of New York Press, 119–30.

Nimni, E.J. (1991) *Marxism and Nationalism: Theoretical Origins of a Political Crisis*, London: Pluto Press.

Nimni, E.J. (2000) 'Introduction for the English-Reading Audience', in O. Bauer, *The Question of Nationalities and Social Democracy*, Minneapolis: University of Minnesota Press, xv–xlv.

Norman, W. (1999) 'Theorizing Nationalism (Normatively): The First Steps', in R. Beiner (ed.), *Theorizing Nationalism*, New York: State University of New York Press, 51–65.

Norval, A. (1996) 'Thinking Identities: Against a Theory of Ethnicity', in E.N. Wilmsen and P. McAllister (eds), *The Politics of Difference: Ethnic Premises in a World of Power*, Chicago: University of Chicago Press, 59–70.

Norval, A. (1999) 'Rethinking Ethnicity: Identification, Hybridity and Democracy', in P. Yeros (ed.), *Ethnicity and Nationalism in Africa: Constructivist Reflections and Contemporary Politics*, Basingstoke and New York: Palgrave, 81–100.

Nussbaum, M.C. (1996a) 'Patriotism and Cosmopolitanism', in J. Cohen (ed.), *For Love of Country: Debating the Limits of Patriotism – Martha C. Nussbaum with Respondents*, Boston, Mass.: Beacon Press, 2–17.

Nussbaum, M.C. (1996b) 'Reply', in J. Cohen (ed.), *For Love of Country: Debating the Limits of Patriotism – Martha C. Nussbaum with Respondents*, Boston, Mass.: Beacon Press, 131–44.

Orwell, G. (1968), 'Notes on Nationalism', in S. Orwell and I. Angus (eds), *The Collected Essays, Journalism and Letters of George Orwell, vol. 3, As I Please 1943–1945*, London: Secker & Warburg, 361–80.

Özkırımlı, U. (2000) *Theories of Nationalism: A Critical Introduction*, Basingstoke and New York: Palgrave Macmillan.

Özkırımlı, U. (2003) 'The Nation as an Artichoke? A Critique of Ethnosymbolist Interpretations of Nationalism', *Nations and Nationalism*, 9 (3), 339–55.

Parekh, B. (1995) 'Politics of Nationhood', in K. von Benda-Beckmann and M. Verkuyten (eds), *Nationalism, Ethnicity and Cultural Identity in Europe*, Utrecht: European Research Centre on Migration and Ethnic Relations, 122–43.

Parekh, B. (1999) 'The Incoherence of Nationalism', in R. Beiner (ed.), *Theorizing Nationalism*, New York: State University of New York Press, 295–325.

Parekh, B. (2000) *Rethinking Multiculturalism: Cultural Diversity and Political Theory*, Basingstoke: Palgrave Macmillan.

Parker, A., M. Russo, D. Sommer and P. Yaeger (1992) 'Introduction', in A. Parker, M. Russo, D. Sommer and P. Yaeger (eds), *Nationalisms and Sexualities*, New York: Routledge, 1–18.

Peled, Y. and J. Brunner (2000) 'Culture Is Not Enough: A Democratic Critique of Liberal Multiculturalism', in S. Ben-Ami, Y. Peled and A. Spektorowski (eds), *Ethnic Challenges to the Modern Nation-State*, Basingstoke: Palgrave Macmillan, 65–92.

Pietersee, J.N. (1995) 'Globalization as Hybridization', in M. Featherstone, S. Lash and R. Robertson (eds), *Global Modernities*, London: Sage, 45–68.

Pollock, S., H.K. Bhabha, C.A. Breckenridge and D. Chakrabarty (2000) 'Cosmopolitanisms', *Public Culture*, 12 (3), 577–89.

Poole, R. (1999) *Nation and Identity*, London: Routledge.

Putnam, H. (1996) 'Must We Choose between Patriotism and Universal Reason?', in J. Cohen (ed.), *For Love of Country: Debating the Limits of Patriotism – Martha C. Nussbaum with Respondents*, Boston, Mass.: Beacon Press, 91–7.

Rée, J. (1998) 'Cosmopolitanism and the Experience of Nationality', in P. Cheah and B. Robbins (eds), *Cosmopolitics: Thinking and Feeling Beyond the Nation*, Minneapolis: University of Minnesota Press, 77–90.

Reicher, S. and N. Hopkins (2001) *Self and Nation: Categorization, Contestation and Mobilization*, London: Sage.

Renan, E. (1990) [1882] 'What is a Nation?' (trans. by M. Thom), in H. Bhabha (ed.), *Nation and Narration*, London: Routledge, 8–22.

Ripstein, A. (1997) 'Context, Continuity, and Fairness', in R. McKim and J. McMahan (eds), *The Morality of Nationalism*, New York and Oxford: Oxford University Press, 209–26.

Ritzer, G. (1993) *The McDonaldization of Society*, Thousand Oaks, Cal.: Pine Forge Press.

Robbins, B. (1998a) 'Introduction Part I: Actually Existing Cosmopolitanism', in P. Cheah and B. Robbins (eds), *Cosmopolitics: Thinking and Feeling Beyond the Nation*, Minneapolis: University of Minnesota Press, 1–19.

Robbins, B. (1998b) 'Comparative Cosmopolitanisms', in P. Cheah and B. Robbins (eds), *Cosmopolitics: Thinking and Feeling Beyond the Nation*, Minneapolis: University of Minnesota Press, 246–64.

Roberts, B. (1999) 'Time, Biography and Ethnic and National Identity Formation', in K.J. Brehony and N. Rassool (eds), *Nationalisms Old and New*, Basingstoke: Macmillan, 194–207.

Robertson, R. (1990) 'Mapping the Global Condition: Globalization as the Central Concept', *Theory, Culture & Society*, 7, 15–30.

Robertson, R. (1992) *Globalization: Social Theory and Global Culture*, London: Sage.

Robertson, R. (1995) 'Glocalization: Time-Space and Homogeneity-Heterogeneity', in M. Featherstone, S. Lash and R. Robertson (eds), *Global Modernities*, London: Sage, 25–44.

Roseberry, W. (1996) 'Hegemony, Power, and Languages of Contention', in E.N. Wilmsen and P. McAllister (eds), *The Politics of Difference: Ethnic Premises in a World of Power*, Chicago: University of Chicago Press, 71–84.

Rustow, D.A. (1968) 'Nation', *International Encyclopaedia of the Social Sciences*, 11, 7–14.

Sassen, S. (2000) 'Spatialities and Temporalities of the Global: Elements for a Theorization', *Public Culture*, 12 (1), 215–32.

Scheffler, S. (1997) 'Liberalism, Nationalism, and Egalitarianism', in R. McKim and J. McMahan (eds), *The Morality of Nationalism*, New York and Oxford: Oxford University Press, 191–208.

Scholte, J.A. (2000) *Globalization: A Critical Introduction*, Basingstoke: Palgrave Macmillan.

Scruton, R. (1999) 'The First Person Plural', in R. Beiner (ed.), *Theorizing Nationalism*, New York: State University of New York Press, 279–93.

Sen, A. (1996) 'Humanity and Citizenship', in J. Cohen (ed.), *For Love of Country: Debating the Limits of Patriotism – Martha C. Nussbaum with Respondents*, Boston, Mass.: Beacon Press, 111–18.

Seoane, J. and E. Taddei (2002) 'From Seattle to Porto Alegre: The Anti-Neoliberal Globalization Movement', *Current Sociology*, 50 (1), 99–122.

Seymour, M., J. Couture and K. Nielsen (1996) 'Introduction: Questioning the Ethnic/Civic Dichotomy', in J. Couture, K. Nielsen and M. Seymour (eds), *Rethinking Nationalism* (*Canadian Journal of Philosophy*, supplementary volume) Calgary, Alberta: University of Calgary Press, 1–61.

Skurski, J. (1996) 'The Ambiguities of Authenticity in Latin America: *Doña Bárbara* and the Construction of National Identity', in G. Eley and R.G. Suny (eds), *Becoming National*, Oxford and New York: Oxford University Press, 371–402.

Smith, A.D. (2001) *Nationalism: Theory, Ideology, History*, Cambridge: Polity.

Smith, W. (2001) 'National Symbols', in A.J. Motyl (ed.), *Encyclopedia of Nationalism*, vol. 1, San Diego, Cal.: Academic Press, 521–30.

Smith, P. and B. West (2001) 'Cultural Studies', in A.J. Motyl (ed.), *Encyclopedia of Nationalism*, vol. 1, San Diego, Cal.: Academic Press, 81–99.

Spencer, P. and H. Wollman (1999) 'Blood and Sacrifice: Politics versus Culture in the Construction of Nationalism', in K.J. Brehony and N. Rassool (eds), *Nationalisms Old and New*, Basingstoke: Macmillan, 87–124.

Spencer, P. and H. Wollman (2002) *Nationalism: A Critical Introduction*, London: Sage.

Spillman, L.P. (1997) *Nation and Commemoration: Creating National Identities in the United States and Australia*, Cambridge: Cambridge University Press.

Stalin, J. (1994) [1913] 'The Nation', in J. Hutchinson and A.D. Smith (eds), *Nationalism*, Oxford: Oxford University Press, 18–21.

Stargardt, N. (1995) 'Origins of the Constructivist Theory of the Nation', in S. Periwal (ed.), *Notions of Nationalism*, Budapest: Central European University Press, 83–105.

Suny, R.G. (2001a) 'History', in A.J. Motyl (ed.), *Encyclopedia of Nationalism*, vol. 1, San Diego, Cal.: Academic Press, 335–58.

Suny, R.G. (2001b) 'Constructing Primordialism: Old Histories for New Nations', *Journal of Modern History*, 73, 862–96.

Tamir, Y. (1993) *Liberal Nationalism*, Princeton: Princeton University Press.

Tamir, Y. (1996) 'Reconstructing the Landscape of Imagination', in S. Caney, D. George and P. Jones (eds), *National Rights, International Obligations*, Boulder, Col.: Westview Press, 85–101.

Tamir, Y. (1997) 'Pro Patria Mori! Death and the State', in R. McKim and J. McMahan (eds), *The Morality of Nationalism*, New York and Oxford: Oxford University Press, 227–41.

Tamir, Y. (1999) 'Theoretical Difficulties in the Study of Nationalism', in R. Beiner (ed.), *Theorizing Nationalism*, New York: State University of New York Press, 67–90.

Tamir, Y. (2000) 'Who's Afraid of a Global State?', in K. Goldmann, U. Hannerz and C. Westin (eds), *Nationalism and Internationalism in the Post-Cold War Era*, London: Routledge, 244–67.

Taylor, C. (1994) 'The Politics of Recognition', in A. Gutmann (ed.), *Multiculturalism: Examining the Politics of Recognition*, Princeton: Princeton University Press, 25–73.

Taylor, C. (1999) 'Nationalism and Modernity', in R. Beiner (ed.), *Theorizing Nationalism*, New York: State University of New York Press, 219–45.

Thompson, J.B. (1990) *Ideology and Modern Culture: Critical Social Theory in the Era of Mass Communication*, Oxford: Blackwell.

Tilly, C. (1994) 'A Bridge Halfway: Responding to Brubaker', *Contention*, 4 (1), 15–19.

Tölölyan, K. (1996) 'The Nation-State and Its Others: In Lieu of a Preface', in G. Eley and R.G. Suny (eds), *Becoming National*, Oxford and New York: Oxford University Press, 426–31.

Tyrell, M. (1996) 'Nation-States and States of Mind: Nationalism as Psychology', *Critical Review*, 10 (2), 233–50.

van Dijk, T.A. (1998) *Ideology: A Multidisciplinary Approach*, London: Sage.

Verdery, K. (1993) 'Whither "Nation" and "Nationalism"?', *Daedalus*, 122 (3), 37–46.

Walby, S. (1996) 'Woman and Nation', in G. Balakrishnan (ed.), *Mapping the Nation*, London: Verso, 235–54.

Waldron, J. (1995) 'Minority Cultures and the Cosmopolitan Alternative', in W. Kymlicka (ed.), *The Rights of Minority Cultures*, Oxford: Oxford University Press, 93–119.

Walker, B. (1999) 'Modernity and Cultural Vulnerability: Should Ethnicity Be Privileged?', in R. Beiner (ed.), *Theorizing Nationalism*, New York: State University of New York Press, 141–65.

Walker, R. (2001) 'Postmodernism', in A.J. Motyl (ed.), *Encyclopedia of Nationalism*, vol. 1, San Diego, Cal.: Academic Press, 611–30.

Walzer, M. (1997) *On Toleration*, New Haven: Yale University Press.

Walzer, M. (1999) 'The New Tribalism: Notes on a Difficult Problem', in R. Beiner (ed.), *Theorizing Nationalism*, New York: State University of New York Press, 205–17.

Waters, M. (1995) *Globalization*, London: Routledge.

Weber, M. (1994) [1948] 'The Nation', in J. Hutchinson and A.D. Smith (eds), *Nationalism*, Oxford: Oxford University Press, 21–5.

West, L. (1997) 'Introduction: Feminism Constructs Nationalism', in L. West (ed.), *Feminist Nationalism*, New York: Routledge, xi–xxxvi.

Wilde, O. (2000) [1891] 'The Soul of Man Under Socialism', in S. Ledger and R. Luckhurst (eds), *The Fin de Siècle: A Reader in Cultural History, c. 1880–1900*, Oxford: Oxford University Press, 185–91.

Willford, A. (2001) 'Anthropology', in A.J. Motyl (ed.), *Encyclopedia of Nationalism*, vol. 1, San Diego, Cal.: Academic Press, 1–23.

Wilk, R.R. (1993) 'Beauty and the Feast: Official and Visceral Nationalism in Belize', *Ethnos*, 58 (III–IV), 294–316.

Wilson, R. (1998) 'A New Cosmopolitanism Is in the Air: Some Dialectical Twists and Turns', in P. Cheah and B. Robbins (eds), *Cosmopolitics: Thinking and Feeling Beyond the Nation*, Minneapolis: University of Minnesota Press, 351–61.

Wodak, R., R. de Cilia, M. Reisigl and K. Liebhart (1999) *The Discursive Construction of National Identity*, Edinburgh: Edinburgh University Press.

Wood, A.W. (1998) 'Kant's Project for Perpetual Peace', in P. Cheah and B. Robbins (eds), *Cosmopolitics: Thinking and Feeling Beyond the Nation*, Minneapolis: University of Minnesota Press, 59–76.

Xenos, N. (1996) 'Civic Nationalism: Oxymoron?', *Critical Review*, 10 (2), 213–31.

Yack, B. (1999) 'The Myth of the Civic Nation', in R. Beiner (ed.), *Theorizing Nationalism*, New York: State University of New York Press, 103–18.

Yiftachel, O. (2001) 'The Homeland and Nationalism', in A.J. Motyl (ed.), *Encyclopedia of Nationalism*, vol. 1, San Diego, Cal.: Academic Press, 359–83.

Young, I.M. (2001) 'Thoughts on Multicultural Dialogue', in 'Review Symposium on *Rethinking Multiculturalism: Cultural Diversity and Political Theory* by Bhikhu Parekh', *Ethnicities*, 1 (1), 116–22.

Yuval-Davis, N. and F. Anthias (eds) (1989) *Woman–Nation–State*, London: Macmillan.

Yuval-Davis, N. (1997) *Gender and Nation*, London: Sage.

Yuval-Davis, N. (2003) 'Belongings: In Between the Indigene and the Diasporic', in U. Özkırımlı (ed.), *Nationalism and Its Futures*, Basingstoke and New York: Palgrave Macmillan, 127–44.

Yuval-Davis, N. (forthcoming) 'Human/Women's Rights and Feminist Transversal Politics', in M.M. Ferree and A. Tripp (eds), *Transnational Feminisms: Women's Global Activism and Human Rights*, New York: New York University Press.

Zernatto, G. (2000) [1944] 'Nation: The History of a Word', in J.

Hutchinson and A.D. Smith (eds), *Nationalism: Critical Concepts in Political Science*, London and New York: Routledge, 13–25.

Zubaida, S. (1978) 'Theories of Nationalism', in G. Littlejohn, B. Smart, J. Wakefield and N. Yuval-Davis (eds), *Power and the State*, London: Croom Helm, 52–71.

Index